ANGELS

THE MYSTERIOUS MESSENGERS

ANGELS

THE MYSTERIOUS MESSENGERS

Edited by Rex Hauck

BALLANTINE BOOKS · NEW YORK

Copyright © 1994 by American Artists and First Light Films

All rights reserved under International and Pan-American Copyright Conventions.
Published in the United States by Ballantine Books, a division of Random House, Inc.,
New York, and simultaneously in Canada by Random House of Canada Limited, Toronto.

Grateful acknowledgment is made to Becky Hobbs and Don Goodman
for permission to reprint the lyrics of "Angels Among Us."
Copyright © 1993 Beckaroo Music and Richville Music.

LIBRARY OF CONGRESS CATALOGING-IN-PUBLICATION DATA
Angels: the mysterious messengers / edited by Rex Hauck.
   p. cm.
  Includes index.
  ISBN 0-345-39301-5
  1. Angels I. Hauck, Rex.
BL477.A54 1994
291.2'15—dc20   94-29248
                                    CIP

Text design by Holly Johnson

Manufactured in the United States of America

First Edition: September 1994

10 9 8 7 6 5 4 3 2 1

*This book is dedicated to the memory of
Chris Deal, Tara Moore, and Mallory Shrieves.*

CONTENTS

CONTENTS

ACKNOWLEDGMENTS

From its genesis, *Angels: The Mysterious Messengers* has been nurtured and guided by many people, each bringing individual talents and points of view, each with a profound respect for the ongoing exploration.

The initial idea came from the heart of Melissa Forth. That idea was crystallized by the generous support of Dr. Dan Holloway and Dr. Glen Warren.

Steve Brown, Vivian Walker Jones, and Eric Van Atta listened, and led through the maze of pragmatic details that allowed the conversation to begin and then to grow.

Sally Allen, Dr. John Boyd, Ian Edwards, Karen Hauck, and Candace Apple were the project's unseen angels who provided the light that shone in the darker moments.

Dr. Ray Moody, Guy Martin, Karyn Martin-Kuri, Malcolm

ACKNOWLEDGMENTS

Godwin, and Eileen Freeman helped us follow where the angels led.

Sophy Burnham lent her honesty, Thomas Moore his vision, and Joan Borysenko her courage. Terry Lynn Taylor was our North Star, guiding when we dared uncharted skies.

Tanya Parks, Bill Shrieves, Sandy and Kirk Moore, Andy Lakey, Kathy Faulstich, Steven Maxwell, and Ron Kennedy opened their hearts to us so that we might better understand our own.

Craig Haffner, Steven Lewis, Donna Lusitana, Rob Kirk, and everyone at Greystone Communications proved to be partners that were heaven-sent.

David Sinrich provided the furnace in which we forged our ideas.

Kevin Holloway was, simply, the heart of the project.

My wife Deborah was and is my own angel; throughout the many months of this passage, her love inspired and calmed.

Thanks to all.

FOREWORD

The impulse that eventually grew to become this book began as the simple notion to understand the resounding interest in angels that is alive in the world today. Why were people from all walks of life and from all religions reporting direct contact with angels? And if this contact was real, why were angels choosing to reveal themselves in such unprecedented numbers at this particular time?

For the better part of a year, we traveled the country compiling film footage for what would become a television series— "Angels: The Mysterious Messengers." Cameramen and editors more accustomed to passing the hours talking sports could be heard pondering angelic questions of wings, halos, and personal guardians.

The months became a pilgrimage. We interviewed hundreds of people. Questions that had seemed straightforward at first glance were not. The answers and the experience of angels were seldom uniform. The only constants were the emotional charge and the conviction with which people spoke.

Some of the people who honored us with their ideas are professionals with impressive credentials. Their experience in the exploration of spiritual matters totals hundreds of years.

Authors Thomas Moore, Sophy Burnham, Terry Lynn Taylor, and Joan Wester Anderson openly discussed their research and investigation into sacred realms. These are courageous people who were speaking their hearts long before it became popular to do so. Their words and thoughts provided the structure within which we framed our conversations.

From the medical community, Drs. Raymond Moody, Joan Borysenko, and Sherwin Nuland added the voice of reason, balancing our need for answers and solutions with a deep respect for the mysteries that enrich this life, and allowing imagination and faith to expand our perspective and understanding.

Theologians Rabbi Baroff, Father LeBar, and Father Sobosan shared their religious views and educated us in the rich history of angels throughout most doctrines of faith.

But many of the people we met did not have professional training in any formal field of study. They came from all walks of life: secretaries, youth counselors, musicians, real-estate salespersons, computer consultants, a United States Marine, mothers, fathers, and children. Their only credentials were their faith and certitude that their lives had been touched and forever altered by a momentary encounter with an angel. Speaking in simple terms, they offered their accounts with both candor and astonishment; their angels created as many questions as they answered.

Not everyone we met was willing to accept that angels watch over us or even exist at all. For many people, the world begins and ends with what their eyes can see or their hands can touch. For those predisposed not to believe in angels, no evidence is possible. But for those inclined to believe, no proof is necessary.

Ultimately it is a matter of faith—even of imagination, to borrow Thomas Moore's meaning. What are we willing to allow space for in our world?

Many will say this current interest in angels is only a knee-jerk reaction to the violent, complicated times we live in—that it is only human nature to hope for a gentler life, to seek refuge in the comfort of angels.

But the angels do not call us to heaven. People are not giving themselves over to an esoteric notion, but rather are taking inspiration and responsibility for the shaping of their lives. It is a life that calls for vigilance and compassion and understanding and courage. I have been among these mysterious faithful who have cast their lot with their faith. And the work is being done. There are beings out there building a better world. And many of them are angels.

—Rex Hauck

ANGELS
THE MYSTERIOUS MESSENGERS

Sir Joshua Reynolds,
Angels' Heads.

JOAN WESTER ANDERSON

Joan Wester Anderson began her writing career in 1973 and has published over a thousand articles and stories in a wide variety of magazines and newspapers. A lecturer and teacher, Anderson is the bestselling author of several books including Where Angels Walk, An Angel to Watch Over Me, *and* Where Miracles Happen.

QUESTION   How did you become interested in angels?

JOAN WESTER ANDERSON   I have to admit, I never really was interested in angels. I've had a very firm spiritual life all my life, and I was raised as a rather traditional Catholic, and in that background there are angels. But they were presented to me when I was a little girl as a kind of legend-lore-type thing. The guardian angel was a sweet concept, but by the time I was twelve or fourteen, it didn't apply to me anymore. I always figured that if you are going to pray seriously, you should just go right to the top; you don't need all these extraneous beings around. But then, in 1983, our family had an experience that changed all that for me.

One of our sons was driving from Connecticut to Chicago to spend Christmas with us. In the days leading up to the drive, we here in the Midwest started experiencing this terrible cold snap. Christmas was on a weekend that year, and I believe it was Wednesday when my husband called the kids and said please don't drive; they are warning cars off the expressways. Of course, the weather warning did not apply to twenty-one-year-olds. The kids decided to come anyway, and my worst fears were realized. They broke down right outside a little town in Indiana, in the middle of the night. It was thirty-two degrees below zero. The windchill was, I believe, ninety below, and they sat there realizing that they were probably going to die. All of a sudden there was a flare of light directly behind them—headlights from a tow truck. This guy got out—as improbable as it sounded at two in the morning— asked them if they needed help, and if he could take them back to this town that they had passed. So, he did. When they got out in front of this place of safety and turned around to ask this man how much it was going to cost, there wasn't any truck there, and there weren't any tracks either. My son's car was just sitting there all by itself, as frozen as it had been twenty minutes before.

When my son got home he didn't tell me the story in just that way, and that's the first clue that I had of the way people re- act when they've had a heavenly touch like this; we try to second-guess it and make it fit into what we already know. That's the process that Tim was going through. He was thinking in his own mind about how this could have happened. But after four weeks he just couldn't fit it into any mold anymore, and that's when he told me.

Now the interesting part was that I said to him, "What time

did that man come?" and he answered, "*That* I know for sure. I'm not sure of much of that night, but I do know that he came at a quarter to two." Well, at quarter to one my time (it was the same time, actually, because my son was on Eastern and I was on Central), I had been standing at the window waiting for him; he was five hours late by then. And I had felt this lifting of my spirit. I heard myself saying, "God, you've got to send someone. Please send someone. Because I don't think I can bear what might be happening here. So send someone." That was not a prayer that I had ever prayed before. So, of course, I was left with the reality that I had asked God to send someone, and God did.

Whom had God sent? In the following months I tried to trace this tow-truck driver. I called the state police, and they said there hadn't been any rescue vehicles out. I called a couple of private tow-truck companies, and nobody knew anything about it. It just didn't fit: Why would a tow truck be leaving the safety of a town on a very frightening night? So, eventually I chalked it up to angelic interference.

A couple of years later I met someone who had a similar story. She sought me out and sat next to me in an airplane. I thought, "Am I wearing a sign? Why is she telling me this?" She said, "I just feel as though I need to do that." It was an exquisite story. Then, a year or two later, the same thing happened in an airport waiting room. Someone came up and sat down next to me and asked, "Do you believe in the Holy Spirit? The urgings of the Holy Spirit?" And I said, "Oh, yes, I do" to this perfect stranger. The stranger said, "Well, I do, too, and I hope you won't be too embarrassed, but I need to talk with you about something." And she did, and it was another wonderful story. So, after that I said, "Okay, God. What's going on here? What do you want me to do?" And that's when I began to feel that I had to start seeking out more stories like this.

Q Was your son religious before that experience? Or after this rescue happened, did he start thinking, "Now, wait a minute."

JWA Well, he was religious to the point that he took God and his faith very seriously. But he was a lighthearted, fun, party kind of guy, and I can't really say that that has changed. He does believe more deeply now that there is a loving presence out there that cares for us that is not God—that God might very possibly be sending angels. He did have another experience where he lost control of his car on ice. He saw himself entering a freeway with cars going seventy miles per hour, bumper-to-bumper, and he thought, "Well, I'm going to die here." Then, all of a sudden, that traffic opened and he kind of slid in until he got on solid ground. So, he told me, "I think the angels did that, too." And I said, "Well, I think you might want to consider slowing down slightly, because you're giving them too much work."

Q When you were working on your book, *Where Angels Walk*, how did you receive the letters that you included in the book? Where did they come from?

JWA I have been a magazine writer for the past twenty years now, and I free-lance frequently for the same publications. So readers familiar with my byline knew, or at least I hope they did, that I was kind of an ordinary, normal person. Some of these are little religious magazines, some are large secular magazines—women's publications, parenting, and so forth. I decided to write to the letters-to-the-editors columns, and just explain that I was working on a new project and that I was looking for people who believed they might have had an experience with an angel. I then explained what an angel was—not the next-door neighbor who helped you, but really more of a spiritual entity.

Now, I was taking a risk doing this because in 1989 angels were not as popular as they are now. People forget that those of us who were working at the beginning were not jumping onto an already-established trend; we were breaking ground. We didn't see it that way, however, because none of us knew that anybody else was doing this. We all thought—the original four or five of us—that we were alone. I kind of worried about people snickering or saying, "What happened to her? She used to be okay!" But I'd had enough confirmation in my own spiritual soul to decide that this was good. This was something that I needed to do. And so I did.

Five or six magazines ultimately published my letter asking people to recount their angel experiences, but at the time that it began, only one did so. And I remember standing outside of my post office box that first time, with my key in my hand, thinking, "Well, now you're going to find out if people are ready to tar and feather you, or snicker at you, or if there are others." I opened up the P.O. box and it was stuffed, just stuffed, with mail. And there was a little note from the postmaster in there that said, "We would appreciate you picking up your mail more frequently; we have more in the back."

I still have those original letters. I believe I had around two hundred fifty when I decided there was a book here. Choosing from them was mainly a matter of getting as many stories across as broad a spectrum as possible. I wanted men in the book. I wanted children in the book. People seem to think that this is a little-old-lady thing—or at least they might have at the time. I wanted people of all faiths and no faith. Unfortunately, I was not able to get a Moslem. I would have loved to have a Moslem in the book, because angels are very strong in the Islam faith. That was probably my only lack. All the other categories that I wanted, God sent.

Q When you're writing your books, are you aware of an angelic influence, something that surrounds you, while you work?

JWA   I am a "make-your-deadline-by-the-seat-of-your-pants, do-it-no-matter-what-happens" kind of writer. I raised five children while I was writing, and I was always carrying spiral notebooks to soccer games to get a deadline out. I'd written seven books before *Where Angels Walk*, all in spiral notebooks. Writing was always difficult.

This angel book was difficult, too, in the sense that it was a project that needed to be completed. But there was something different about it in terms of my own sense of responsibility. I exercised a keen and very overwhelming sense of responsibility in the choice of the people, and in my handling of them, because I had to give them a safe place to be. Otherwise, they never would have talked to me. You know, once people began to open up, they would weep. Sometimes I conducted my interviews over the phone, and you could just hear them sobbing, and trying so hard not to do that. I found myself becoming a kind of counselor in a way. This was okay, because when you are touched by heaven, I always maintain, that's where goose bumps come from. You know, we have a God-shaped hole within us. And it can't be filled with anything but God. That's part of the loneliness in the world; people try to fill it with other things. And yet, when God does touch us, sometimes we know it first physically—through goose bumps or a wash of tears. So I always said to people, "It's okay to cry. You're touching something precious here, so go ahead." It was that sense of responsibility that I found difficult; the writing itself was very simple because it was their stories, not mine.

Q   You're working on a new book now, aren't you?

JWA   Actually, I have just completed two books. One is *Where Miracles Happen*, which is about answered prayers. The other is on children's experiences with angels, and it's called *An Angel to Watch Over Me*. This second book came mainly from the reader response to *Where Angels Walk*. Children wrote and said, "We're reading your book" and their parents wrote, too, and said, "We're reading your book to our children at night, and they don't have nightmares anymore. They seem much more serene. But we're wondering, some of the stories are a little old. Would you have anything in the works just for kids?" I thought, "Well, why not?" So I did a book just about children's experiences though it's not only for children readers.

I find that today children are having mystical experiences in a way that the rest of us are not familiar with, and in a way that did not occur years ago. I find that some children seem to have a memory from heaven, and it frightens me just a little because I'm not sure that it's authentic, and yet what else could it be? They come to Earth retaining a slight connection to heaven. Things that we would have passed off five or ten years ago, I now am beginning to take a lot more seriously—such as stories of children running down the hallway with their arms up, as if someone is coming towards them by whom they want to be picked up and swung around. And yet there is no one there. These are children of a year to eighteen months old, maybe. I hear of children of two and three being adamant about an imaginary companion, describing the "pretty lady that comes in my room at night." Children of five or six are telling their parents of things that happened before they were born. It says in the Scripture, "In the last days I will pour out my spirit upon all mankind. Your sons and daughters shall prophecy. Your young children shall see visions," and I'm wondering if maybe that's connected to it.

Q You know that children have incredible imaginations.

JWA Yes, they do.

Q So I'm wondering if you've talked to a few very creative children. Do you believe that some children who claim to have little spirit guides or angel guides might be dreaming this and confusing it with real life, or do you think that their stories are genuine?

JWA I think the answer to both questions is yes. Sure, they could be imagining it, but they could also be in touch with something that we don't know about. I think that when children get to Earth they are probably still in connection with heaven for a while. It's been said that there's a veil that draws over us more and more as we become more involved on Earth. One person said to me, "Maybe we're not born with language because we would have too many wondrous things to say and the world couldn't accept it." I don't know. My job is, I think, not to promote anything, but simply to chronicle. That's what I see myself as doing. I need to discern correctly, to be sure that everything that I write about fits my own spiritual life so that I'm not being insincere or accepting things that I don't believe in. On the other hand, as a chronicler, you're simply sharing what others are telling you and it's up to the individual reader to decide if he or she wants to believe it or not.

Q Why has this sudden burst of interest in angels come at this moment in history?

JWA I agree with those who say that the world is in a very dark place right now. And being a Catholic, I have a little more definite viewpoint, because in Catholicism we have a strong faith in the Blessed Mother, as a guide, as an intercessor. She has allegedly been appearing much more frequently in the world over the past fifteen years or so. She's been coming as a loving warning to people. In effect, what she's saying is that we're going to have to start cleaning up our act, or there will be great punishments and chastisements yet to come. These are not messages from a vengeful, angry God, but from a God who is trying to get our attention. He should be first and everything else should follow, but actually the way our country is at the moment, He's kind of at the bottom, after everything else.

I don't believe in every single vision—neither does the church and neither do most people—but there's enough consistency to make me take it seriously. And yet, it's a sign of hope as well, because with the more dire pronouncements, there's also a constant awareness that people of the light, people of God, don't need to fear—that the angels are there, that all the help we need will be there for us, and so we don't need to be afraid.

And so that may be one reason why the angels are coming. It's a response, and a way of giving us the confidence that we need in whatever will happen.

Q You mentioned recent warnings from the Blessed Mother, signs of upheaval. Can you point to any specific events in history or in nature that we should pay heed to?

JWA In America we had the largest natural disaster we've ever had, Hurricane Andrew, and that same year the largest man-made disaster, which was the rioting in L.A. People shrug these off as coincidences, but here again, I'm not so sure. Yet I know that we don't have anything to worry about if we're walking with the Lord. That's my opinion. And I think He's sending angels to remind us of that.

Q What is an angel?

JWA From my perspective, an angel is not a person who has died and gone to heaven. Many times we hear someone say, "I lost my dad last year, but now I feel his presence in our home and I feel that he must be our guardian angel, watching over our family." Well, it's a nice thought, and I believe that it's probably true in terms of her dad watching over her family, but technically speaking, angels are a separate creation. It says in Scripture that they were created before God created the earth and humankind from the earth. Therefore, they were around at the very beginning, and they are a separate creation, purely spiritual. They have three basic functions: they worship God, they act as a liaison between heaven and Earth, and they guard us.

Now, people will say, "Well, can't God deal with us directly? What do we need angels for?" Yes, God can and often does deal with us directly but I don't question why we need angels; if He decided we needed them, that's good enough for me. And in order to guard us or to bring messages, they sometimes need to take on human form; that's why we sometimes see them as a little old lady or a figure of great splendor, or perhaps a child with a word of reassurance or comfort for us. But basically, they don't have genders, they don't have bodies.

Q   Do we all have guardian angels?

JWA   My own belief is that yes, everyone has a guardian angel. You can't have it both ways; either all of us do, or none of us do. It says in Scripture, in Psalm 91, "I will send my angels around you to guard you in all your ways." It doesn't say, "I'm going to guard you only until you are eleven years old or only if you need it." It's just "in all your ways." Lots of people believe that means from the beginning, for all time, and that angels bring us home to the throne in heaven when our life is done. It's a very comforting thought, and I've chosen to believe that we all have guardian angels.

Q   Do you feel that the angels are giving us a specific message?

JWA   I'm thinking they're giving us the same message they always gave us. Think about the Christmas angels who came to the shepherds on the hillside—they gave the message, and then they pointed to the stable and they left. The stable is where it all begins. I think the angels come to point to God. Their function is not to become an end to themselves, a religion in themselves, a cult, or something that people worship, but to come to say, "He's here, He's with you, fear not"—just as they always did.

Q   Do you think angels play a major part in healing?

JWA   I do, but I don't think that was their major function years ago. I think that they are becoming more active on Earth now—in all of human needs, and that would include healing. My own belief, though, is that healing comes directly from God. And He heals on His timetable, and not ours. The angels could intercede for us if we ask them to help with healing, as they could intercede in anything else, but the ultimate decision always rests with God.

Q   One hears so many incredible stories of people whose prayers for divine intervention come true in amazing ways. Have you touched on this in your writing?

JWA   I have some of that in my book *Where Miracles Happen*. I decided to offer stories of people who had had heavenly touches other than angels. I was concerned about how much mail I was getting from people who said, "I believe in angels, but I've never had an angel experience." And underneath those words I often heard the unasked question: Does God love me as much as He loves these other people?

A lot of these people were coming off of a tragedy. They'd heard of people pulled out of the way of a speeding car, while they might have gone unaided through a hit-and-run that happened to their child. They were suffering from cancer, and yet they had heard how angels had marvelously released someone else from cancer.

This silent question began to bother me. And so I began writing back to these people, asking them if they'd ever had an experience from heaven, if they'd ever felt graced by an answer to prayer in any way? Then, people began to reply, "Oh yes, well I have. Oh, I see." And I thought, "We haven't made this clear enough." So, *Where Miracles Happen* is written with other aspects of answered prayer, as well as more angel stories, because they, too, are a wonderful answer. One of the sections involves some healing. These are not all people who are instantly healed of grand maladies; a couple of times their diseases don't go away, but they receive a different kind of healing, which is sometimes the healing that they needed. We don't always get what we ask for. But we always get something, and sometimes it's better.

Q Do you believe that angels can appear in different forms, whether it be physical manifestations or light beams?

JWA I think they come in whatever form is necessary to communicate the message to us. Yes, they can come in light. They can come as children, as elderly ladies, as people of another race—I find that last example I mentioned extremely interesting. When I first started doing my research, I was finding that Asians were reporting Asian angels. Black people were saying that their angel was black. And I thought, "Well, angels probably come in a culture, a color, a gender that would not intimidate you so that they don't worry or concern you." But now my mail is shifting, and I'm finding people having cross-racial experiences. People point this out to me because it is so unusual. They say, "This little Asian lady came to us, and isn't that interesting that she was Asian?" And I say, "Well, why do you think that happened?" They don't really know, but I'm thinking, "Isn't this neat?" It's kind of a unity thing—God drawing all of his children together. I find it fascinating to see the guises that angels come in.

Q Do you think angels really help to answer prayers? Do you hear of people not only praying to a higher power but also praying to the angels?

JWA   Well, yes I do. Pope John XXIII had a little ritual that he used to perform. He was in many high-level meetings where there was the potential for misunderstandings or heated debates, and when he remembered, he would tell his own guardian angel to go to the angels of all of the people who were going to be meeting that day and just get together with them to kind of mellow out the situation—to open up everyone's hearts so that they would all be willing to come to the right conclusion. He said that when he remembered to do that, the meetings were always beautiful.

When I began telling that story people said to me, "You know, I started doing that when the kids went off to school," or,

Francesco Albani,
Allegory of Water,
ca. 17th c.

"I started sending my angels when I knew that someone in my family was in a difficult situation." So, yes, I do think that angels can be used as emissaries.

Q   How do you respond to quantum physicists and other scientists who insist that they can't really define an angel or question whether they could possibly exist? A few quantum physicists have said that if you believe in angels you're nuts because they just can't be proven.

JWA   Well, you can't prove matters of faith. You have to either accept them or reject them because faith requires a response from us, otherwise it's dead. How can you respond in your heart to something that's already spelled out for you? You need a lifting of your spirit in order to respond to God, and this doesn't necessarily come about through quantum physics. The saying, "To those who believe, no explanation is necessary. To those who do not believe, no explanation is possible," says it all.

And my role, as I see it, is not to respond to people's objections. My job is not to convince people. God will work with everyone in His own way. My job is simply to put information out there and hope that it might give someone like a quantum physicist, who might want to read up on it only to debate it, a little nudge. If he opens the door of his heart just a little bit, then I have full confidence that God will come in and work.

Q   Are children more likely than adults to see an angel?

JWA   I don't think they're more *likely* to, but I think they might be a little more open to the possibility. An adult will second-guess a situation that's happened. An adult will replay it in his or her mind and try to get a natural explanation for it. That's because we're suspicious. We don't think we're good enough, that God would actually come down to Earth or send an angel to tell us that He loves us. We kind of throw all these disclaimers into an angel experience, where a child is simply free and open.

Jesus said that you have to be like a child with your heavenly father, and what does a child do? *He loves his father.* He puts his hand in his daddy's hand and he walks with him. The word "Abba" that Jesus used in Scripture is translated as "daddy." That's the kind of relationship we're supposed to have with our father, and you find that children do. But we adults don't because we've already had so much pain in life, and maybe we haven't had a good relationship with our dads, or there's been something there that's made us miss this significance.

I learned about this when I had my own children. I looked at my children and I realized that although part of my loving them meant allowing them to reap the consequences of their own behavior, still there was nothing that my children could ever do that would make me stop loving them. Nothing. And I saw then in a little, tiny way that if I could love that intensely and that unconditionally, then God must feel that way about me, too. I could be brokenhearted over my children, I could be angry with them, but I could never stop loving them. And that's why I believe so strongly that God will do almost anything to get our attention.

Q   We've talked with so many people who have that same intense feeling of love when they're blessed by their angel or touched by their angel—that feeling of comfort, warmth, and light, a feeling beyond compare. You've had many stories told to you. Do you have a favorite angel story—other than the one with your son?

JWA   I have lots of favorites. I always say my favorite story is the one I've just heard, because I find myself gasping, but then I'll read another letter, or someone will call, or I'll be doing a radio talk show and someone will call in with a story and I'll say, "That is by far the best story I ever heard."

But I think one of my favorite stories was probably the man in white. A young woman wrote this to me after an episode with her son. They lived in Florida, and her son, who at that time was thirteen, went out to play. Their area was lightly populated, and there were a lot of snakes in the area. Children knew to be careful. Her son Mark was out with his rifle and his dog, and he somehow stepped on a huge rattlesnake; it bit him on the ankle in a main vein. Well, his mom was in the house when he staggered through the front door and fell on the floor, unconscious. As he fell he gasped, "I've been bit." That was all she had—no other knowledge. But already she saw that his ankle was two or three times its normal size. It was a terrible time getting to the hospital, but they made it. Mark lapsed into a coma, and they felt that he would lose the leg. Then they felt that they would lose him completely.

They didn't. For some strange reason he came out of the coma, and a couple of days later the doctor and the family asked him what had happened. Now, his first explanation was that he'd been bitten by this snake about two hundred to three hundred yards from the house, but the doctor said, "Oh no, you could never have been bitten that far from the house because you immediately had so much venom in you that you could not have covered that distance to get back to the house." Mark said that he hadn't walked that distance. A man in white had come and picked him up, and held him very tenderly and carried him. Now Mark was a long, lanky teenager, heavy, but this man carried him to the house and told him that he was going to be very sick, but that he would be all right. They asked Mark if he had seen the man's face, and he said no, because his cheek was on the man's shoulder. But he felt so wonderful and so loved, and he remembered that message all the time when he was trying to cope with this pain and fear in the hospital. The man had simply carried him up these thirteen steps to the house, opened up the front door—which had been locked—and deposited Mark safely in the house. I always loved that because I thought that is the essence of an angel experience: the tenderness, the comfort, the reassurance, and the protection.

Q   Did Mark ever say that he thought it could have been an angel?

JWA   Mark said that he thought it could have been Jesus. He had a rather difficult situation after that, though, because when he told people about it he was made fun of. (This was a little earlier than what has happened now with the angels.) I think if this had happened to Mark today, he would have found a very ready and a willing-to-believe audience. He was hurt by the response of others. He found this to be such a precious thing that he didn't want to have it belittled, so he stopped talking about it after a while.

Q   Why do you think that maybe ten, fifteen, twenty years ago people were not as accepting of angels as they are today?

JWA   Angels have become very "in"; they're very trendy. We have two levels going on in the country right now. We have people who are wearing angel pins and talking about angels because it's part of a trend. And that's okay, because my theory is that God will get you no matter what door you open, and maybe by wearing an angel pin you're a little more aware of heaven. That will be a helpful thing for you. But then underneath we have all the people who have always wanted to believe in something special. These people are the ones who are buying the books and beginning a tentative touching upward. I get a lot of mail from people who have not thought about things spiritual in ten to fifteen years. Maybe they were wounded as children, or given the wrong messages, or perhaps they were not cared for at all that way. And they've come into adulthood with no fixed set of principles. They flounder and they float, and they have this hunger within them, of course, as everyone does, and now, all of a sudden, angels are a way to open up the door. It's a tentative, nonrisk way to begin to touch God. Angels don't require anything of us. They just bring us love. But I believe that angels should not be the stopping point. Most people who have been touched by angels have a hurdle they have to get over. The question they ask themselves is, "Do I want to go on? Do I want to go where the angels are pointing, or am I still afraid that God will expect too much of me?" And I always want to say to them, "No, go. Because there's where all the freedom and the peace really are."

Q   You mentioned that angels are a trendy thing. We've even heard the term "angel-mania." And the demographics show that on a lot of rock-and-roll shows, people come on and speak about angels. The kids at these concerts are called Generation X. Do you think these kids are looking for something spiritual? Do they really believe, or are they just latching onto angels because that is the "in" thing to do?

JWA   I love this age group. Four of my children are still in Generation X, and I have always regarded them as being hilarious and so filled with life and fun. There have been dire prophesies for their generation, which I don't think are going to happen. But this is a group that has, on the whole, rejected organized religion. As soon as they get to college they stop going to church because Mom and Dad are no longer there to watch them and they can do without God. And yet, because things are not as well developed and spelled out for them, these kids find themselves quite a bit more in a floating mode than their older brothers and sisters who had a firmer job market. Kids who are graduating in the nineties are really at sea. For this reason they are going back into a spiritual interest a little earlier than their older brothers and sisters did.

We used to say at our church that there must be something in the water because at age thirty there would be this huge influx of people coming to sign up and get involved in church. It finally dawned on us that thirty is the age when a lot of people have a three- or four-year-old who's beginning to ask questions. "Do we believe in God, Daddy?" And all of a sudden the dad is thinking, "Gee, maybe we should get back into a church."

Q   You have five children. Did any of them come up to you when they were young—six, seven, eight years old—and say, "Mom, what's an angel?"

JWA   No, and I didn't educate them as to angels. We never had any guardian angel pictures hanging in the house or anything like that. Now I look back and see how I missed a key thing. My first four children are boys, and they were born within a five-year span, so I was very nervous; I was always waiting for someone to leap off of a roof. They were constantly getting into trouble, and they used to play a lot of jokes on me. But they had an imaginary companion—I think his name was Peter—and when I would be slinging hash out in the kitchen, getting sandwiches together, I would say to this little group of preschoolers, "Is Peter here to-day? Does Peter want a sandwich?" This was always my way of getting in on the joke, but what I never realized until just recently was that all four of them would answer in unison, "Yes, Peter is here." Or "No, Peter is not."

Now, if I had thought, I would have wondered, "How did they all know that?" They didn't confer with one another. They didn't signal behind their backs or anything. I've asked a couple of them about it today, but they have no idea what I'm talking about because, once again, most children don't remember these things as they get older. And I'm thinking, "Aw, you missed it. You weren't aware of what might have been going on."

Q If a young child did come up to you right now and asked, "What is an angel?" what would you tell them?

JWA I would say an angel is a spirit that lives with God. Angels have different roles to play. Some live in heaven and just hang around God, and others come down to Earth to help you. And when you were born God told the angels, "Take care of this child. I love this child." And that's what the angels do. So you probably have one special angel that's with you all of the time, and then you have other angels who come around you when you need some extra love or some extra help. And you don't ever have to be afraid of an angel, because they're wonderful. You may never see one with your own eyes—this is an example of what your mom and dad call "faith." Sometimes we have to believe in things without seeing them. But it's a wonderful thing to believe. You can talk to your angel your whole life and he or she will always be there for you.

Q You obviously have a great love for children.

JWA I do. I have a great heart for children at this time in history because so many have been abandoned by us. They need to know that they aren't alone. We have so many emotionally homeless children. Children who have no one to nurture them. Children who perhaps have been given a lot of material things, but there's no one there who will just talk about things with them. Many children have been sacrificed on the altar of materialism. That may sound harsh, but I don't place guilt trips on parents because of this. I think a lot of parents were emotionally homeless, too. And I'm not saying, "Gee, in my day we did things better." No, we just did as well as could be expected, and there are a lot of parents today who are doing as well as can be expected. But that still means that a lot of our children need more than they are getting.

Q   How do you feel about the fact that so many people are now asking the angels for help?

JWA   Asking is very important. Asking is a form of humility. It means that we have acknowledged that we don't have all of the answers. It was pouring rain here last night, the winds were flying around, and, of course, the first thing I did was ask the angels to surround our house with protection so that we would not be blown away. You see, in the asking I was acknowledging that I am totally powerless before a storm. My relationship with God is that He's the God and I'm just one of His children. And when you put yourself in that relationship and you ask, it's no wonder that you receive help. You've acknowledged that you're needy, and God would always respond to a needy person.

Q   So angels are coming so frequently now because more people are asking?

JWA   Yes. More people are sensing the darkness. We're sickened in our spirits over a lot of things that are going on, and yet we tolerate a lot in the name of tolerance. Things that may have been considered wrong years ago are no longer considered wrong. And yet, our spirits know. We see all the violence and all the pain, and we know there has to be an answer. And our spirits know where the answer is. Sometimes we're just not willing to take the step yet. We think that being more openly spiritual will diminish us in some way, while it actually frees us.

So angels are coming to say, "Look up. You've tried to do all of this on your own. It's not working." You can only do this up to a point, and then you have to acknowledge that God has got to do the rest.

Q   What is your favorite story of a child experiencing an angel?

JWA   One of the dearest stories in my book about children and angels hit home with me because I had a child who had learning disabilities. In those days people didn't understand it as well as they do now, and he felt as if there were something the matter with him. This story concerns a little girl who has the same problem. When she is in class her foot keeps tapping, and she can't make it stop. The teacher would say, "Stop that wiggling!" And she would say to herself, "Foot, stop tapping," and then, in a couple of minutes, it'd be bouncing back. You can just feel how hyperactive this child is. The lines in the book look squiggly to her: all the other kids can make sense out of them, but she can't. It's a form of dyslexia, but she doesn't understand that she's got a problem there. She just knows that she must be an awfully stupid person.

One day the teacher gets angry with her and sends her out of the room, and she goes over to the library. She just puts her arms down and her head down on her arms and starts to cry. She's telling herself she's stupid and ugly and all these things. And then, all of a sudden, she feels a hand on her shoulder—a little kind of a massage—and a male voice saying, "It's all right, little Laura, you'll be fine; don't worry about it." And she begins to have this infusion of strength and love and confidence. And she turns around, finally, with the tears still wet on her face, and there's not a soul in the library. But it soothes her, and she just feels that things won't be the same anymore. It does work out that way, too, because a year later, some wonderful person comes in and tests her and finds out what her problem is, and teaches her a new way to learn.

Throughout her life she never forgot that hand, the feel of

that hand. And, of course, she believes—and I do, too—that that was her guardian angel at a time when she needed him.

Q   Your stories are so moving—and so real. Do you have any others that have really meant a lot to you?

JWA   One of my all-time favorites is not a stunning story that you catch your breath over; it's a smaller story, and I like it because I think God often works in small ways, and sometimes we overlook those; we call them "coincidences." But I myself don't think there is any such thing as a coincidence.

This involved a story of a woman who, with her husband, tried to have a child, and it just wasn't happening. This woman was part of a singing group in Kansas, and they would go around and sing for different events. And the other women in the singing group started telling this woman, "When we get to the part in the program where we introduce ourselves and tell a little about ourselves, you ought to tell people that you've been trying to have a child. Ask people to pray for you." These were not religious singalongs, necessarily—they'd be doing something for a school—but this woman decided to do that. She asked everyone she met.

One day, she and her mom had driven to Kansas City to spend time with her sister, who was a student there. It had been raining all day. They had been in and out of the car all day, and every time they got out, this girl always pressed the automatic door lock because, "hey, this is Kansas City, you gotta be careful." So, at the end of the day, she pressed the door lock. At night, there was rain, all night long. The following morning it was still drizzling, so they ran across the parking lot and got into the car. As her mom got into the backseat, there was a knitted pink bootie lying on the seat. Her mom asked, "Where did this come from?" They all started reasoning about it: Could someone have put it in the car? But how could they have done that; we know you locked the door, and it was an automatic. Well, maybe someone saw it on the ground and picked it up—but how come it wasn't wet, then.

They kept sitting in the car looking at this bootie, and the woman said, "It was on the seat as if it had been placed." I loved that.

That weekend happened to be Mother's Day weekend, and she was pregnant. In fact, she had been pregnant when she went to Kansas City, but didn't know it. Nine months later, she had a daughter, of course. Because, as she said, would God have sent a pink bootie for a boy?!

I love that story because I had the image of these prayers rising from the Kansas plains, and all I could think of were all these prayers just going to heaven, all these people and, possibly, all their angels interceding for this one woman. That bootie was put there as a sign for her. That always gave me goose bumps.

Q Do you think that we're going through a major shift in consciousness, that we are attaining a higher level of vibration?

JWA Well, I wouldn't put it in those terms. Harkening back to what I said earlier about the possible chastisement or upheaval of nature and man against men, after that happens, traditionally, there is supposed to be a period of great peace, when people will live in harmony with one another. This is all very scriptural, as well as being something that the New Agers believe as well.

I think that no matter what name you call it by, it's a very real possibility. We can look back in history and see that there has always seemed to be an outpouring of angelic activity during times of great crisis, and that this leads to a better period. I hope the better period comes soon. I think we're now in the middle of the "dark time."

Q Many people think we are near the end of time—that

the final days are coming, and that the heralds are war and famine and people dying and AIDS.

JWA Yes, a plague. People can call it what they want, but at the turn of the century, I believe at least 40 percent of the people in one part of Africa will have AIDS. If this is not a plague of epidemic proportions, I don't know what is. I have heard people say, "One of the prophecies is that new strains of diseases will afflict the human race in the next few years and we will have no cure for them." We think AIDS is difficult, but there may be more. I don't say these things in a dark sort of way, because we have a promise that this is being done to call our attention. And I firmly believe that whenever our attention is called, things will stop. It may very well be that this is the age you're referring to. That may be what we are leading up to.

Q What hand do you think angels will have in it?

JWA I think the angels will be here ministering to us, protecting us in many ways. We will get through our difficulties with the assistance of the angels. I have been moved enough to ask parents to write down things that small children say about their own experiences, because I think that will be significant in years to come as a consolation or a guide. I've said to parents that we have this false-memory syndrome surfacing now, with people insisting that memories have been planted in their minds or in the minds of others. You don't want to take that chance years from now, when you bring this stuff up. So write down at the time what Johnny did, and put a date there. He probably won't remember, and you'll be able to say, "Yes, when you were eighteen months old, this is what you said and this is when you said it." This could be valuable knowledge for us.

Q Is there any way we can learn to contact our own angels?

JWA You have to remember that, at least from my perspec-

Abbott Handerson
Thayer, *Angel*, 1889.

tive, the angels are God's servants, not ours. They operate on His
timetable, at His bidding, not ours. So to me that would mean
that we could always ask them for their protection and help, but
I don't think we can contact them in the sense that we can have
them do for us what we want or have them manifest themselves
to us in a way that we choose. They do what they do on God's
authority, so our job is just to say, "If you're here, and I hope that

you are, I'd love to know that you are. Could you let me know in some way today? Could you give me a little heavenly hug and just let me know?"

Sometimes when that answer comes, it might come on a bumper sticker or a letter from a friend. Someone said recently she had lost a child—a grandchild—and she was devastated over this. And at the funeral there were pink roses all over the place. The pink roses had not been a part of the child's life, but they served as a way of saying good-bye. And for the next week or two pink roses were in people's houses, and people brought them to the grieving couple. A good year and a half later, this grandmother had a conversation with her angel and she said, "I'm still grieving a little, and I need to know that everything is okay and that you're near me and that she is well." That night, she and her husband went to dinner at a very crowded restaurant, and when they came out, theirs was the only car with a pink rose lying on its windshield. Now people would say that was coincidence, but I say she prayed, she asked, so why should we be so surprised that she was answered? And she was answered in a way only she could recognize as being from heaven.

Q What is the most important concept, the key word we have received in the presence of the angels?

JWA Hope. People today are very lonely, and they're looking for something in their life they can hold on to. And hope is what we all need. Hope that this world is not all that there is. Hope that if we hang in there and try to do what God asked us to do, that there is a plan that He sees but that we don't, and that everything is going to be okay. I'm reminded of a Dutch missionary named Corrie ten Boom who once said that our life here is like the back of a tapestry. If you've ever looked at the reverse side of a tapestry, it has all kinds of random threads in it. There are knots and stuff hanging, and the red kind of juts out and then it stops, and there's all this chaotic color. It's a mess, but when you turn it over, you see this magnificent pattern.

Well, that's the heavenly view of what's going on, but here on Earth we just see the back of the tapestry with all the confusion. Once in a while we get a little vision, but it's a little touch—like the rose on the windshield—and it doesn't last long. If we kind of go with what He's asking us to do, all of a sudden there will come a time when we will see the front of the tapestry, and it will be explained, and it will all be glorious. I have no doubt about that. None whatsoever.

Q   What do you think about the angels coming to us in our dreams?

JWA   I do get letters from people who relate angel experiences to me, and then they put a caveat on it by saying, "I know it wasn't a real experience because it happened while I was dreaming." I always tell them to go back and read their Scripture a little bit. Look at St. Joseph, the foster father of Jesus. There's no record anywhere that he ever saw an angel during his waking moments, but on three separate occasions, an angel came to him in a dream and told him just what to do: first, to marry Mary; second, to get Jesus and Mary out of the area because Herod was sending his troops to kill all the children; and third, to go home because it was safe. Those experiences were obviously all from heaven, and Scripture does not record any evidence of Joseph ever having an angelic experience while he was out plowing or working in the carpentry shop. So if they can happen to Joseph in a dream, why can't they happen to anyone else?

Q   Do you know of any contemporary instances in which an angel has come to someone in a dream?

JWA   People have said to me that angels come to them in dreams and tell them things about themselves. Many times it's an advance warning, when they feel something is going to happen.

One woman told me of a dream she had right before the family set out on a trip. They had spent a lot of time planning it all. And yet, she had a dream the night before that they got lost on an expressway and the car blew up. And she knew to turn around and unhitch her child's safety seat—it was the first thing she did—and take the child out the front door of the car. This dream repeated itself all evening. She would wake up, and then she would go back, and there was an angel in this dream that was kind of around the car.

She was exhausted by morning and now they were going to have to go on this trip. She's thinking about all this as they're driving, and all of a sudden the front of their car exploded. It burst into flames on the expressway. She turned around as if she had been programmed. She didn't think, she didn't get upset or excited. She simply turned around and unhitched the safety seat and moved out this door that, for some reason, was open. And she said that she would never have thought to do this. She would have panicked and screamed and discussed it with her husband—you know, the distracted things you do in a crisis. She knew herself well enough to know that's what she would have done. But this dream had repeated itself over and over again that night, so she was almost programmed to unsnap that baby seat and take him out through the front.

That was one of the best dream stories I've heard. A lot of them are simply consolation dreams. Some people also have dreams regarding loved ones who have died. They will come to them in a dream and say, "Look. Everything is fine. Don't mourn me anymore." One woman had a dream about a relative who said, "I have so much to do in heaven, and I can't get on with it when I feel that you're holding me in some way. So lighten up." It's just the kind of thing her aunt would have said to her. But the woman said what was so interesting about it was that the dream was so real and when she awakened, she no longer had any grief. And grief, as we all know, isn't something that ends like that. We have to work our way out of grief, and we think it's going and then it comes back. We grieve a little and then it comes back in a huge wave. So the fact that she was over this and never again thought of her aunt in anything but a marvelous way was an indication to me that this was an angel dream, even though her aunt wasn't an angel. It was a spiritual kind of thing. A dream sent from heaven.

Q Most of the stories we've heard have been about rescues from death or major catastrophe. But do angels also come to help people in quiet, unobtrusive ways?

JWA Yes. Many just come in ordinary ways. One of my favorites involves a mom who said she was at the top of a long escalator in a large shopping mall, and she was going to go down one flight. She has a child of eighteen months over her arm, and her shopping bag and her purse, and she's wearing high heels. She's pulling her three-year-old child onto the escalator. The three-year-old is afraid of the moving stairs and does not want to get on. So this is a situation ripe for disaster. In another minute, this mother would have lost her footing and fallen. She says, "All of a sudden, as I'm at the top of the flight, I saw a hand come down on my daughter's shoulder. That hand belonged to a dapper-looking gentleman of perhaps seventy, seventy-five years, in a dark suit, with white hair. He was a very well dressed, very serene sort of person. I liked him right away, and he kind of looked at me as if to say, 'I've got your daughter under control now,' and I kind of nodded back—thank you." They didn't exchange any words. This was such a short little thing, just one flight of stairs. They got to the bottom and there was a little flurry trying to get off the escalator, and she took her eyes off the gentleman for a minute. When she looked up, no one was there.

She said the mall was really empty at that time. There weren't a lot of clusters of people. He was a very significant figure in his dark suit and white hair. She should have seen him moving away. The escalator was transparent so there was no way he could have popped behind it. Then, all of a sudden, it dawned on her that her daughter had not reacted to this at all. She said, "Tammy, did you see that man behind you?"

And Tammy said, "No, Mommy."

"That man, that man with his hand on your shoulder. Didn't you see him?"

Tammy said, "No, Mommy, I didn't feel any hand on my shoulder."

And then this mother, who was very intuitive, said to me, "It was then that I realized I had been given a glimpse of Tammy's guardian angel. And the message that he was sending to me in the wordless moment was: 'As you see me now, with my hand on your child, is the way I always am. So just relax. Relax. Enjoy your children. Your job is to love your children. You cannot add one day to their lives and you cannot take away one. While you have them in your care, your job is just to love them. And we will take care of the rest.' "

This was very significant for her because she had been a nervous mother. She said it was a life-changing moment for her. And that is a story I like because it is so ordinary. God comes to us in so many ordinary moments of our lives. Angels don't always come to us with trumpets. Sometimes they come in the softest ways there are.

RABBI RICHARD M. BAROFF

Rabbi Richard M. Baroff is a rabbi of Temple Beth David in Snellville, Georgia, and president of the Atlanta Rabbinical Association. He attended George Washington University and Hebrew Union College–Jewish Institute of Religion in Jerusalem and is currently collaborating on a book concerning the relationship of Judaism and Christianity.

QUESTION   Can you describe the history of angels in the Jewish religion?

RABBI RICHARD M. BAROFF   In the Apocrypha, there was a great elaboration of the role of angels. Angels took over many of the forces of nature, of the wind and rivers, and they acted much like pagan deities. Angels acted as a buffer between us and God, who was seen as being further away from us, more transcendent. Thus we needed intermediaries, a whole edifice of intermediary beings between us and God.

On facing page:
Crypt. Père Lachaise
Cemetery, Paris.

My guess is that there's a Greek influence, which would make sense, because early Judaism was profoundly influenced by Greek culture. When you get to the period of the major commentaries, the Talmud and the Midrash—say about 200 C.E. (as Christians say A.D. 200) to about 800—angels are there and are taken for granted. There is no preoccupation with angels as there is in the Apocrypha and, to a lesser extent, in Ezekiel, Daniel, and Zaccariah. They're present in the Talmud and the Midrash, but they're just taken for granted as part of the structure of reality.

Q   What role do angels play in the various Jewish literary traditions?

RMB   In Jewish mysticism, in the Zohar particularly, there's a great deal about angels. Angels seem to reflect large-scale cosmic forces, light and darkness, good and evil, male and female. At one point, each individual is said, I believe, to have a good and bad angel with him or her at all times, and so angels are seen as part of the fabric of the universe. And they're definitely seen as a part of a giant hierarchy of both the positive and the negative sides of the cosmos. There's also a place for angels in Jewish philosophy, but here angels become more abstract. Among those medieval Jewish philosophers who follow Aristotle, angels are seen as kind of separate intelligences, celestial intelligences. As angels become more abstract, perhaps they're angels only in name.

In Jewish liturgy, in the prayer book, there's much about angels. In Chapter 6 of Isaiah, you have the seraphim, which have six wings. They come to Isaiah and say, "Holy, holy, holy is the Lord of hosts; the whole earth is full of his Glory." That's part of the daily Jewish liturgy called the Kedushah—holiness. We have a song which is normally associated with Shabbat, with the Sabbath, called Shalom Aleichem—peace unto you—which talks

Tycho Brahe,
Planisphere of the World,
ca. 16–17th c.

about ministering angels coming to us. So angels are there in Jewish liturgy as well.

Q   Do you feel that angels and the afterlife have been devalued today?

RMB   The devaluation of angels in modern times is, in my opinion, a function of the Enlightenment. The Enlightenment came to Europe, starting with Locke and Newton, and then shifting to France, particularly with Voltaire, Rousseau, Montesquieu. It was an attack on Christianity, an attack on the belief in the transcendent and the supernatural. In France, Germany, England, and to a large extent America as well, there was a movement away from the belief in this rich, almost medieval idea that angels and the afterlife have a real ontological status, that they really exist, and that you really can go up and down, from world to world, as Jacob did on the ladder.

This belief ended in the Enlightenment and people began to view the world strictly through reason. This is reflected in science and democracy—the notion that we've built a better world here on Earth and that's it. Judaism to a large extent accepted the Enlightenment because it meant some very good things for Jews. The ghetto walls were torn down by Napoleon, and Jews were able to participate in France and England and in what is now Germany, and so most Jews accepted much of the Enlightenment.

So Jews came to devalue the belief in the afterlife and the transcendent and angels, and I think that can be seen reflected in the philosophies of the conservative movement, in the reform movement, and even more in the reconstructionist movement, where this belief in the transcendent and the supernatural is, if not rejected outright, deemphasized to a very large extent. I don't think there's any question about that. That's why you don't hear much about the Jews talking about angels.

Q Did the bubonic plague that swept through Europe back in those times weaken the belief in angels or undermine the church?

RMB It has been said that the plague was one of the things that fostered the Renaissance. I think the plague was one of those seismic events that helped destroy the medieval consensus and led to the modern world.

Q How has this great shift in consciousness affected the world? Have we become richer or poorer?

RMB I think that the effect on Judaism is to take away much of its transcendence, its spirituality, its ability to exalt the Jews. In both Judaism and Christianity, there is a split between those who believe that angels and the afterlife are real and represent God's revelation to the world and those who believe that they are symbolic. I guess you could call that a difference be-

Dante, Virgil, and Those Stricken by the Plague. Manuscript illumination from Dante's *Divine Comedy,* ca. 14th c.

tween a conservative theological position and a liberal theological position. In Judaism I would say theologically most people are more on the liberal side, in that they believe that these entities or these ideas developed historically rather than represent a real being with ontological status created by God. But I do believe that within my own religion, we have to recapture the transcendent, the afterlife, God's role in our lives, and the place of angels in our lives. We must reconnect with that whole belief that there is a realm beyond this one in order for Judaism to regain its spiritual power.

Q   What would bring that about?

RMB   In Judaism, particularly, there's a belief that life can be elevated from a lower level to a higher level—to exaltation—and that spiritual lift comes from our belief in the higher life, higher realm. Judaism is about going from lower to higher, and in order for that to happen in the lives of Jews individually and collectively, I believe we have to have a sacred vision of God in a realm above us that we can rise up toward. Angels may be a part of that realm.

Q   When you say lower to higher exaltation, what exactly do you mean? What aspect of us goes from lower to higher?

RMB   It's a feeling, a psychological, emotional response to the holy. It's my theory. I'm trying to flesh it out in the introduction to the book I'm hoping to write about the afterlife—that that is the essential feeling of Judaism, the cardinal spiritual feeling. Our response to the ultimate or the holy is the sense of uplift, but for that to occur, you have to believe in a certain structure to the universe. I believe that the structure has to be beyond this world of space and time that science measures.

Q   What about the notion that you can build a big enough telescope to see God?

RMB   There are parapsychologists and other people at the fringes of science who believe that some paranormal events or beings can be measured, really measured, and it's just that we: a) don't know where to look or how to look, and b) don't have sophisticated enough equipment. But they're trying. It may be that these paranormal phenomena, including angels, are real and can be understood in scientific terms. It may be they're some kind of radiation or electricity, something like that. These beings may or may not represent a realm beyond ours, or maybe they're part of the world we know but are too ephemeral for us to measure right now. All this is possible but unproven.

Q   Is there any value in trying to measure them?

RMB   Oh yes. I think it's very important if we could prove that there are paranormal phenomena and if we could prove that these phenomena point to a transcendent realm beyond ours. That would be tremendously important as we try to chart out what it is that life is and what we're supposed to be doing, which we don't know. Those are big ifs, and I don't know if we can ever do that, or if perhaps belief in God, in angels, and in the afterlife is always a question of faith. I think it's worth giving it a shot. We really don't have much to lose—maybe a little money dragging all the equipment around—looking for ghosts or angels or auras. None of it, as far as I know, has been proven, but we have to keep an open mind—skeptical, but open—that it's possible.

Q   In my upbringing, it was always drummed into me that belief in God had to be hinged on faith. In other words, that there was really no point in trying to prove it.

RMB   I don't agree with the point of view that faith itself is the whole point. I think if you knew for sure that there was a God, that there was an afterlife, if these things could be proven—

and I'm not at all sure they can be, but if they could be—then we could amend our lives, we could change and be fuller human beings because we would have more knowledge about what the universe is and our part in it. I think that would be a good thing and a broadening thing, an ennobling thing. In other words, I am not absolutely convinced that science might not be the gateway to spirituality. It's possible. So if a few scientists are on the fringes studying the paranormal, I think it's worth the effort.

Q   These days there are a lot of people experiencing angels, going to angel classes, reading angel books. What's your feeling about that? What are they looking for? What's behind all this?

RMB   They're looking for a connection with God. It's possible that for many people, God is too awesome, too powerful, too overwhelming to come face-to-face with. God, of course, says to Moses, "Man cannot see Me face-to-face and live." I think angels, at the very least, represent a psychological need to have a buffer between us and God. That was particularly evident in the apocryphal period and in Jewish and Christian mysticism. But this need for a buffer is still true today. Remember the movie *The Bishop's Wife*? God didn't come to David Niven; Cary Grant came in the form of an angel because that's much more human. Angels are more human than God. I think that's what's going on psychologically. Now whether all this is really true and there really are angels who come representing God rather than God Himself, that I don't know. That would be interesting to find out.

Q   So it's difficult to say whether angels are a projection of the mind or an actual entity, but God is an absolute—God exists. Is that what it comes down to?

RMB   I believe that. Obviously, there are people on the left wing of theology in Christianity and in Judaism who think of God as a process or a category of mind as well. But within Jewish tradition and in all the major movements, there is a belief that God exists as a real being, the Creator of the universe, and we can reach God through prayer.

My personal belief is that God exists. My belief is that all conceptions of God are inadequate and the reality of God is beyond anything we can say or talk about or think about because human beings are finite and God is infinite, and so God may ultimately be beyond what we call being or state of being. Imminent and transcendent, all these theological categories we use to describe God are limited, but God is infinite. So the best we can do is grope toward an understanding of the holy and that's a journey, a constant journey, as we come face-to-face with God.

Q What is your definition of soul?

RMB The big question is whether the soul is an epiphenomenon of the brain, of the mind, something that comes out of the neurological complexity of human beings, or is the body a house for the soul? In Judaism, in the Bible, it looks very much like the soul and the body are intertwined, so that you can't differentiate between the soul and the body in a clear way. In rabbinical literature, the soul separates from the body after death and goes to some realm we call the Olum Habal, the afterlife. According to some, the soul comes back into the body at some point during the time of resurrection when the Messiah comes and the world is judged. The definition of the soul is a big question and I don't really have an answer to it. But my deepest instincts tell me that if there is an afterlife, then some part of us would have to separate from that part which rots in the ground and go to another place. So I would say that there is a soul within us, a spark that will leave us at the point of death and continue on.

Q   Can you explain the Jewish concept of the Shekinah?

RMB   The Shekinah is God's presence in the world among the righteous. It's sometimes considered God's feminine aspect. It might be where the Christians got the idea of the Holy Spirit residing amongst us. God is transcendent and also imminent among part of us. The Shekinah is that imminent part that dwells in our midst.

Q   Does the Shekinah appear more vividly on the Sabbath? Is this a time of welcoming or recognizing it?

RMB   The Sabbath is considered a bride that comes to us, and that's related to this whole idea of Shekinah. Spiritual life is amplified at the time of Shabbat—at the time of the Sabbath—as we welcome the Sabbath bride amongst us. It is a time when we communicate with God on a more intimate level than during the rest of the week.

Q   Could you translate "Shalom Aleichem"? How does this apply to angels?

RMB   It means, "Peace unto you" (which refers to the angels of peace). It's a song we sing on the eve of Shabbat. I believe it has to do with the ministering angels coming to us. It is an aspect of this whole spiritual amplification which is part of the Sabbath.

Q   Is there something angels want from us? Do we owe them something?

RMB   In Judaism, angels represent a supernatural force which is in some ways greater than human beings but, in some ways, ironically less than being human. They're not flesh and blood and they don't live as fully as we do. In Judaism, they don't really have minds of their own so much as they just represent God's will in an intimate way, in a scaled-down way, so we don't have to see God face-to-face. We can reach God through this messenger. I don't think we owe anything to angels. We owe allegiance to God, and to try to the extent that we're able—the limited extent that we're able—to make the world a little warmer, a little kinder than it would be otherwise.

$\mathscr{A}$ $\mathscr{T}$ransformation
of the $\mathscr{S}$pirit

MELISSA DEAL FORTH

On January 6 of 1981, my husband, Chris Deal, was diagnosed with acute lymphatic leukemia. At the time, we were living in Nashville.

He had started getting ill before Thanksgiving, in 1980. He was a session musician and they played odd hours all the time—their sessions would go on well into the middle of the night. He got in this habit where he started to take naps. He would come home and fall asleep before I could even cook dinner; he was sleeping all the time.

This was strange because Chris was very athletic; he would run five miles a day, but now he just slept, and he began to run a low-grade fever. I tried to get him to go to the doctor, but he wouldn't; he kept putting it off, saying, "Let's wait until after the holidays; it's no big deal."

I believe that Chris knew he was very ill; I think that he knew that it was serious and wanted to wait until the holidays were over so *as not to darken our holidays. I finally convinced him in January to go and see a doctor. We went in to see a general practitioner for a checkup, and I waited for an hour, then two. It was over four and a half hours before I saw him again. I knew that something terrible was going on. When Chris came out, the doctor was with him. The doctor told me then that Chris's white cell count was extremely high and that they suspected leukemia. My heart fell immediately. Chris went to the hospital for more tests, and, indeed, he was diagnosed with acute lymphatic leukemia.*

We were told the only way he could survive was with a bone-marrow transplant, so we went to M. D. Anderson, the cancer hospital in Houston, Texas. Back then (in 1981), they would not do bone-marrow transplants unless you were in remission (I understand that now they do so). We had a perfect match in his brother, so basically we were waiting to get Chris back in remission. They were bombarding him with all kinds of chemotherapy trying to get him back, but he would not come back. Several months passed and he became weaker and weaker; it just really turned into a downhill situation for him. It was pretty obvious he was losing the battle.

His room was on the eleventh floor, which was the leukemia floor of M. D. Anderson. The nurses' station is an island in the middle of a round ward. This is so the nurses can see all the patients all the time. Chris had just finished another series of chemotherapy, and his body was really in terrible shape. He was not eating, he slept a lot, he was under a lot of stress, and he was very depressed. He had to have help to just go to the bathroom. After the chemotherapy series, they bombard you with vitamins and a lot of other things to try to keep your body going. At this particular time Chris was connected to two IV poles on either side of his bed. On January 4, 1982, I was sleeping in my cot next to Chris's bed; when laid out for the night, my cot was about eight inches away from his. I was awakened at 3:00 A.M. by a nurse who was shaking me and saying, "We cannot find Chris." She was very upset. I couldn't believe Chris was gone. I was very confused, and I panicked. I jumped up, took off down the hall, and instinctively ran toward the elevators, looking for Chris. All of a sudden I looked and saw the chapel. The chapels are on each floor at M. D. Anderson and they are very small—about the size of a large walk-in closet. There were three rows of chairs on either side with an altar at the back wall, and there's a long glass pane at the entrance to the chapel. I went to the glass pane and looked in. There was Chris and he was sitting with a young man. They were sitting across from each other, knee to knee, and they were talking. I couldn't believe it. I thought, first of all, how did he get his IV poles past me and around the nurses' station without being seen? It was also unusual because I usually sleep, as anyone with a loved one in these situations does, with one eye open; I was up if a pin dropped. But I must have slept as if I were in a coma; he managed to get out of that room with two IV poles and not wake me up!

So I couldn't believe he was in there talking to this guy; it was so strange. I opened the door, walked in, and said, "Chris, where have you been? I was so afraid!" And he looked up at me and he was so calm. He said, "It's okay, Melissa, I'm okay. You need to go back to the room." I said, "Chris, what's going on? Where have you been? Everybody's upset; you scared everybody to death!" Just as calmly as could be, he said again, "Melissa, it's okay; you can go back to the room. I'll be back soon; don't worry."

In the meantime, I'm looking at this young man he's sitting across from. Where did he come from at three o'clock in the morning? What was he doing there? I had never seen him before. When I first looked at him, he looked down at the ground, like he didn't want to make eye contact. Immediately I began to check him out, because I was worried; I didn't know if he was dangerous. I noticed that his hands were white and transparent. At one point he did turn and look up at me. Our eyes caught. The only way I can describe his eyes is like ice blue, like huskies', but even clearer than that; he had this light in his eyes. But I wasn't frightened by them. I was mesmerized by them. Then he looked straight through me—no expression on his face. His skin was so white, almost transparent, and there was not one line on his face. I couldn't take my eyes off of him. He looked like a youth, like a teenager, but there was some wisdom, something old about him. The look and the feel that I got off him were not the same.

Then I started really looking at his clothes, and I realized he had on a flannel shirt, Levi's, and lace-up work boots. Chris was a musician, and this was an attire that he wore a lot, and I think, in an odd way, this man was trying to dress in a way that would make Chris feel comfortable. The odd part about his clothes was that they were all brand-new—like they had just come off the shelf. They even had wrinkles in them.

At this point, Chris interrupted us, because I was just standing there, mesmerized by this guy. Chris looked at me again and said, "Please, Melissa, please go back to the room. I'm okay. I'll be back soon." I said, "Are you sure?" and he said, "I'm sure." I was reluctant, but I could tell he really wanted me to leave, so I did. I went back to the nurses' station and told the nurses that I had found Chris in the chapel. They were very relieved. Then I went back to his room and sat on his bed and just waited for him.

I sat there a long time until, about thirty minutes later, he comes. He's got hold of his poles, he's walking by himself, he's smiling, he's energetic, he's strong; it was unbelievable. This man had gone to bed not being able to get up—and yet here he comes, rolling two poles down the hall, smiling. I can't take my eyes off of him; the man that I had fallen asleep with and the man that came into the room were not the same man. When I had seen him before he went to bed, he was a man carrying around the weight of a terminal illness. He was someone who was extremely depressed and his body was physically wiped out by all the medicine they were bombarding him with. The man that came back into the room after he had been to the chapel was like the young healthy man I had married. He had changed.

I asked, "Who was that guy?" He said, "You're never going to believe me," and I said, "Yes, I will." He said, "He was an angel."

"An angel?"

"Yeah, he was my guardian angel."

He told me—these were his very words—that I was "put to sleep" and he was "called." He said he just jerked awake in his room and had this overpowering feeling to go to the chapel. So he just got up and went. He was spiritual, so I'm sure at points he prayed, but religion was not something we ever talked about. In the chapel, he kneeled down and started praying. The next thing he knew, he heard this voice say, "Are you Chris Deal?" He turned around and that young man was standing there. He said, "Yes, I am."

And the young man said, "Well, I've come to talk to you." The young man or the angel asked him if he had anything he wanted to be forgiven for, and Chris said yes. He wanted to be forgiven for hating his stepfather. He had had a really rough childhood with his stepfather, but he just didn't want to take that hate with him. So the angel told Chris, "Well, you have been forgiven."

Chris was worried about me, and the angel told Chris not to be worried, that I was going to be fine. That was the word he used—fine. They talked about things in there that Chris didn't share with me; he said he'd rather not discuss them. Evidently a lot of conversation went on that he wouldn't tell me about. He did say that the angel asked him if he wanted to say the Rosary together. He had never told the angel that he was Catholic; the angel just knew. So they said the Rosary together, prayed together, and then Chris left.

At this point, I jumped up and took off down the hall; I wanted to get another look at this guy. But he's not in the chapel, he's not any-where on the eleventh floor. I go down the elevator. Being a nuclear, experimental hospital, M. D. Anderson has real heavy security. Family members have to carry an ID card to get in and out of the hospital after nine o'clock at night. I went down the stairs and there was a security guard at the elevator. I described this young man to him and asked, "Did this guy come down?" He said no, he hadn't seen anybody like that all night. Well, I went back up to the eleventh floor and back to the room, and I told Chris, "No one's seen him; maybe he got off on another floor."

Well, Chris just busted out laughing, like, "Okay, Melissa, if that makes you feel better."

Anyway, that night he slept sounder, more peacefully than he had slept in months and months and months. Two days later he died—one year to the day after he was diagnosed. But I spent those two days that we had left with the healthy Chris. Chris had returned to himself. He was smiling, he was eating, he was laughing, he was telling jokes, he was visiting other patients in the ward. It was like he was not sick at all. He had this unbelievable energy; it was like all the weight of the ter-minal illness was gone. Everything had changed, other than the fact that we were in a hospital; that was the only thing that made us realize that he was sick. He was like he had been when I first married him. It was an unbelievable transformation. When he died two days later, I believe that though Chris's physical body did not survive, his spiritual body was healed. Whatever journey or adventure he was on the threshold of, he really went into it whole, strong, and ready for it. Chris was totally free of all fear, of all pain. Whatever went down in that room that he didn't tell me about, whatever that angel told him or showed him, it took away the pain, it took away the fear. This was a miracle of a different kind.

To all of us, death is so scary because it's final, it's over, it's the end. But that angel gave Chris something that totally changed him, that totally transcended the illness of his body and the depression of his mind.

It was a total transformation of the spirit. He saw something in the future for him that must have been wonderful.

And I've gone on not worrying about Chris; I've been able to go on in life knowing that he still exists, that he is still out there, that he's still . . . alive.

JOAN BORYSENKO, PH.D.

Joan Borysenko, Ph.D., is cofounder and president of Mind/Body Health Sciences, Inc., Boulder, Colorado, and the bestselling author of numerous articles and books including Minding the Body, Mending the Mind, *and* Fire in the Soul: A New Psychology of Spiritual Optimism, *and* The Power of the Mind to Heal. *She received her Ph.D. from Harvard Medical School, and cofounded the Mind/Body Clinic of the New England Deaconess Hospital. One of the architects of the new medical synthesis called psychoneuroimmunology, Borysenko is a cell biologist, a licensed psychologist, and an instructor in yoga and meditation.*

QUESTION   In one of your books, you tell a wonderful story of a woman who prayed for healing. Can you talk about the deeper significance of this?

JOAN BORYSENKO   Through the years that I've worked

On facing page:
Agostino di Duccio,
*Angel of the
Annunciation.*

with people who are sick and people who are dying, I've heard a lot of remarkable stories. Many of them have involved a story of light. People lying in bed at night will typically have a light come to them—often a light in the doorway that will ask their permission to enter the room—and then proceed to bring about a physical or emotional healing. Author Melvin Morse told a story in one of his books about a woman who had been diagnosed with cancer, a nonserious form of skin cancer, but to many people cancer is cancer and always sounds serious. So she went to bed in a moment of terrible panic and terror. As she was lying there in bed, indeed a light came to the door and she said to herself, "Oh, I know I'm in the presence of something holy." She figured this was a great opportunity to pray, and she did. She prayed for the cancer to be removed. And the light spoke to her and said, "Hey, essentially what you usually think of as praying is more like complaining. If you really want to pray, think of your own worst enemy and send to that person the kind of light and love that you're experiencing yourself right now."

I love this story. She did that. She sent this tremendous light and love out from her mind to her own worst enemy and she said she felt it bounce back at her like it was a mirror. And so, that sense of light and love was magnified a thousandfold, as if all her entire being was really on fire. She found herself laughing and crying and that's when the light said, "Ah, now you've prayed for the first time."

Now when she got up the next morning to go in for surgery, a remarkable miracle had happened—the cancer had disappeared, there was nothing there to remove.

Q   What about the feeling of interconnectedness?

JB   Through the years, people have related, oh, five hundred or six hundred near-death experiences to me. When people come back out of that experience of light, they'll often say that they have a sense that everything is interconnected. In some way that's hard to put into words, we're all the same. We all share one mind. And it doesn't stop with people, it has to do, too, with trees and plants and living things.

One fellow in particular said that when he came back after he'd had a heart attack, he realized for the first time what it was to be happy. And he said happiness consists, number one, of recognizing that everything is interconnected. Everything in this universe is dependent on something else. And if you send out

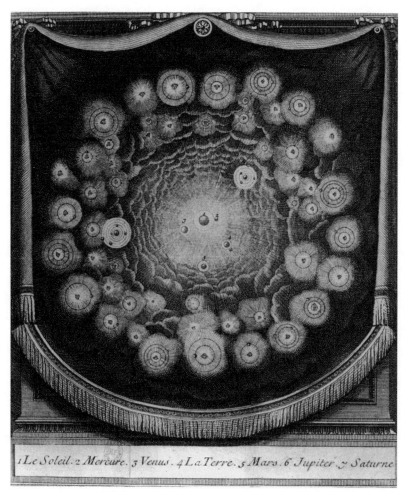

1 Le Soleil. 2 Mercure. 3 Venus. 4 La Terre. 5 Mars. 6 Jupiter. 7 Saturne

Fontenelle, *The Solar System*, 18th c.

love along those connections—if you truly see and acknowledge the beauty of the tree, or truly see and acknowledge the beauty of another person—then that love you send out is what you feel internally as happiness.

Q Does your scientific training and educational background clash with what you're saying about interconnectedness and experiences of light?

JB My training as a scientist has been a wonderful background for me. One thing I've learned from being a scientist is that life is extraordinarily beautiful and well ordered. It's given me a sense of tremendous awe when I look down an electron microscope and I see the structure of the cell and it looks like a solar system. It's like the old spiritual wisdom, "as above, so below."

My training as a scientist has taught me to continue to have an open mind and to look around and say, "What are the unexplained things that I might be able to get some sense of explanation for?" A scientist is somebody who approaches life with a sense of mystery and a sense of wonder. And for me, when I left the laboratory and began to work more with patients, particularly people who were critically ill, there were many unanswered questions. Questions like, why, given the same illness, does one person die very quickly and another person live ten or fifteen years beyond their prognosis? What makes the difference? That to me is a mystery.

And it led me into looking at the mind/body connection and matters of spirit. When people started to tell me, "Gee, I was prayed for by my prayer group; I think that might have had to do with my healing," or somebody came back from Lourdes and had experienced a miracle, my sense was, well, this is not antiscientific. This is a great opportunity to see what science can bring to bear on some of the oldest mysteries that have intrigued humankind.

You can study prayer scientifically . . . there have been some great studies. One of the most commonly cited ones was done by a cardiovascular specialist, Dr. Randolph Byrd at the University of San Francisco. He studied four hundred people who had had heart attacks who were assigned by a computer either to be prayed for while they were in the intensive care unit or just have regular intensive care. They didn't know they were being prayed for, and the staff didn't know they were being prayed for, so it wasn't the placebo effect. And at the end of the study the prayed-for group had done significantly better. They had fewer cardiac arrests and fewer cases of fluid collecting in the lungs and fewer deaths. So here's a case where something that seems intuitively right to some people can be validated by science.

There are other cases where that may not be so. I have had many patients who've had experiences of light and have had physical or emotional healings that stem from those experiences. There's no way that science can possibly study these things. And so are we to say they're unscientific because there's no method? No. I think these things stand on their own, and the final judge of their utility is whether they've helped the person to become more loving, more whole, more functional in some way, and we don't need science to prove that.

One experience that I had which science will never be able to validate concerns the death of my mother. The night that she was dying I was sitting by her bedside in the hospital. It was about three in the morning. My son Justin, who was twenty at the time, was sitting on the opposite side of the bed. We'd both been meditating and praying for my mother and the room was very still.

Suddenly, I had a vision—and believe me, I'm not the sort of person who's prone to visions. And in that vision I was a pregnant mother giving birth to a baby, but I was also simultaneously the baby. That's an amazing thing: to find yourself conscious of being two people at once. And as the baby, I was coming out through a dark tunnel, and I came out into an experience of ineffable light—just like the light that people talk about when they have a near-death experience. And in that moment, my entire life with my mother made sense, and it seemed perfect that she had birthed me into this world, and it seemed that I had just birthed her soul back out of the world. And I felt such gratitude for her.

When I opened my eyes, the room was literally filled with light. You could see it. You could see particles of light. And I looked across the bed and there was my son weeping, tears just pouring from his eyes. And he looked at me and he said, "Can you see the light in the room?" And I nodded and he said, "It's Grandma; she's holding open the door to eternity for us so that we can have a glimpse."

Now, you take an experience like this; what is science going to say? When a person has an inner experience that's transformative, we don't need any proof to know that that experience had a validity to it.

Q   Is it possible to describe what a "direct experience of the sacred" is?

JB   When people try to describe the direct experience of the sacred, the first thing they say is, "This is indescribable." There aren't any words for it. After having heard so many near-death experiences and other experiences of light that people have had, I've gone on to have four experiences of light personally. And all I can tell you is that it's indescribable—but I'll try.

In the case of a light experience, you feel that a living light which is warm and is created totally of wisdom and of love is shining at the same time from somewhere beyond you but also is coming out of you, is coming out of your own heart. And you feel bathed in a sense of mercy and compassion and forgiveness and tremendous wisdom. Somehow you feel, "Oh, everything does make sense," and anything you think of when you're in an experience of light somehow seems to fit into a larger whole—even the frightening or difficult experiences you might have had and not been able to understand before. Everything falls into place, everything makes sense, and you know that the universe is really benevolent.

Q   When you speak of an experience of light, are you really speaking of an angelic encounter?

JB   Over the past five years, there's been a resurgence of interest in angels and of people having experiences that they ascribe to the angelic. And my own sense, when I've talked to people about this, is that they appear in different ways.

Oftentimes people will say what they see in an angelic experience is a kind of swirling light, a sense of light, but more than that, there's a particular feeling, a physical feeling, almost of being enfolded or enveloped in wings, a sense of being directly comforted. Sometimes it is a brush along the body—or more a sense of having fallen into a state of grace. It's a feeling that you're no longer alone in the room but that you're being spoken to or cared for or looked after.

Q   Is there a difference between our higher selves and what we refer to as angels?

JB   Nobody really knows what an angel is. At some level the Buddhists tell you that everything you see around you is a projection of your own consciousness, so that all of the angels and all of the devils are there in you, but projected outward. Other people would say, "Ah, no, they have a reality that is independent." The truth is, I don't think we can answer that question.

It fascinates me now that modern psychology and the ancient wisdom through many spiritual traditions have come together in a description of the higher self. For example, we know that many people who were severely abused will form multiple personalities. They'll literally learn to become beside themselves when they're traumatized as children and disassociate from what's going on.

Several years ago, a psychiatrist by the name of Ralph Allison was treating multiples by regressing them hypnotically to the source of the trauma. And he'd find that each personality would tell you the story of how it was born, how it came into being. But there was always one personality that had a distinctly different story to tell. It would say things like, "I have been with the person from before the time that they were born and I will remain with them after they die." And frequently it described itself as a conduit for higher wisdom or even as a channel for the love of God. Regardless of the person's religious beliefs, or lack of them, the description would be the same.

When I read Allison's description, I said, "Wow, that sounds exactly like the *Upanishads*." Some of the old wisdom traditions of the East say that within each one of us there is a core self, a higher self, and this self is in fact birthless and deathless, and regardless of what happens to us in our lives it can never be sullied. It can never be dirtied. It cannot be cut by the knife or crushed by the rock. The Buddhists have a phrase for this, too; they call it one's *rigpa*, your own true nature, and they say it's like a mirror—it reflects the fantasy and the spectacle of life but itself remains completely pure.

And I think that is what people come across when they have the near-death experience. They find the purity of their soul, which is there behind all of the difficulties that they have experienced in this lifetime.

Q So, the soul might just be another word for the higher self?

JB I would say that the soul and the higher self certainly seem to be the same thing.

Q We've spoken about light and angels—but what about darkness? Does darkness also figure in the higher self?

JB We're a country, in general, that loves good stories. We love happy endings, we love the stories of light, but we like to re-press the darkness. It's very one-sided, I think. Jung had a great quote; he said, "You don't get enlightened by imagining figures of light. Essentially, the way to enlightenment is to go back out through the darkness." And I think this is true. You don't get to the point where you even come to recognize what happiness is—that it's something internal, not something that comes from the outside—until you go through a period of darkness.

One thing that I really appreciated in the years that I ran a mind/body clinic and the years that I saw weekly dozens of people with cancer, dozens of people with AIDS, was they were going through a real dark night of the soul. Suddenly the bottom of life had dropped out from under them, and when that happens, you come face-to-face with the big questions: Who am I; what is the meaning of life; what is a life well lived? Usually it isn't until we get to that really dark moment that we ask these big questions. We're too busy making a living and getting on with our lives. And generally, in that moment, people will either say, "I'm a happy person. I've come to some kind of peace inside myself," or they'll say, "I now recognize that my priorities weren't quite right, that I don't know what it is to have peace of mind." And through that darkness they'll then begin to ask, "What do I need to do in my life to heal? Is there forgiveness that needs to happen? What's important to me?"

People often say that what they recognize as most important at the time of darkness were the three F's: their faith, coming to peace with what their idea of God was, their soul, the universe; their family; and their friends, because that's where the love is—it's within relationships. And that's where the light comes in, but not until we face the fragmentation that may be in our family of origin, the fragmentation that we feel about not loving ourselves. That's the value of darkness: it puts us face-to-face with what needs healing in our lives.

Most people's lives are ruled by fear, but we don't want to get in touch with it. People often will do everything they can to repress the gnawing sense of fear and anxiety. For years, the biggest-selling drug in this country was Valium, and, in fact, all of our pharmaceutical dollars really go largely into producing drugs that are antianxiety and antidepression—that have to do with helping us live with the fear intrinsic in being human. Unfortunately, most people would rather take a drug, take a drink, go to the refrigerator, do *anything* to distract themselves from taking a look at the roots of the fear that they're feeling and how it can lead them to grow.

I found that for me personally, and for many people, fear has been one of the greatest teachers. It's only when we get to the point of being really uncomfortable and not running from it anymore that we find, "This is what needs healing in my life"; this is the way that we transform ourselves and transform our culture.

Q What is your perception of the existence of goodness and evil?

JB The existence of good and evil is one of the most intriguing quandaries that humankind has ever grappled with. If God is all-good, all-benevolent, all-powerful, is evil a force distinct from God? Or is evil in fact created by God somehow or other to help us to grow, to train us in wisdom? These are the unanswerable questions of theology, the fascinating questions.

I think there's no doubt that evil exists. All you have to do is look around the world; every time there's a holocaust, that's evil in action. Every time you see greed and exploitation where people's rights are taken away, that's evil in action. Whether or not some greater good accrues to somebody's soul because of this, I think evil is an absolute fact and cannot be overlooked. My own sense, though, is that everything in the universe has a balance: without above, there's no below; without male, there's no female; without your right hand, there's no left hand; without good, there is no evil. There are many teaching stories that Joseph Campbell used to tell about good and evil, about God and the devil, about one needing the other in order for the "great drama to unfold." I do agree at some level. But at another level, we have to be aware of evil and to be aware that each of us daily makes the choice moment by moment for love or for fear, to do good or to do evil, to try to seek for wisdom or to remain in ignorance. And that has to drive our search for goodness—that personal sense of wanting to find the best within ourselves.

Sandro Botticelli, *Annunciation*. Detail of the Virgin, 1489–1490.

Q   Can you describe your personal sense of God?

JB   My own personal experience of God is very much like that of the medieval Christian mystic Mechthild of Magdeburg. What she said essentially is that her experience of God was a great paradox. That, on the one hand, God is a great impersonal mystery; it's all that is, everything that's formed. And, on the other hand, the experience of God is uniquely personal, uniquely intimate.

That's my own experience. On the one hand I think of God as so much beyond my understanding, so mysterious, that I appreciate God mostly in the little things—like my grandson's smile, or a flower that's unfolding, or the way that the stars are arranged in the sky. I think with great awe, "What an amazing thing this mystery is—through which everything was created." And that impersonal mysterious sense is very important to me.

On the other hand, I have a very intimate, personal relationship with the divine in a number of aspects or forms. I have a very personal connection to Jesus, which is very interesting for a Jewish woman. People often do forget that Jesus was a great rabbi—that we do have a Judeo-Christian religion. And I have an enormous sense of closeness to Mary. To me, Mary is the divine-feminine. And so I might pray to Mary and use a particular form of prayer that comes actually from Tibetan Buddhist practice. I would, in a personal sense, see that personification of God before me and feel myself drenched in the light of God and cleansed by the light of God. Eventually I feel myself merging with that in a very personal sense. So, that's it: both intimate and mysterious.

Q   Can you return for a moment to the dark side, the shadow side of the human soul?

JB   Author and poet Robert Bly had a great metaphor that I love. He said, "We are born as 360-degree balls of radiance, and then we come and we give this great gift to our parents, and they look at us and they say, 'I didn't want that, I wanted a nice little girl, or a nice little boy.'" That, he said, is the "first act of the human drama." All the things about our uniqueness that either our parents don't like, or society doesn't like, or our teachers, our peers, our clergy don't like get pushed off into our shadow. Bly calls the shadow "that long bag that we drag behind us containing all the discarded parts of ourselves that somebody said weren't good enough."

And what happens is that for most of us, all of that doesn't get looked at. It kind of composts there in the bag and it builds up a head of steam. That head of steam is what we hear in our minds as the self-critical judgmental voice that's always saying,

"You could have done that better, you're not good enough"—the voice of unworthiness.

Part of healing is going back and owning the part of us that's the shadow, owning the part of us that's the darkness, and recognizing that most of our creativity, most of those underground forces of our subconscious, are there in the bag. To empty that bag again is to become an authentic and whole, healed human being. Bly puts it beautifully; he says it "takes us until we're about twenty to load up all of our stuff in the bag, and it takes the rest of our life to empty it out again."

Q What about the "Angel of Darkness" and the story of Satan's fall? Do these still live as vital metaphors?

JB Just as there are many stories of creation, the way that God created the earth, there are also many stories of Satan's fall from the light. There are maybe seven different stories, in fact, of how Satan fell. My sense is that they're all great metaphors for ourselves—how do we fall into darkness?

We all do have that higher self, that core self, that's been described by psychology and philosophy. When we're in it, we feel totally connected with the moment—we're so wise, we're so loving, our hearts are compassionate. But the fact is that most of us are not in that part of ourselves very often. We tend to spend most of our lives behind various masks that we learn to put on so that we'd be pleasing to Mother, or pleasing to Father, or pleasing to Teacher. We forget who we really are. We lose our authenticity. We fall from the grace of our own brightness into some far more limited version of who we really are. So each one of us undergoes a personal kind of fall, if you will, into darkness. And all of our lives, we're tempted by our own darkness. We're tempted because it's familiar, because it's comfortable. It's hard to move into the light, it's hard to heal, because to do that, old pain comes up. You have to reevaluate your beliefs, reevaluate your life. And that is one of the old roles of Satan: Satan is the tester of souls. So, if Satan is the darkness within ourselves, it's also part of our salvation.

For example, the word *Satan* in Hebrew actually means "the adversary"; it's only used about four times in the Old Testament to mean "an actual being with dark purposes." In a certain sense I would say that all of the darkness, all of the difficulties of our life are testings by the adversary, testings by that part of the universe that wants us to wake up and become self-aware. This may not be evil in any sense, but it certainly makes us stop and ask the big questions.

Q   Each day you make contact with one of the angels. Can you tell us how you do that?

JB   My own practice of meditation is informed in part by Jewish mysticism. And Jewish mysticism has a belief in the angels. I grew up Jewish and I never knew that Jews believed in angels. My Catholic friends had guardian angels—my Jewish friends, no angels. Several years ago I was leading a women's retreat, which started on a Friday night. And I thought, "Let's welcome in the Sabbath." In Judaism, when you welcome the Sabbath, you're welcoming the Shekinah, the feminine principle of God. And there's a song that one sings called "Shalom Aleichem/Welcome to Peace." As I researched this, I found it was a song of welcome to the angels—which come in to help you keep the Sabbath, to protect you for this holy twenty-four hours during which you pull yourself out of the world and you come in to the "divine presence." And so I found an old meditation which really changed my spiritual practice.

It has to do with the invocation of the four archangels: Uriel, Gabriel, Raphael, and Michael. And, first of all, I want to say that oftentimes when you talk about angels, people go, "Oh damn, they're all men, the patriarchy has taken over again here." But in Hebrew, those names are neither masculine nor feminine—they're all aspects of God. Uriel—*ur*, in Hebrew—means "fire." And you invoke this as it comes up in the east. So, if I am facing east, as you would in prayer, I invoke Uriel in the space in front of me. The fire of God is all about clarity, so I'll ask Uriel, "Please give me clarity in this day. How can I best be of service?" Or, if I'm going through some problems, I'll ask specifically for clarity on that problem.

Then I'll move to my right, which would be south, and the angel of the south is Gabriel. Gabriel in Hebrew means "the strength of God," particularly the strength to face and overcome one's fears. And so I'll think, "What are my fears and where do I need strength?"; and I'll ask for Gabriel's help.

To my western side, in the back of me, I invoke the angel Raphael. In Hebrew, Raphael means "the healer of God." And the west is the gate of death and rebirth—this is very much like the "medicine wheel" of Native American culture. And the guardian of the western gates is Raphael. So if there's particular healing I need—physical healing or emotional healing—I'll ask Raphael for that. But I'll also think about what's dying away in my life so that something new can be born, and I'll ask for illumination or help about that thing.

The last angel would be directly to my left and that's the northern side and that's Michael. In Hebrew, Michael means "how like unto God" and is the energy of wisdom and of love. In the Native American tradition, the north is "the great frozen lakes of winter." You look in that lake and it allows you to have a mirror of your life—to get insight on the meaning of your life, to reflect deeply on things. So that's what I'll do: spend a moment or two reflecting on my life, and if there's something I really feel I need some more insight on, or true wisdom about, I will ask for the help of Michael.

The last part of the ancient Jewish practice is that after the invocation of the four angels, one is supposed to imagine the light of the Shekinah, the "divine principle of God," and that is everything created by the feminine, the nurturing, the womblike aspect of God. And you imagine that washing over you— washing over you and pouring through you. As all my own negativity and doubt wash away, I imagine my heart becoming lighter and lighter and lighter and expanding to encase me in an egg of light, which interweaves with the light of the divine. That's how I start my meditation every morning, and then I just sit in that divine presence for a period of time afterward as the bulk of my meditation.

Q Are you aware of angelic presence throughout the day?

JB Definitely. And let me tell you, I was surprised by this initially. I started to do this practice and almost immediately I became aware of presences around the different sides of my body during the day. I'm frequently aware of the presence of Michael to my left, and I find particularly, if somebody says something in conversation that I should really take note of—or if I'm reading something that I should really take note of—I feel almost not a tapping on my shoulder, but a sense of the presence moving really closer, a sense of "pay attention!" And when I find myself afraid of something, some old fear coming up, I'll consciously call upon Gabriel. Or if I find that I am totally confused, I'll call upon Uriel. Or if I feel that I'm emotionally ragged, or if I have a headache, I'll call upon Raphael. It has become a very important part of my daily life.

Q Could you comment on mysticism in the light of science?

JB   The question of how science interfaces with mysticism is a fascinating one, and people usually bring up quantum mechanics and Einstein's theories. This chair that I'm sitting on, for example, sure does look solid, but the fact of the matter is that the space between the atoms in this chair is much larger than the atoms themselves. It's like the distance between the earth and the sun. Between every atom in this chair, I'm sitting on space. In fact, if you were really to go one step further, all of those little atoms are just made of light. I'm just sort of sitting on a small mass of light here. So that's one reality. We talk about what is scientifically observable to the naked eye or even to our measuring instrument, but we see "but through a glass darkly." What seems to us to be observable and experiential really is a very different matter from what it seems to be.

Oftentimes, mystics will tell you that they actually would see this as a mass of energy. When Buddhist scholars look at quantum mechanics, they tend to go, "Aha, aha, this is what we've been saying all the time. Phenomena are all interdependent." What looked to be isolated phenomena at an energetic level aren't isolated at all. Everything's related to everything else. On the other hand, I think you can take this too far. I don't think necessarily that quantum mechanics proves mysticism. But what fascinates me most is that many of the very fine physicists, after a while, talk like mystics. They begin to become mystics. Take a look at Einstein, for example; he had the most wonderful things to say. For one, he said the idea that we are separate from one another is an "optical delusion of our consciousness." Is that Einstein the scientist speaking, or Einstein the mystic speaking? In a certain sense, they do converge.

There does seem to be a neurophysiological basis for mystical experiences. For example, there's a part of the brain called the right temporal lobe. People who have temporal-lobe epilepsy will often have mystical experiences. They'll have light experiences. Oftentimes they'll have spontaneous discharges of energy in their body and might even find themselves taking certain yoga poses that they'd never even heard of before because their bodies naturally will move into that position. It is likely that some of the great mystics might have had temporal-lobe epilepsy.

Near-death experiences also seem to be mediated in this part of the brain. Neurophysiology doesn't mean we can reduce everything to, "Oh, gee, these things are meaningless discharges of our neurons." There's a group of scientists who have tried to say, "A near-death experience is nothing; it's essentially a discharge of dying brain cells." The fact is, anything we experience is bound to have a biological substratum, but I don't think it ends there. For example, many people who've had the near-death experience, when they feel this great sense of peace and then they separate from their body, suddenly they'll find themselves at a distant site. They'll be able to see what their family is doing at home, for example. And if the family is queried later, you can validate that the person actually did see what was going on at a distance. So in addition to something going on in the physical body, something's going on *out* of the body, too. So, yes, there's a circuit board for mysticism, and we have to be careful not to reduce mystical experiences to biochemistry.

Q Are we programmed before birth to be prepared for the near-death experience?

JB The fact that we have this area in our brain that predisposes us to mystical experiences is important for a number of reasons. First of all, having mystical experiences talked about in our culture is quite a new thing. Up until about a decade ago, people didn't tend to share their light experiences or their mystical experiences. Now there have been so many more of them because we have great technology. We can resuscitate dying people and they come back and they tell us what happened. Somewhere between eight and twelve million Americans—about one in twenty people—have had a near-death experience. What these experiences do for the people is make them think about the meaning of life, and truly give credence to the old adage that "we are not human beings who are having an occasional spiritual experience, but we're spiritual beings who at this moment happen to be having a human experience." And as more people report this, it sets up the culture in general to think in a more spiritual way. So I think it's very important that those experiences are there and those experiences are shared.

In terms of further meaning, there's one school of scientists who actually believe we're evolving as a species and that our whole body is shifting—particularly that area of our brain that mediates mystical experience—so that more and more people are having this experience. As that happens, and as we begin to take responsibility for being spiritual beings, I think what we'll see is a lot less violence in our culture and society, and a lot more interest in healing our wounds so that we can truly be of service to other people and express more loving-kindness to ourselves and to others. So there's a reason for all of these shifts taking place.

Q Please comment on the expression, the "joyous nature of death."

JB Our culture, as many Western cultures, has avoided death. There's fear of death. You know, I've been in the medical profession for many, many years. The medical profession views death as an enemy. Somebody dies and this means there has been a failure. So oftentimes, right around the time of death, doctors and nurses don't even come into the room of the patient. They sometimes don't want to face their own fear or the fact that, "Well, I failed this person because they're not living." We've lost the appreciation for two things.

One of them is that death is the natural end of the cycle of life—that life is not linear. First, we're born, and then we fall off the end in death. I think the Native Americans have it right when they say, "Life is a circle," and that, "Birth and death are one." And second, if we can listen to the accounts of people who have had near-death experiences, there is the sense that they have not died at all at the time of death, but in fact, they've been freed. People say there's the most wonderful sense of leaving the prison of the body and then going into the presence of the light. They're in the presence of a great being of light, which some people say is an angel, some people say, "It's Jesus," or some people say it's some other aspect of the divine. They see this whole drama. And people will say, "You know, there wasn't a missing beat; nothing happened in my life for any other reason than for schooling me in love and for helping me to accumulate wisdom in my soul."

Q Do you feel that individual transformations are part of an expansion of global consciousness?

JB At the risk of sounding painfully optimistic, I have to say that when I look at the global crisis that we're in the middle of right now—the holocausts that are going on, the epidemic of AIDS, the gross inhumanity toward human beings that we see—the sense I have is that it is a big dark night of the soul. I'm a fan of the dark night because I believe in what Meister Eckehart, the Christian mystic, said: "At the darkest moment, that's when the dawn is going to come." And I think we're right there. There's a physicist whose name is Ilya Prigogine, who won the Nobel Prize for what's called the Theory of Dissipative Structures. And that is [about] the way that progress happens, the way that transformation occurs: it is always when the old system just explodes and goes to pieces. At that moment, we can have a quantum leap as the energy comes forth in a new way and jumps to what he calls "a higher level of organization." I think that that's where we are right now: we're in the middle of one of these quantum leaps to a higher level of organization, and what is going to fuel that leap, I think, is the emerging spiritual sense that so many people have. This is not to say that there's not a lot of darkness coexisting with this; we live in a society where violence has become endemic and pandemic and is really very frightening. But that's a dark angel, too, because what it has done is make us aware that there must be a better way to live. And what we keep coming back to, individually and as a nation, is the need for tolerance, the need for compassion, the need for greater understanding.

To me, the greatest role model for that has been His Holiness the Dalai Lama. In Tibet, his native country, there was a terrible holocaust. When the Chinese overran Tibet in the 1950s, they killed about a sixth of the population. They burned down about six thousand monasteries. They killed most of the wildlife in Tibet. They raped the land. They made it into a nuclear wasteland, burying China's nuclear wastes there. Oftentimes the Dalai Lama is asked, "Well, aren't you angry at the Chinese? Don't you want revenge?" No, he doesn't want revenge. What he actually tries to do in his own meditation practice is to take on the ignorance of the Chinese that would allow them to act with such inhumanity and return to them his own happiness and his own wisdom. What a wonderful role model he has been. That's why he won the Nobel Prize.

But if we look even a little bit more broadly, thirty years ago nobody really knew very much about Tibet. Nobody knew about all of the ancient meditation practices for learning to be compassionate. Now, because they've been driven out of their homeland of Tibet, which of course was a terrible crisis, thirty years later we see the up side of that. So, that's part of the global transformation.

Q Can you comment on new ways of healing on the horizon?

JB Several things are going to happen in terms of the nature of healing. I think we are going to lose some of our preoccupation with the physical body and with the belief that if only we ate right, if only we had the best genes, if only we thought right, our bodies would last forever. People often make themselves miserable by saying, "I'm guilty; I caused my own illness." They try to use mind/body techniques so that they won't age or so that they'll live forever. They're going to be terribly disappointed. Redd Foxx had a great line—he was a wonderful philosopher. He said, "All these health-food nuts are sure gonna feel foolish when they're laying there in the hospital dying of nothing." And the fact is, all of us are going to die. Even the great saints and mystics died—people who had the sense of living their lives imbued with being in constant contact with the divine presence. Oftentimes, they even died young.

Saint Bernadette, who saw the vision of the Virgin at Lourdes, made herself the laughingstock of the town by digging in the mud because the Virgin said, "A healing spring will arise here." A healing spring did arise. There've been many miracles, documented miracles of healing, that have happened at Lourdes. But Bernadette herself died in her early thirties from a very painful case of bone cancer. Now, what are we to say? Gee, she didn't meditate well enough? She thought wrong? She didn't heal herself? We have to say that Bernadette's life was *whole*—that the circle of life must have been complete in thirty-two years. We need to stop judging a life well lived as a life that's gone on for a certain number of years. I've always felt that some people's lives are complete in two months, and some people's lives are complete in a hundred years. It's not about your physical health, it's about how you've *lived* your life—whether you've been able to open your heart, whether you've been able to have a sense that your life has had a purpose. And if you've had the courage to live your purpose, that is really what healing is all about. When we get to the more limited sense of physical healing, we are, of course, able to extend life span now. We have some marvelous medical treatments that allow us to live longer than we ever have before.

But I want to stress again, the real healing is the healing of our soul. The body is a temporary vehicle, and at some point it's gonna go. The real healing that we get if we use mind/body healing is what we have learned about ourselves: how we've learned to be aware; how we've learned to be loving. The fact that your physical body benefits from that is, I think, a nice add-on, but not the main value.

S O P H Y   B U R N H A M

Sophy Burnham is currently serving as manager of the Fund for New American Plays in Washington, D.C. She is an award-winning play-wright, novelist, screenwriter, journalist, and nonfiction writer. The bestselling author of A Book of Angels, Angel Letters, *and* The President's Angel, *Burnham has taught at the Writers' Center in Washington, D.C. She is currently at work on a new novel.*

QUESTION   Can you describe how you came to write and publish *A Book of Angels?*

SOPHY BURNHAM   I'm a professional writer, and I was be-tween books. I had written *Revelations* and I didn't have anything to do. I thought that I would write down—just for myself or my children, not for publication—all the magical, mysterious, and im-possible things that had happened to me in my life, or to people so close to me that I knew they weren't lying. And I would write

On facing page:
Melozzo da Forli, *Angel Playing Music,* ca. 15th c.

them down and turn them like stones in my head and see what truth they made—because they didn't make sense in the logical, rational, reasonable, scientific, college-educated kind of way that I was brought up to believe was the way that the world worked.

So, there were all of these things and I kept thinking, "Is this really true or is this my imagination?" Now, Joan of Arc was asked once, by her inquisitors, "You say you've heard the voice of God?" She said, "Yes, I've heard the voice of God." They said, "Oh, how do you know it wasn't your imagination?" And she said, "It was my imagination." And they said, "But you just said it was God—which is it, is it your imagination or is it God?" And she said, "That's one of the ways God speaks to me—through my imagination." Well, that's how it was with the early version of what became *A Book of Angels*—not knowing if these were true experiences or my imagination.

I got to be halfway through the whole project and I showed it to some friends, who were all very, very moved by it. And I was, too. Now, when you're a writer, you know when you've done something good and when you haven't. Lots of the stuff I do is not good. But in this case, I just felt that it had a lot of power. So I decided to see about getting it published. I gave it to my agent. And my agent held it for four years. He could not sell it. And then I got a new agent, and she managed to sell it over-night. The reason she did this was because times had changed. Every artist is a little bit ahead of the time, a little bit ahead of the public, in order to get the work done.

Q Can you talk about some of the changes that occurred while you were waiting for *A Book of Angels* to be published?

SB In the 1980s, I wrote six books in eight years—a huge amount of work. And I couldn't get any of them published. These were all books about the spiritual life, the spiritual search.

I couldn't get any of them published because people at that time were not interested. This was the most materialistic time of the Reagan years—the yuppie generation, as the newspapers called it. And I think that as we shifted into the new decade, something happened; there was a shift of consciousness. People discovered that they could not get satisfied. The hole in the heart was still there—no matter how much money they threw into it, or how many marriages, how many fur coats, how many BMWs. There was still no peace at the heart, and what we're looking for *is* fulfillment and peace. We're approaching the millennium, and we've had these ninety years of horror, and we realize that something is missing, and people are starving, spiritually starving.

Q When we speak of angels, what exactly are we talking about?

SB There are these spiritual beings. They apparently are a different species from us. Many people say humans evolve into angels after we die, or after many lifetimes of living and dying. Other people say that angels are a separate species, created by God at the beginning of time. With the first break of light, with the first moment of song, the angel appeared. We don't know. What we do know is that there are these beings that we call angels, that they're on our side, and that they come with warmth and light and a great sense of glory and colors—just magnificent colors. When you see them, you experience warmth and unfathomable love. They are loving us beyond our wildest imaginings that it is possible to be loved. The compassion with which we're held by the universe is beyond imagining. And most of the time we don't know it. Occasionally, you get a little crack in the shell, a little breaking through of the veil, and then you can see it. And then it closes down again.

The angels come, but they don't like to be seen. They want

disguise. They're not going to break in and intrude on our sense of reality. And so they will come in ways that will not interfere with our perception of how reality is supposed to work. They'll come as visions, as voices, as intuition—the little tap on your shoulder that says, "Go here, don't go here." And everybody has had this experience of saying, "I *knew* I shouldn't have gone down that road, and I didn't listen." So, that little intuition is an angel voice whispering, or the guidance of the angel wing. They'll come as animals. I have wonderful stories of them as animals.

My favorite story of an animal concerns a woman on a bus. Actually, this is a story from Hope MacDonald's book, *When Angels Appear.* The woman is on the bus late at night, going home. And there's only one man on the bus with her. She knows suddenly that the man is going to get off with her at her lonely stop and follow her. And she is very frightened. She says a prayer. And sure enough, when she gets off, the man gets off with her. But just at that moment, a big white Great Pyrenees dog comes up, puts his head under her hand, walks along to her house with her, and the man disappears. The dog stays until she puts the key in the lock, then trots on. She lived in the neighborhood and had never seen the dog before and never saw it again. That sort of thing comes as an angel. You don't know what that dog is; maybe it's a real dog. But we'll call it an angel because it took the form of an angel. It did the angels' work.

Sometimes they come as humans. I will come to somebody and say just what they need to hear. You will come to me and say just what I need at that moment. Accident? Coincidence? Coincidence is God's way of doing a miracle anonymously. And then, [there are these] little serendipitous moments—invisible hands that pull you from burning cars—all of this stuff that we just don't understand. And sometimes, rarely, and occasionally, they will come in their full effulgent glory, as an angel—but this is most unusual, and generally children see them—people who are very innocent, who are full of wonder, and who can still see with the heart. You don't see an angel with your mind. You see an angel with your heart. And it's very hard for us to open to this because it's dangerous. You can get hurt if you have an open heart.

Q   What, physically, do angels look like?

SB   I think that the reason that artists paint angels as little cherub babies, or as glorious and magnificent creations with wings, or with fiery swords of passion and righteousness is because that's the way they're seen. Now, angels are formed of light. We're formed of light, too, but we have a very heavy vibration, so it looks like we have mass. But angels are formed of light and they can take any form they want. They can be male or they can be female, they can be big, they can be small, they can be children, they can be gigantic. And because the light is falling in kind of ripples down them, it gives an impression of wings, of flowing. The wings are also a metaphor for the speed with which angels move. They move swift as thought, but they do not need angels' wings, obviously, to move. You do not flap your shoulder blades to get someplace. They move by *thinking*, and by thinking they are instantly a child or instantly a young girl or instantly a magnificent male sword-bearing fierce angel.

I imagine that cavemen—Neanderthals—saw angels. Australopithecus, the first ape-man, saw angels. If everybody in every religion has this concept—that there is a spiritual dimension with spiritual helpers—then maybe it's true. Mystics say it's true.

Q   Do you think we are living at a time when spirituality is being redefined?

SB   A lot of people wonder, "Why is there so much em-

Lucas van Leyden, *The Just Awaiting Their Assumption*. Central panel of The Last Judgment triptych, ca. 1526–1527.

phasis on angels?" And one of the reasons might be that we have this concept of a punitive, righteous, jealous, mean-spirited, patriarchal, white God, who is watching over us and knows when the slightest feather falls from a swallow. And we don't like that.

Nobody wants that. An angel, on the other hand, or our relationship with the angel, is always tender, always compassionate.
When it comes, you fall back into it with a sense of home or
mother or safety.

Angels are pointing to something else. They're pointing to
what we call God, but not this righteous, jealous, watchful deity.
But rather, a source of energy which is even more unfathomably
loving than the angel. And this ocean of love is us, and we come
from it and we go back to it, and all the cells of our bodies are
composed of it.

Now, whether people are, all over the place, redefining their
relationship to God—that's up to an individual. And that's a lifetime's process. But it is the question that's behind all of the major
questions of, "Who am I? Why am I here? Is there life after
death? What happens when I die? Why did I get born?" All of
these questions are really saying, "Are you there, God? What is
God?" And it's in that that the angels are helping. It's that knowledge that they are presenting themselves, to help us to reach and
to help us through daily life.

Q So, everyone is attended by angels?

SB Everyone is attended by angels. Everyone is attended
by more than one angel. I am told, and I have no reason to
doubt it, that when we decide to be born—when we're spirits
on the other side and decide to be born—we have already chosen the companions that will be with us for our entire lifetimes and that we knew those spirits on the other side. And
when we die, which is to say when we go back to living, we
will be with those spirits again and they are our friends.
We have many more than one angel or two angels; we have
dozens. And any angel that you call on can bring forth thousands more.

Q Was there a time when you felt an angelic intervention in your own life?

SB My mother and I had a very loving and a very stormy relationship—she's been dead now for many years. When she was dying of lung cancer, she was in the hospital in Baltimore. And I was living in Washington. I drove over every day to see her in the hospital. And then some of the time I'd be staying in Baltimore, near my father, who had had a stroke. And it was really painful. It was very, very hard to be there. I threw myself into work to stop thinking, because it was very clear my mother had only a few more weeks to live, or a few more days to live; you didn't know.

She had an oxygen tube up her nose, and she would take it off and wave it around like a pasha and make pronouncements. And one of the things that she did when I'd come to visit her was to pick on me. She would say, "Your skirt is dirty." And, "Why are you sitting like that?" And, "How could you write the things you write?" And, "When did you last see your father?" And, "Why are you behaving the way you behave?" Just little nagging, picking at me all the time. She was doing this once, and these little pickings hurt. I didn't want to answer her back. She was sick. I didn't want to fight openly. I've never wanted to fight openly with her—I never *did* fight openly with her. And so, I was sinking lower and lower in my chair, thinking, "Why am I here? I should just leave. We should be discussing important things. There are really serious things to talk about when your mother's dying." And at that moment, in the hospital, there came this black Jamaican maid with a mop, and she's mopping the hospital floor vigorously. My mother's picking on me, I'm sunk in my chair—a scowl. And she says, "I love to hear the mother talk." I sat up in my chair—I hadn't quite understood her—and my mother and I both said, "What?" She said, "I do love to hear the mother talk. My own mother died when I was twelve years old. It's been so long since I heard mother talk. It is so good to hear." And then she went away. But we were changed; my mother and I were absolutely changed. From that moment she stopped picking on me, and we began to talk sweetly, from the heart, deeply. I always felt that that woman came like an angel at that moment, to reconcile my mother and me—to place this awareness before us of what was happening. All she was doing, my mother, was cuffing the cub—loving me in a really hard way, but loving me. It was wonderful that the maid could tell me that before my mother died.

My mother died about two days after that, but we did talk a lot about her dying and about what would happen when she died. I asked her to come back and tell me what happened on the other side. She said, "Oh, I couldn't do that. Not even Houdini could do that." And I said, "Well, you and I have this very close relationship. You can do it." And she did. She came back three times. But I couldn't ask her what it was like on the other side because it's too hard to do.

Actually, my parents came back to me not long ago—my mother *and* my father. I was watching television and I was very, very disturbed about a dear friend of mine who's had a stroke. And my father'd had a stroke. I was really upset that I couldn't do more with my friend who'd had this stroke. I felt miserable about myself. And so I'd been pacing around the house, walking up and down and thinking, "All right, where are you now when I need you? I need you to tell me what to do and you're not anywhere around, and you've been dead for years and years and I'm all alone." And then I went in the kitchen and I was watching television—a dumb movie—and all of a sudden, out of the corner of my eye, I saw these shadows on the wall by the dining room. (It's important to note that the peripheral vision is where you often see this.) So these shadows were there and I could look at them and see them and they stayed, waiting. There was no light that could make a shadow, and there was no moving car or anything else. But I knew when I saw the shadow, [that] that's my mother and father—both of them together as they had been together in their lifetimes. And they didn't say anything and I didn't learn any information about what it's like on the other side. I don't think the whole experience lasted more than thirty seconds to a minute, but when they had faded away and the shadows were not playing there anymore, I knew what I was supposed to do with my friend who had had a stroke. It was so simple. It was to love him. That's all. It didn't matter how I behaved. It didn't matter at all. The bottom line of all of this is, "How do we love each other more deeply? How do we love and how do we express our love for one another?"

Q   If we all have angels and guardian angels, why do bad things happen?

SB   It's a terribly important question, and it's one that I don't think any of us have any answer to. But I do have one thing that I find acceptable now. Angels appear to be able to help us in all forms; they create miracles; they can interfere with physical laws of the universe; I even have stories of cars going through each other. But the one thing that they cannot do is to interfere with our free will.

There is a story in *A Book of Angels* of a woman named Sarah who's in a very perilous position in Greece. And she says a prayer: "Lord Jesus, have mercy on me. Lord Jesus Christ, have mercy on me." She is terrified. And being Christian, of course she prays to Christ. But it would have been the same thing if she was Muslim; she could pray to Allah. It doesn't matter. But in this case, she prayed to Christ, and she felt these two hands come up behind her and pick her up at the ribs from behind. And she felt all of the manifestations that I was talking about earlier—of settling back into these arms of warmth and comfort and enormous love and safety. And the hands carried her down the road and across a bridge, and then dropped her. So she fell and skinned both knees. And she gets up and she runs off to the village and pounds up the steps to her pension and bursts into the room where her friends are. And they all say, "Sarah, Sarah, what's happened?" And, she says, "Nothing, nothing, I got spooked out there. It's just absolutely nothing." And one of them says, "No. You're shining with light; you have seen God."

Well, years later, she's raped, and all during the rape she's thinking, "Now my guardian angel will come and save me. Now my angel will come and save me." And there's no angel. There's no one there at all and she's raped. So we were talking about this and she said that it was okay, because by undergoing that, she'd learned another level of forgiveness; she had to learn to forgive her rapist. And I thought that the fact is that the angels can do everything, but they cannot stop the murderer's hand from plunging the knife into your heart. They can't stop the war. They can't stop the free will of one human being to harm another.

Q   Is there some way to notice or contact your angels?

SB   I hear this all the time: "How do I contact my angel? How do I see my angel? How do I get in touch with my angel?" The fact of the matter is we don't have to do that. All we have to do is to recognize the blessings of our life and say, "Thank you." And the more we say thank you, the more blessings will pour into our lives and the more open we will be. It's not up to us to see angels. It's up to the angels to reveal themselves to us. Ultimately it doesn't matter if you see your angel. It matters whether when you come to the end of your life, you look back and you say, "Did I lead my life well? Did I hold out the cup of compassion to someone else?"

I have a story of a little girl who had a near-death experience. She was twelve years old when she died. She had all of the experiences that people do with near-death experiences—she goes down the tunnel of light, and there are spiritual beings or angels on the other side. There is a barrier that she cannot cross—a meadow, or a fence, or a river—but she can go right up to the edge. And then she's shown her life—her whole life passes before her eyes, as we say, and the reason we say that is because apparently it does when you die. And she noticed that it was being shown to her in dashes—like Morse code, but just blips with empty spaces. And then she realized that she was being shown only those moments when she had loved unconditionally. And so she chose to come back, because she had not loved enough unconditionally.

Now, I think that is what we're being called to do: higher and higher vibration, higher and higher calling, higher and higher spiritual life. It is extremely painful. How can you love the person who has just insulted you? How can you love, unconditionally, the person who just bruised your feelings? And how can you release your resentments? Well, Buddha spent two hours a day doing a forgiveness exercise. Two hours a day he would spend just getting himself into a state of forgiveness and sending out a forgiveness wave to the world. Well, we're doing it. People are praying all the time and people are forgiving their enemies all the time and people are holding out the hand of help, to strangers even, all the time.

Q It's interesting that when Saint Thomas Aquinas talked about angels as "beings of light," he described, intuitively, physical laws that quantum physics has now seemed to have proven true. Can you explain this?

SB   You know, you see things in meditation. Meditation is the way to see your angels. You may have to be taught meditation, but when you meditate, you see things. Lucretius was a Roman poet and philosopher and he was the first person to put down the atomic theory—the theory of atoms. He saw them in meditation and he said, "Chairs and tables are made of atoms with space in between—[like] human beings." Now, this is what—first century B.C.? Something like that. How did he know that? He knew because he meditated and he saw it in the meditation, which is where you see angels. So, the scientists, with all of the exploration into quantum physics, end up at the very mountaintop where the mystic is sitting and where he has already seen it. But now it can be proven. It can be demonstrated by building three-billion-dollar reactors with hovered cyclotrons.

Q   Why do some of us try to deny the experience of an angel encounter that we have had?

SB   After people have had an experience with an angel— after you've had your life saved by an angel, after you have looked into the eyes of an angel—nothing is the way it was before. It creates great conflict. After the angels saved my life when I was just a young girl, I didn't want to believe it. I wasn't ready to have my life turned upside down. I didn't believe in God at that time and I was not ready to embrace the responsibility that it would entail. And so I simply put it out of my mind and said, "This didn't happen." Years passed, and during the years I had a lot of other experiences, and as more things happened I was forced to go back and reexamine that particular experience and recognize it for what it was—for what I had been afraid to recognize it as.

It is not something that you really want, to see an angel. It may be that you would like it, but it is not a silly little moment. It's a moment of enormous power and you will carry that mo-

Mathias Gruenewald,
Concert of Angels.
Isenheim altarpiece,
ca. 1512–1516.

ment all through the rest of your life. And you may never tell anybody about it all, and it will be one of those Maslow peak experiences that you do not scatter around. But you will look at it and touch it and remember it and be comforted by it, healed by it, and have the faith that something else will happen.

Q   Do we owe the angels something?

SB   Yes. We owe the angels thanks and praise, and particularly adoration to God. But the angels do very well with kind words, softness, and loving thanks. Just say "thank you" all the time to angels. They're very light. They play. They want you to laugh. You can give them laughter and they'll be very, very pleased with that. Angels go lightly because they take themselves lightly.

Q   Are we growing more compassionate? Are we learning?

SB   I think that that's the task. And the question is—can we take the dare to love one another instead of to hate? We seem to be doing it. Can we teach our children that there are angels ready to help them? Can we dare to teach them that it's all right to pray for what we want, and when we do, we get what we need? Do we dare to admit to ourselves, not just in church, but actually in the events of our lives, that we live in a world much larger and much grander than we may be cognizant of? Do we take the dare? I don't know if it's an individual choice. You can drive in your heels and put your head back and balk, but you're not going to be able to withstand it. You have to go where it is taking us. And where it's taking us is to this light, more loving plane. But we still have free will. We can stop anytime.

A Bright Light

RON KENNEDY

In October of 1984 I was just returning from Bristol, England, where I had given a seminar. I was in a lousy mood: it was a ten-hour flight and I was really tired. I arrived at the airport about 12:30 in the afternoon. My secretary, Paige, picked me up there, and we arrived at my home in San Francisco about 1:30. We parked the car in the garage, and I was bringing my luggage in through the door from the garage to the foyer. Sitting on the stairs was my friend Abdul, who had been house-sitting for me during that week I was gone. Paige had told me that he was in pain from some sort of toothache, and so I was concerned about him. I noticed that he was beading sweat across his brow. I had just reached up with my hand to touch his brow and asked, "How are you?" when he screamed at the top of his lungs, "That's it!"

I hadn't noticed before, but he had a steel tennis racket in his right hand. He swung the tennis racket and struck me with it on the left side of my head. It spun me around back toward the door; he had incredible strength. I had no idea he was that strong, and I could only ask myself, "What's happening? Why this?" I spun myself back around and asked in an equally loud voice, "What are you doing?" Well, he did it again—same place—and spun me right back around toward the door. I turned around again and one more time said, "What are you doing, Abdul? I'm your friend!" He hit me again.

By that time I didn't question anymore what he was doing; I knew what he was doing, and I thought I should get out of there. I was fumbling with the doorknob, but I couldn't figure out if the doorknob went 'round and 'round, or if you pulled it out . . . I suppose I had sort of an early concussive syndrome.

Then there is a break in my memory, and I don't remember anything until waking up on the floor a few moments later. I suppose he had knocked me out from behind. At any rate, I woke up and I was not really sure of where I was and what was going on. I can remember struggling with someone and then being on the floor again. I suppose he was knocking me out over and over again. About the third time I got up, everything began to come into focus, and I realized who he was and who I was, and what was happening. I noticed, also, that there was a lot of blood on the walls . . . at least, there was a lot of red stuff on the walls. Then I noticed he was swinging what turned out to be a dagger. It was a really long steel blade, and I put it all together: this is my friend, and for who knows what reason, he is trying to kill me. And it appeared to me that I really didn't have a chance; he had gained the upper hand and I was going to die, and there was no turning back. I could feel his intention to put that blade into my heart. In fact, I learned later he had already put it through my neck and it had come out the back. So he was dead serious about getting the job done.

I was holding his shoulders in a kind of death grip, and time *seemed to slow down. I remember that he took a swing of the knife, which turned out to be the thirteenth strike of the knife, and that happened very slowly in my experience. As it happened, I accepted the fact that I was going to die, that there was no turning back, that there was no way out of it for me, and that it was okay. I came to the conclusion, "Well, this is not a pretty way to die—I had something different in mind—but if this is it, okay, I'll accept this." And as I looked over his shoulder I could see a kind of hallway . . . and you know, I don't have a hallway in that part of my house. Nevertheless, it was a hallway, and at the end of the hallway there was this dead end: there was no way to turn right or left, or go up or down. It was a dead end, and I thought to myself, "Well, this really represents the end for me." I felt very peaceful, and totally relaxed.*

As Abdul drew back to swing his knife one more time and came around halfway, at that moment time stopped . . . or, in my experience, the action stopped. Nothing in the external world was happening. And over his left shoulder, where the hallway had been, there appeared a light. I can only describe it as a light, but it was brighter than light, really.

It was shaped in a kind of triangular shape with rounded corners. It was about the size of a man, but it was just a light. It was so bright and beautiful, and I felt so at peace. I was admiring the beauty of whatever it was, when it began to take on the characteristics of a kind of personality. The first thing that struck me was this infinite love: love that was huge . . . bigger than the universe. Enormous love. I never experienced anything similar to that in my life, and then I realized that whatever this light is, it also knows everything: it has infinite knowledge as well. I realized that it knew everything about me.

The next thing I realized was full, complete acceptance—in spite of knowing everything about me, every single mistake I had ever made, every dumb thing I had ever said or done, all the people I had ever hurt in my life. I was, in a way, overwhelmed with ecstasy, and I thought, "Well, for sure I am going now."

And then—I have to say it this way—it shot a question into me, like an arrow into my chest. It wasn't with words, but with the heart of the thought itself. The question was, "Will you come now, or later?" When he . . . it . . . she . . . whatever asked me that, I realized that the ball was in my court, and I could choose to live or die. On the one hand, I was very curious, and I wanted to know what might be next; on the other hand, I could see aspects of my life that were just clearly unfinished. My son, Houston, was three at that time, and what I considered to be my real work in life was, in a way, only a few years old. My son's presence and the presence of my work in my life really made the decision. And so I gave an answer back as directly as the question was given me: "I stay." As soon as I gave the answer, the light was gone and the passage of time resumed, and the swing of the knife continued around to my back and entered my back and I fell to the floor.

As I fell I heard something else hit the floor, and lying there just beside me was the handle. The blade had broken off the handle! Well, I hadn't known how I was going to survive, but that question was very quickly answered (although I was certain I would survive, from the very instant that I was given the choice and gave the answer). Well, to make a long story short, I was in a condition of ecstasy. I had lost about 50 percent of my blood volume at that time, but it didn't matter. I jumped up to my feet, and I charged into Abdul and pushed him back across the room. And I was laughing—not at him, not at the situation, but because I was incredibly happy. I was in a great state of ecstasy.

Well, I had forgotten about the steel tennis racket. He still had that, so he whacked me on the head a few more times. The police arrived then. Paige had managed to find someone at a nearby home and had called the police. They took him away, and he spent many years in prison for what he had done.

I was taken to the hospital, and I was still excited about what had happened. Well, I didn't know if I was going to make it out of surgery. The light didn't tell me how much longer I was going to live—maybe it would only be for a couple of hours—and so I thought I had better tell someone about my experience. I called Paige over to the gurney, and I related the story as quickly as I could to her, just before I went into surgery.

I woke up from surgery five hours later no longer in a condition of ecstasy; in fact, I was enraged that anyone could have done such a thing to me. I would say from that moment until about two and a half years later, I was in very bad shape. I was in the kind of condition where all I wanted was revenge, all I could think of was revenge. In my view, it was a very good thing that Abdul was in prison; if he hadn't been, I probably would have been in prison soon after that! There is nothing in my life which I ever experienced which was more painful than wanting revenge on that man. At the same time I realized that I must have this feeling for some good purpose. I had a real challenge: it seemed that if I could overcome my revenge and forgive this guy, it would transform me. I would be, in a way, a new kind of person. That was the real growing aspect to this, and forgiving somebody did me good.

It has occurred to me that the love from this light was so overwhelming that this life must have something to do with learning to love like that, or perhaps learning to be loved like that—to actually experience the love that people have for us. It is plain to me that there is an enormous amount of love that people have for us, and somehow we miss it, somehow we go through life as if it's not there. If we do recognize that it's there, we discount it and it doesn't really mean anything. We think our self-deprecating thoughts about ourselves, despite the enormous quantity of admiration and love that people have for us.

It has also occurred to me that if this light could appear to me as I was being murdered, and yet I was not going to die alone but in a sea of enormous love, then those people you love who have died, and maybe in the most extreme circumstances, did not die alone as you would fear that they did: they died with great love around, and peace as well.

Phillipe de
Champaigne, *The
Concert of Angels*, ca.
17th c.

EILEEN ELIAS
FREEMAN, M.A.

Eileen Elias Freeman, M.A., is director of The AngelWatch™ *Foundation, Inc., a nonprofit organization that serves as a major resource center on the topic of angels. A former teacher of theology at the University of Notre Dame, where she received her master's degree, Freeman is the bestselling author of* Touched by Angels, Angelic Healing, *and* The Angels' Little Instruction Book, *and the publisher of* AngelWatch™, *a journal devoted exclusively to angels.*

QUESTION   Would you tell us about your first experience with angels?

EILEEN ELIAS FREEMAN   When I was a child of five, I was a very, very fearful little girl. I was afraid of almost everything in my small world. And when my grandmother died, it escalated my fears almost beyond my bearing. My grandmother's death was like a light going out in my life. I couldn't bear the thought of her being trapped underground forever. I thought because she loved me so much, she would come back and take me with her. And as a result, when nighttime came, I was much too afraid to go to sleep.

One night I was sitting up in bed, and I remember how cold I felt; I can still feel the cold plaster wall up against my back. All of a sudden I saw a light that was beginning to grow at the foot of my bed. At first I thought it was the hall light, but the hall light wasn't on. And as I watched in fascination this light became brighter and thicker until I couldn't see the wall behind it. It was a color I've never been able to describe, as if a diamond were made of silver and the sunlight were shining through it. And as I looked at the light a figure began to emerge out of it—a humanlike figure. I remember the eyes most of all because they were piercing and also compassionate. And as this being looked at me my fears began to fade. He said, "Don't be afraid, Eileen, your grandmother is not in a cold grave. She's happy in heaven with God and the people she loves."

All the fear just drained out of me as the being spoke those words. And I remember saying, "Who are you?" And he replied, "I'm your guardian angel, child. Always remember there's nothing to be afraid of."

Before I could ask any more questions, he began to fade back into this light. And the light itself was withdrawn back to the heavenly realm from which it came. And the room was just the way it was except with one important difference: I found that I was no longer afraid. Not of my grandmother's death, not of the dark, not any of the other fears I had. I was never again scared of the sound of the telephone ringing or the sound of the vacuum cleaner. Or of trucks on the street or of my father going to work or of going to school. Those fears had all gone away because of the words of the angel. And I went to sleep normally;

I woke up the next morning feeling fine. And as the day progressed I realized the angel had actually changed me—that I was no longer afraid of anything. I was able to grow up as a normal child, without being obsessed with all sorts of fears. I realized that all of those fears were less substantial than an angel's wing.

Seeing my angel when I was a child stirred up a great longing inside of me to learn more about the loving God who had sent the angel. And it filled me with a sense of peace and reassurance that I was being cared for—not just by the people who loved me, but by God, who looked after me from heaven by giving me this wonderful angel to watch over me and offer me guidance.

Q How has your childhood encounter with an angel continued into your adult life?

EEF I'm the founder and director of a nonprofit organization called the AngelWatch Foundation, whose purpose is to search for evidence of angelic activity in the world, and then to disseminate that information to as wide an audience as possible. And I do that through a bimonthly magazine about angels that gives people's own stories of having seen angels, and also through books and through speaking about angels in the United States and abroad.

I'm interested in talking to people about angels because angels are one of the means that God has placed in our lives to help us grow in our wisdom and understanding, to help us learn more [about] love, to help us care for this beautiful planet and to preserve it. I do it in thanks to God for the angel who came to me when I was a child. I want people to know just how wonderful these angelic beings are.

Q You've talked about your first encounter with an angel when you were a child. Didn't an angel come to you again when you were in college? Can you share this experience?

EEF One day I went to meet my friend Victor. We had planned to discuss a Mass that we were going to have the next week. As I approached Victor's building something very unusual happened. I put my right foot on the first step leading up to his apartment building. As I did so, I felt a hand on my shoulder that pulled me back. I looked around, startled, because I wasn't with anyone. Nobody was there. I thought I had imagined it. And so I started to go into the building again, and as I put my foot on the step up, the hand, unseen, pulled me back again. And I heard a voice that said, "It would not be wise for you to go in there just now."

I decided to go across the street to a little church where I was accustomed to go to Mass, so I could sit inside and think about this, and try to understand what it meant.

Suddenly I began to hear sirens. First one, then another, until I heard several and I became curious. I opened the church door and looked out. My friend's apartment building was surrounded by emergency vehicles: police, fire engines, rescue squad, ambulances.

I wasn't able to keep my meeting with Victor that day. Later that evening, when I was back in my dorm, I called him—just so I could apologize for missing our meeting. And he said, "You know what those vehicles were for? A woman was stabbed to death in the elevator. She was murdered by a drug dealer."

Q What is your definition of an angel?

EEF An angel is a spiritual being fundamentally different from humans. I believe they were created by God a very long time ago before the earth was created. These heavenly spirits are organized in a society whose purpose is the worship of God and the carrying out of God's commands on Earth.

Q And what is a guardian angel?

EEF I believe that for every angel in heaven there is a

guardian angel on Earth, a being whose duties are not solely the praise of God in the heavenly sphere but the actual care of human beings and other forms of life on Earth. A guardian angel is assigned to each of us when we are conceived and watches over us through our growth in the womb, through our birth, through our life in this world, until the angel guides us from the confines of this world into the glory of heaven.

Q   When did angels first arrive?

EEF   According to much of the ancient traditions, angels were created long before the earth, and they have been a part of our history ever since we've been here. The earliest writings about angels go back to ancient Sumer some five thousand years ago, and angels have been intertwined with our history ever since then. They have been a part of most of the world's great religions, both the Eastern and Western traditions. But I think they're best known through the Judeo-Christian and Islamic traditions. In these traditions, the angels are all servants of God, created by God to carry out God's designs both in the heavens and on Earth.

Q   In all the thousands of years in which people have seen angels, has their appearance changed? What do angels really look like?

EEF   The truth is, we really don't know. We only know how they appear when they come to us or [when] they appear in physical form on the earth. Angels can take any form they want, which suggests that angels are spirits with no particular bodies. But we're not sure of that either; it's possible angels have bodies which we simply can't see. Perhaps they exist in a certain color spectrum which is invisible to the human eye.

Maybe angels' bodies are made of infrared or ultraviolet. Maybe they're so microscopic we've never discovered them. Maybe they're so macroscopic that we could all fit on an atom on an angel's finger. We simply don't know. Maybe angels have no consistent shape and they're shape-shifters; they can be any shape they want. We certainly know that when they appear to us, they can take any form that is necessary. An angel can look masculine or feminine or both or neither.

An angel can come in animal form. An angel can look like any human being you care to name. And in fact, many angels come in the guise of other human beings just so they won't disturb the person they've come to help.

Angels do not have wings, although they're portrayed in art with wings. That's just a convention, and it's a very ancient one. The first winged angels go back a good four thousand years, and there are representations of divine beings with wings on cylinder seals and on ivory carvings from a number of sites in the ancient Near East. We paint angels with wings because the wings represent the speed of their thought, or the grace of their beings.

As far as an angel's halo goes, we tend to confine it to the head, but in reality the halo is the aura which surrounds the angel. It surrounds the whole being. When I saw my angel as a child, I saw the angel totally enveloped in light. And that's the description that most people give of angels. In art, at first, the artists did paint halos that surrounded the whole being. But as time went on they cut it down further and further, until today we tend to see angels in art with simply a little aureole of light around their heads.

Q What about the orders and categories of angels? Do these reflect differences in the types of angels?

EEF The scriptures of Judaism, Christianity, and Islam mention angels, archangels, princes, dominions, powers, seraphim, cherubim, and many others. Does this represent fundamentally different kinds of angels? We don't know. There's been a lot of speculation on that. A famous theologian known as Dionysius the Areopagite wrote a large treatise in the fifth century about the different choirs of angels, and how they were created, and what they did. All of this is just speculation; we truly

Melozzo da Forli, *Musical Angel*, ca. 15th c.

don't know. For myself, I think what we're really talking about is job descriptions, not different kinds of angels. So angels may be what we call the rank and file. And archangels might be middle management, for all we know.

I do tend to think that the cherubim and seraphim might be fundamentally different from the garden variety of angels. The way they are referred to in all the scriptures and many other ancient literatures seems to indicate that their duties are confined to the heavenly regions—the other realm, the other dimension, if you will. In fact, in Islamic tradition, particularly among the Sufi mystics, it's said that the cherubim are so enthralled with the face of God, they don't even know God has created an earth or people known as human beings.

Q   What purpose do you think angels serve in our lives?

EEF   One of the most important things we need to realize about angels is that when they come into our lives, it's not simply to have a pleasant word and a cup of tea. They come to bring us an important message. They come to bring us the possibilities of change. That's one of the major reasons I wrote *Touched by Angels*: to show the many ways the angels touch our lives. They come into our lives when we're children, when we're young adults, when we're old. They come to men and women and children, to people of all races and all cultures, to people who are religious or not, to people who are in distress or to people simply beginning their day's work. And they come to tell us that we can grow, we can change. That there is hope. That we can make progress in love, wisdom, and enlightenment. That we can heal and be healed. And that's why I wrote my second book, *Angelic Healing*, to show that one of the specific reasons angels come into our lives is to help us heal. Not that they wave wands over us like fairy godmothers, but they teach us wisdom, by sharing with us the grace of God, the enlightenment which comes from heaven.

They show us ways that we can heal our own lives, and not just our own lives, but the lives of the people around us. And not just the lives of the people around us, but the world itself.

Angels want us to be whole, as God is whole. Angels are whole beings without hurts or wounds in them, [and] they want that for us very, very much. And so they work with us in whatever ways they can to help us heal our lives. Not usually by doing the work for us, but by showing us what we need to do, and supporting us with extra love, wisdom, encouragement, and peace.

MALCOLM
GODWIN

Malcolm Godwin is the author of Angels: An Endangered Species.
An artist and a designer, Godwin has written extensively on esoter-
ica, Eastern philosophy, and alternative wisdom traditions. Most re-
cently, Godwin, who lives in Dorset, England, has completed a book on
lucid dreaming.

QUESTION How far back does the history of angels go?
When did people first write about them?

MALCOLM GODWIN The first recording of angels is really
from the time of Zoroaster, about fifth century B.C. An angel
called Good Man came to him, came to the prophet as a messenger from God. Angels always appear as messengers; this is their
function. They basically have no essence, but they have a function. And the function is always inseparable from God Himself.
The angels we're talking about are those of Zoroastrianism, Juda-

On facing page:
Crypt. Père Lachaise
Cemetery, Paris.

ism, Christianity, and Islam. These all share pretty much the same image of the Western angel, the species of beings that we know of as "angels." Before the fifth century B.C., there were Egyptian, Syrian, and Babylonian mythical creatures—the original ancestors of angels—with wings and heads of humans but bodies of lions.

Q   So even the drawings of the first angels had wings?

MG   Well, it's difficult to say because it wasn't until the eighth century A.D., after the council of Nicaea, that angels actually could be represented at all. Up until then the angels were considered both too ethereal and too close to heresy to be manifested in form. After Nicaea, angels were allowed to be painted and depicted, which brings us to the great golden age of angels, which really started about the eighth century and ended about the fourteenth century. These are the angels we know of: the angels with wings, the angels who look human.

The angel as we know it today is almost like an insect caught in resin. It's a time-encapsulated creature. From the fourteenth century onward, basically after the plague, angels never really changed their shape. They never evolved after that.

The classical angel—the angel we all know of and see in paintings and on postcards—is a fantasy created by a collaboration of the artist and the theologian. In the Middle Ages and the Renaissance, there was actually a demand for this sort of mystery, which somehow the church had lost. The church was very dry at that time. It was an incredibly corrupt, male-dominated organization with no counterbalancing female presence or essence. Even the priesthood itself was divided. In this atmosphere angels gave an extra spark, a female sense of really caring and healing, and a luminous quality which was otherwise sadly lacking in what appeared to be a cruel and heartless religion based on unthinking obedience.

Q   Can you explain how the system of nine choirs works?

MG   The nine choirs [of angels] work in three triads. It is a system based on a cosmic image that God who is the unknowable and the unknown exists at the center of all and everything. From this center He radiates the Divine thought (some theologians equate this with the Word). This vibration spreads outward, becoming light which, as it gets further from the Divine source, becomes heat, and finally congeals into matter. The choirs are arranged in concentric circles of ever-diminishing energies. Thus, the first choir, closest to God, are the three purest and most powerful. These are the incorruptible seraphim, whose being is love, the cherubim, whose function is knowledge, and the thrones, or wheels, who are like all-seeing eyes. The second triad of angels are the dominions, the virtues, and the powers, while the third are the principalities, the archangels, and, finally, your run-of-the-mill angels who exist at the very edge of this great sphere. The archangels and angels are moving into that area which is very close to human beings, which is matter. They are the shock troops right at the edge nearest to evil and to human beings, who are known to be sinful. And often those angels are the ones who get corrupted most easily. For angels do supposedly get corrupted by human intervention.

Q   At what point in history did this hierarchy come about?

MG   Historically speaking, the hierarchy stems from two sources—Dionysus, a legendary character who was later proved to be a fraudulent creation of overenthusiastic theologians, and Thomas Aquinas, who was the epitomy of medieval Christian scholarship. Between them was created the main school of angelography—the study of the finer points of angelic law and behavior.

Q   Are the angels in Christianity, Judaism, and Islam much the same or are they completely different?

MG   The three religions of Judaism, Christianity, and Islam share pretty much the same pantheon. The Judaic angels were, of

Angel of the Annunciation. Russian icon.

course, the originals. But Islam absorbed the most renowned Christian angels, Gabriel and Michael. In the Islamic tradition there are only four archangels, whereas Christianity has seven, but that's hardly much of a difference.

Q Are angels present in other religions such as Asian and Native American?

MG They're found in Asia but not like *Angelus Occidentalis*. For instance, the Indians call their angels Devas or Devadasis, who are far juicier creatures than the Western messenger angel. The Western angel has very little between his legs or her legs, whereas the Devadasis are incredibly sensual creatures.

Q Let's talk about angels in the Bible. Exactly how were they created and what is their focus?

MG Curiously, there are only two angels mentioned in the Protestant Bible. In the Catholic Bible, in the book of Tobit, Raphael is mentioned. But otherwise there are only two instances of angels appearing in the whole of the Bible: Michael in Revelation as he defeats the Satan dragon, and Gabriel, who of course appears in the Annunciation. But if one wants to know about angels, then one must seek those writings which have either been removed from the Bible at some time, or have been deemed of questionable orthodoxy by the Church fathers. This body of quasi-heretical work, known as the Apocrypha, is the greatest source of angelography. The apocryphal Book of Enoch, which once enjoyed a high spiritual status amongst both priests and theologians, was removed by the third century as being too heretical in its imagery.

Q So angels were really created in the Bible just to tell stories?

MG No. The Apocrypha actually has a lot of information about angels. But the church was always a little suspicious of angels. The problem is, angels are in direct competition with the

priesthood. I mean, the priesthood was the intermediary between God and man. And if you have the competition of an
angel who is supposedly the messenger, who gives you a one-to-
one message directly from the Divine Source, there's no priest involved, there's no necessity for the church. So in fact the church
was always a little ambivalent in its attitude toward angels. At one
point, it banned a lot of the works and a lot of the writings about
angels.

The Archangel Michael.
Icon.

Q   The seraphim and cherubim appear in the Old Testament, don't they? Could you describe the difference in appearance between seraphim and cherubim, if there is any at all?

MG   The seraphim are called the fiery serpents burning with love. Now, a seraphim was the angel which appeared to Saint Francis of Assisi. Supposedly it has six wings. The whole imagery of it has a curious whiff of mythical dragons. Such great fiery serpents have an obvious similarity to the huge winged creatures of ancient times. The cherubim, on the other hand— the original cherub was a guardian of the temples in Syria, a vast winged creature with a lion's body and a human head. They were obviously seen by the Jews in captivity in Babylon. The Jews are very inventive about their religion, and they have taken from many, many different sources, and so you have the difference between these vast thirty-foot-high guardians of the temples and your little Italian cherub with little butterfly wings.

The cherubim can be seen as embodying knowledge. In Syria, not only did they guard the temples, they also guarded the Tree of Everlasting Life. In their wanderings in Persia, Syria, and Babylon, the Jews managed to gather rich mythical and spiritual imagery to incorporate into their own belief systems. The cherub guarding the Syrian Tree of Everlasting Life, for instance, appears in a new guise as the cherubim who, with burning swords, are guarding the gates east of Eden.

Q   Could you just describe the differences between the archangels Michael and Gabriel?

MG   Michael and Gabriel the archangels are perfect foils for one another. Michael has very male attributes and Gabriel has very female attributes. In fact, Gabriel is probably the only female angel. Michael is the most trusted of God. Whenever God wants anything done, He is sure that Michael will do it perfectly. Michael is the archangel who destroys the fallen angel, Lucifer, or Satan, the great dragon. In many cases, Michael is also called a serpent. Michael is the psychopomp—that is, the guide for the souls when they leave the body. He is also the weigher of the souls. And the source of that probably comes from Egypt. The giveaway is that Michael has peacock feathers for his wings, which are eyelike: they're the same peacock feathers of the goddess Maat, who weighs a heart in Egypt on the scales. Michael also has scales that he uses to weigh the souls of sinners. Anubis is the psychopomp in Egypt and the Prince or Commander of the Stars in Persia. So Michael assumes many of the multidimensional attributes from very different cultures. He appears as guider of the souls, as weigher of the souls, as the champion of God, and as the Commander or Prince of the Stars, or as we might say, Prince of the Angels.

Gabriel, on the other hand, is not so trusted. Gabriel could only appear to Mary in the Annunciation simply because Mary did not see the angel as male. The impregnation of the Holy Spirit at that moment would have been too obvious and lacking purity; Gabriel is linked with the Gnostic goddess Sophia, who was cast out of Heaven to live as a whore. Gabriel was also exiled for a while and supposedly suffered a similar fate, being reviled by her fellow angels. As the only woman in what was essentially a gentleman's club, this is hardly surprising. So Michael and Gabriel are perfect counterparts, at two ends of a spectrum.

Q   Do you believe the current increase in encounters with angels, both white and dark, is related to the Apocalypse as foretold by different religions?

MG   Our time is a time of crisis, a time when all values start sliding and there's nothing that you can really anchor onto. Everyone's desperate for a message. Now, angels are messengers; they bring messages to you. They bring messages from the Divine, from on high. Extraterrestrials also bring messages that we should be peaceable, otherwise the world will blow up, or ecology will go wrong or something. It's always a message. So if there are more reported angelic or mysterious encounters, then it is perhaps because we are counterbalancing the loss of the numinous, the loss of the magical. We seem to have lost some essential mystery—some deeper experience which human beings require. Maybe this need was once satisfied by the tribe with its stories and magic, by the witch doctor or the sorcerer or the shaman who would bring that magical element directly into your life. Now we only have a technological, an informational and scientific environment which does not allow us much in the way of direct religious experience. The religions as they are now are so impotent. They lack that spark which they once obviously had. So we will probably find far more encounters, angelic or otherwise, happening which are necessary in some way to satisfy the need for the numinous.

Q   Tell us how faith can create facts. Do scientists discover what they believe? And does it follow that if science does not believe in angels, it will never prove their existence?

MG   There are probably two ways of looking at anything. You can either *believe* what you see or *see* what you believe. If you see the sun coming up in the morning, you know you've seen the sun coming up in the morning. It's a knowledge—it's a knowing. You don't need someone else's knowledge or belief to tell you that the sun's coming up. If you're blind and you've never seen the sun come up, you have to take someone else's word for it. Now, if you expect to see an angel, there is a pretty good likelihood that you'll see it. If a scientist is hunting for a quark or an atom or a small particle, they will probably find it because they will actually create the equipment to find whatever it is. Now, in one sense, science is hardly likely to find anyone to put up money to look for an angel. And even if you had the funds, how do you look for one? Where do you look for one? Wherever you're going to look, it's probably exactly the wrong place.

Q Do you think scientists may look into it anyhow?

MG It doesn't seem a subject which would immediately bring reward. What is interesting, though, if we go back to the earlier image of a central unknowable divinity, which radiates vibrations which change from thought to light, from light to heat, from heat to matter the further they are removed from the source, it is as though thought becomes substantial when it is slowed down. Then, if you look at modern science, you discover that many scientists believe that thought actually creates objects, that we actually have collectively created a world about us of objects. There are many mystics in the East who can produce anything from Swiss watches to ash to perfume in their hands, and it's not a trick, it really appears to spontaneously happen. Many mystics insist that life is a waking dream, and as a dream we are capable of manipulating it. Much as lucid dreamers claim they can change the outcome of their dreams, so we are possibly capable of changing the nature of what we believe to be our reality. If we really intend to be a millionaire, we can be one; if we really want to see something, it will appear substantial. Now, in the same way, if a scientist really wants to see an angel, he will probably find one. Whether it has an inherent reality or not, that's an entirely different matter.

Q When you think about Superman, doesn't he fit the criteria of an angel in the ability to fly beyond this world, possessing supernatural powers, fighting on the side of good?

MG One of the most fascinating aspects of a resurgence of interest in angels actually comes from the American super-heroes—Superman, Spider-Man, and all the many Captains America. They are all angelic in a way. They stand for good, they stand as good citizens. Here is the ethical and spiritual equivalent of the thirteenth-century angels who appeared on the walls of churches—in many ways so similar to the comic strips of the superheroes of today. Superheroes too have a similar function: they protect the weak and uphold the law, which is exactly what angels do or supposedly did.

Q   If someone asks you how to get in touch with an angel, what would you tell them?

MG   Perhaps the best advice is to go within; it's where the angel is probably to be found. Angels most often appear to us in dreams and in visions which are very dreamlike. Since about 1979, there has been a fascination with lucid dreaming, which is conscious dreaming. When you are asleep you suddenly wake up within the dream and you realize that you're dreaming and then you can do anything within this dream. You can even summon up an angel, if you like. Now, many lucid dreams are so powerful and so real, as real as anything in this room, that you can actually feel, you can touch, you can smell, you can taste: this appears to be a function of the whole brain/mind mechanism. But it appears we're doing something remarkably similar all the time anyway. For we are constantly reconstructing everything around us within our brains. We mostly perceive what we have constructed within, rather than what is actually there. So, in a lucid dream, an angel can be a very real event; it is as real as many of the visions of Saint Teresa, who saw an angel and felt it was totally real. But it could have been an especially powerful lucid dream. So if anyone wants to see an angel, I would say certainly lucid dreaming is a very good way.

Q   Have you ever had one of these dreams?

MG   I've had many lucid dreams, but certainly I haven't chosen angels. Interestingly, one of the first things anyone does in lucid dreaming is to fly. This tremendous desire to fly seems a primal urge in human beings: to defeat gravity, to get out of that iron grip. Anyone in a normal dream will say how enjoyable it was actually when they began to fly. Now does that type of experience, that type of ecstatic joy, have any link with an angelic prototype?

Q   Are children more sensitive to angel encounters?

MG   I would think so, but the beauty of childhood is really that you cannot distinguish easily between what we consider reality and what we consider a vivid dream. Young children seem to experience life as if enhanced, which could be attributed to the intense action of the pineal gland in the early years. This is where, in the East, imagination, fact, and dream all become one. Expand this concept a little further, and one can see that a child could be very impressionable if someone feeds information into that powerful and complex imaginative richness. The child can then create a very real angel indeed if such an idea appealed to him or her, just as many children see what we call "imaginary friends."

That third eye generally starts to atrophy by the time we're about five years old. But I think that it is quite possible that in earlier times, when we weren't quite so blasé about our technical world, many people kept that sort of childhood innocence for much longer and therefore would see angels and actually experience them as fact—see them fully around, see them blazing with light—and yet it could all have been an imaginative process. It shows that the whole subject of angels touches a mystery about which we know very little—simply because we really know so little about the extraordinary power of the mind itself. We use such a very tiny fraction of the brain, and simply don't know what it is *really* capable of. Angels do seem one of those mysterious phenomena which could be far better understood if we used a more scientific approach while at the same time allowing a mystical possibility. It might just change the nature of our science.

The Voice of an Angel

BECKY HOBBS

One December, a couple of weeks before Christmas, I started get-ting premonitions that I would be in a bad car accident. They would hit me when I'd lie down to go to sleep, at that stage when you are just drifting off. All of a sudden, boom!, there would be this big crash and I'd sit straight up in bed sweating, with my heart pounding wildly. And I'd have this awful feeling of despair, like, "But I'm not ready yet; it's not my time to go. I have more things to do." This kept going on for a couple of weeks before Christmas. A friend of mine and I were driving back to Oklahoma to see my mom for the holiday, and we had to pull over a few times because my heart would start pounding. As a result, we got in real, real late on Christmas Eve, and I had to tell my mom, "I'm sorry we're so late, but I just keep having this feeling I am going to be in a bad car wreck and it won't leave me alone." And she understood.

Well, we had Christmas and drove back to Nashville, and nothing happened. So in Nashville I thought, "Wow, it's over. It wasn't meant to be; it didn't happen." Well, it wouldn't let up.

Almost every night afterward, that feeling would happen. My birthday is January 24, and in the wee hours of that morning, I was in the kitchen making some goodies for my party; I was going to have some folks over that night. And I had this feeling of somebody tugging on my sleeve, taking ahold of my arm to take me out to my front yard. And it was something I didn't have a choice about; it was something I had to do. I thought, "What is going on?" Because it was three o'clock in the morning! I looked up at the stars, and I got goose bumps, and I asked, "What do you want me to know? What are you trying to tell me?" And this loud, booming voice—it was as loud as any physical voice I've ever heard—said, "Be careful, this may be your last birthday." The voice in the front yard was so commanding I was just shaking in my boots. But I knew the voice, and I was not afraid of it; the voice loved me. The voice was here to help me and cared about me.

That is all the voice said. And I knew right then that the warning was associated with the premonitions I'd been having about being in a car accident. The key word for me was "may." This may be your last birthday. So I thought, "Then it's up to me. I have to be aware. I have to be careful. I'm in a dangerous situation right now." After that, I tried to ask for more information, but that's all the information I could get. The message had been given and that was all I was allowed to hear. So I went back in the house and that night had my birthday party.

The very next day, January 25, I got into my van with my band and drove to Albertville, Alabama, to play for a police benefit. We loaded up our equipment and were on our way back to the hotel to pick up our things before driving on to Nashville. We were at a four-way intersection on the highway and it was raining and dark.

I was sitting in the back of the van—on the left-hand side in the third seat. I looked out to the left and saw an eighteen-wheeler barreling toward the intersection. I thought, "My God, he's not going to be able to stop." And then I looked over and at that moment our light turned green. Randy was driving the van, and I felt his foot lift off the brake and the car start going. And I knew right then. Boom! It was that feeling, the same feeling I've been having every night, that feeling of, "I'm not ready yet. I'm not ready yet to go."

I yelled at Randy. I yelled for him to stop and he did. The eighteen-wheeler slid into us. We were pulling a trailer and I don't know how many times we spun around. The collision totaled the van—a Dodge Maxivan. And then there was quiet. I didn't know if I was dead or alive, because I couldn't feel anything. We were shaken up pretty badly, and at that moment I thought, "Well, either I'm out of my body or I'm okay." And I really didn't know for a couple of minutes. We were bruised, we were cut, but everybody got out of it alive. And I feel that the warning from the angel saved all our lives because a split second later we would have been completely broadsided. The truck slid into us, but it hit the left front of the van, which is the strongest part. The state trooper said, "You are lucky because you all would have been killed if it was a split second later." We would have been broadsided and, I am sure, killed. The truck was going too fast.

It took me a while to look back and be able to realize that the voice I had heard all those times was an angel. I always thought you have to see an angel; now I realize you can hear angels. The voice was my guardian angel, and ever since then I know those of us who are here are here for a reason or we would not be here. The very fact that we are still here means we have not fulfilled our purpose here on Earth. And I think the angels are with us right now, because it is their number-one thing to help us on this planet. And for those of us who are communicating with angels, it is our number-one thing right now to spread the word and to help others. And that's what I am trying to do.

For a number of years, I have had the title Angels Among Us in my writer's notebook. And I was watching the movie Fried Green Tomatoes, and in the movie, Jessica Tandy says, "I do believe there *are angels among us." And I went whoa, she has been in my note-book!*

And then it just hit me: I have got to write this song. I had a few lines jotted down, but for some reason I hadn't really spent a lot of time on it. So I went home and worked on it for the next week, but I just couldn't finish it. I went home for Christmas to see my mom, and all over her house were angels. My mom is into arts and crafts, so there were beautiful handmade angels everywhere. Once again I had this over-whelming feeling: I've got to finish this song. I came back to Nashville, sat down at the piano but still couldn't finish it. So I called a friend of mine, Don Goodman, and he and I sat down and finished it together. I pitched the song to my friend, Randy Owen, in the group Alabama, and they recorded the song; it is on their new album, Cheap Seats.

Here are the lyrics:

ANGELS AMONG US

I was walking home from school on a cold winter day
Took a shortcut through the woods and I lost my way
It was gettin' late I was scared and alone
Then a kind old man took my hand and led me home
Mama couldn't see him though he was standing there
But I knew in my heart he was the answer to my prayer

> *Oh I believe there are angels among us*
> *Sent down to us from somewhere up above*
> *They come to you and me in our darkest hours*
> *To show us how to live to teach us how to give*
> *To guide us in the light of love*

When life held troubled times and had me down on my knees
There's always been someone to come along and comfort me
A kind word from a stranger to lend a helping hand

A phone call from a friend just to say they understand
Now ain't it kind of funny at the dark end of the road
Someone lights the way with just a single ray of hope

(repeat chorus)

They wear so many faces
Show up in the strangest places
To grace us with their mercy in our time of need
Oh I believe. . . .

(repeat chorus)

What I'm conveying is that yes, I do feel like there're angels right here. There're angels in the human form, there're angels in the nonhuman form, and they are here to show us how to live, to teach us how to give, and to guide us with love. And we all have the power to communicate with our angels; the only thing that is holding us back is ourselves—and maybe fear and maybe not knowing, not believing.

You know, writing songs is a lot of listening—listening to that still, small voice inside the subconscious, the angels, the beings, the spirit world. To be a great writer, you have to be a great listener. I write my best songs when everything's quiet and I'm by myself and I listen to that little voice deep within me. I feel everybody has got that voice, but a lot of people just don't get off by themselves enough to listen to what is going on.

I've learned the hard way. A lot of times I'd be writing a song and I'd feel that it should do something, but then my head would say, "Oh, no, the radio won't play that." So I'd go in another direction. And then, in looking back, I realized I should have just said to heck with what I think someone wants to hear: You've got to follow that small, still voice, you've got to follow your heart. And you can't go wrong *if you do that. Because when you write a song, you're conveying human emotions. So you have to keep the song as honest as possible and not let outside influences come into the writing of the song.*

So I ask my angels, "What do you need me to do? What would you like for me to say? What do we humans need to hear right now?" I do that because I realize the music doesn't come from me; I'm just the vehicle. Everything comes from the greatest force, the power, God— whatever we want to call the Creator. The angels communicate from God to us humans on the physical plane, and we are just channels. That's where the music comes from, that's where all forms of art come from, that's how we communicate with others. A lot of people look outside of themselves for God, for power, for faith, for love. But it's all within. That small, still voice inside connects us to the other realities, to the angels, to God, to everyone. And it's hard for me to even say my song, my music, 'cause it ain't. It ain't mine. I'm just lucky enough to be here to bring it to other people. And that's my mission here in life.

Rosso Fiorentino,
Music-making Angel, ca.
16th c.

K. MARTIN-KURI

K. Martin-Kuri is a professional artist, angelologist, and founder of Twenty-Eight Angels Inc., an organization dedicated to furthering the study and understanding of angels and of the Divine. Teacher, lecturer, and author, Martin-Kuri produced and directed the First International Conference on Angels and is currently working on a book addressing the current resurgence in popular interest in angels.

QUESTION How did you decide to devote your life to angels?

K. MARTIN-KURI When I was a little girl—and I was born many years ago—I found that angels were around my cradle. I could see these angels and I knew these angels were around the people in my family. I saw that many people did not pay attention to the angels around them. I saw much suffering, and I saw that there was a lot of potential for people to ease their suffering if they could listen to this glorious, radiant being who was standing right beside them, who was whispering comforting, nurturing blessings from heaven. I had one experience when I was in first grade and I was walking across a lawn. The heavens opened up behind me and I saw millions and millions and millions of angels. It was like a Dürer painting. And I knew, at that time, that I would not always be able to achieve my work unless I remembered the importance of being here as a human: living and trying to help others.

And so I decided at a very young age that I wanted to help humanity. It became a lifelong path to work with these angels and to understand how they were involved in the creation of the universe. I became an expert in color and the effects of color in altering suffering—meaning changing one's consciousness. Angels work very closely with color. Where we have beautiful flowers, you've seen the imprint of the workings of some of the greatest angels—specifically, the elemental kingdoms that are controlled by the angels above the particular known realm of guardian angels.

But I would add that working with the angels is also working with the force that created the angels. From the very beginning, I felt I wanted to live a life that would honor God. And I try hard. I try hard.

Q Can you define what an angel is and describe the various types and orders of angels?

KMK Well, in the English language, the word *angel* really has the connotation of messenger. But I think angels are greater than just messengers. To me, angels are those aspects of the Divine Creator that have built a bridge between humanity and the Source itself. And this bridge is built upon various gradations of light or formations of consciousness that create the various hierarchies. Closest to humanity we would have the guardian angels. And beyond the angels that take care of humanity we have the angels that take care of nations or cultures, and they are referred to as archangels.

And beyond the archangels we have the Archai. And they are the ones responsible for the whole rise and development and decline of civilizations on a planetary level. Then beyond the Archai, the Dynamis or the Spirits of Motion. They are involved in such things as the rotation of the planets, everything that is dynamic. And next are the Kyriotetes, known as Spirits of Wisdom, that give us the wisdom from which we know there is perfection in the beauty of a rose. And then above these angelic hierarchies we have the three greatest angelic beings. First in this category are the Thrones. The Thrones are responsible for the maintenance of the whole universe. And then there are the Cherubim. And greater than they are the Seraphim. And then [there is] the Godhead.

So the purpose of these angels is to become a transformer, if you will, from the most powerful light of all existence down to a level where we can receive it. We cannot be in the presence of the great one, the Creator, without being filled with that same degree of light, that same degree of purity. Except by grace.

Therefore, we've got to allow for the work of the angel in our life if we would like to be more in harmony with the workings of holy universe.

Q   Why were angels pictured with wings?

KMK   To me angels appear as beings of great light. But they can appear with winglike energy fields that we discern as wings. The wings are an image that reflects the multidimensional levels on which angels operate. It's a symbol of their ability to travel through dimensions. But at their highest level they appear as light. There is nothing but light.

Angels appear to people in a form they can perceive. It might be a man in a three-piece suit with a briefcase, or a truck driver, or a lady in a waitress outfit, or an airline pilot. It doesn't matter what their appearance is—you can always feel an essence of peace around an angel. You always have that feeling of inner quietness and a sense that they are giving you a blessing.

That's on one end of the scale. On the other end of the

Francesco Botticini, *Three Archangels and Tobias*, ca. 15th c.

scale you would have just pure perception of light. Our universe is nothing but energy. Our Creator is nothing but the greatest of all light. And so there would be this experience of a person being so filled with his or her own inner light that he or she could connect with the light of that great angel.

Q   What are guardian angels? Do we all have one?

KMK   It's my belief and experience that we do, in fact, all have a guardian angel. And it's a wonderful miracle. We have this beautiful—and every one of them is beautiful—representative of the Divine to accompany us through life, through its higher moments and its lower moments. The task of this angelic being is really sort of special, because it acts purely out of love. Its responsibility is to always keep the soul of the individual aligned with God. So no matter how an individual might stray away into a period of darkness, no matter how forlorn they may be, or no matter how hardened their heart could become, the angel is always there, faithfully awaiting the moment when the individual will seek to have a greater union with God. But the greatest task always with a guardian angel is to remain faithful to the soul on behalf of the Divine.

The other thing to keep in mind is that there cannot be a birth without the interaction of the guardian angel and there cannot be death without the interaction of the guardian angel. So the role of the guardian angel really begins before birth. Until the child is about seven years of age, they're usually more aware of angels than we are later in life. There's a veil that comes down and the memory is lost. But the action of the angel is always there. As we grow older we find we have a different relationship with the guardian angel. It's more elective. We need to ask, we need to connect with the angel.

The guardian angel holds and protects our destiny. Our destiny is sort of an outline that we can feel in accord with our free will. That general outline is preserved and protected by the guardian angel, and the guardian angel leads us step-by-step through that destiny. The destiny is designed for our spiritual development. So the more that we can open up to the influence of our guardian angel, the more we will fulfill our destiny and the more we will be in harmony with the universe—not only the immediate universe of our life, our family, and our culture, but on a global level. And on an even greater level in terms of our relationship to all the realms of the Divine.

I have this image of how we can see the guardian angel and its responsibility with our individual destiny. It's an image of an angel who is carrying a basket on its arm. And in that basket are the various different potentials we have in our life, and the various different obligations or experiences that we have agreed to go through, according to the will of God before birth. You can call it destiny, if you will. These events are like outlines; there's still a space for there to be changes in response to our free will. For example, when you meet a person you will have the opportunity to recognize that this is an important connection, or you may ignore it and walk on. The angel gives you the wonderful potential to grow closer to God through such experiences.

I would also like to emphasize the need of acceptance in working with one's guardian angel. No matter what difficulty comes into our lives, if we accept the presence and the loving care of the guardian angel, then we are accepting at the same time the love of God, as it is manifest and present in a very direct and personal way in our life.

Q Can you picture the guardian angel as a sort of angelic friend?

KMK Yes. No matter how difficult a task one has to get through, it can be made easier by learning to think of an angel as you would of a friend. If you were going to become a friend with any particular person, you take interest in the things that make them happy; you like to know their music, their art interests. It's the same with the realm of the angels. If you want to get to know your guardian angel, you focus your thinking on those areas of interest to the guardian angel. And what are the areas of interest to a guardian angel? Moral development. Spiritual development. Transformation of the inner nature of mankind.

Q   Can you talk about the role that angels play in various world religions?

KMK   The angels are beginning to unify in such a way that the religions will no longer be as disparate as they are. It doesn't mean that there will be a homogenization, but that there can be a greater sense of peace and unity between the different religious dreams. After all, the belief in angels gives us a common denominator. I'm not one who thinks mankind made religions, I'm one who believes that the angels were involved in the creation of these religions. The angels played a very important part, particularly the Archai and the archangels.

Q   Are the angels playing a new role in the world? Has there been a shift in their function?

KMK   Angels haven't just arrived. They were here before our planet was created. They helped in the development of our planet. They helped in the formation of our flowers and our trees and our mountains and our animals and our dogs and our cats and the music and the wind and the trees. But what's happening now is our consciousness is expanding. So we're beginning to see with new eyes.

Perhaps other people are saying that angels are descending and that they are here on the earth in new numbers. I do not perceive that. They've always been here. It is we who are being given grace in being able to see the angels or to recognize them. And this has a lot to do with the impulse of archangel Michael. It also has a lot to do with the work going on this century of many great spiritual leaders and people who have devoted their lives to trying to bring about a better world. Their prayers have been heard, their prayers have been answered. It does not require a descent of angels; it's more a matter of our opening to the awareness of angels.

On the global level, we're beginning to remember heaven. We had forgotten; we had gotten lost in matter. We'd gotten immersed in the material age. We have become inundated in the worries about our expense accounts or payments of bills, or traffic problems, or snow-removal problems. Whatever the little problem we have, we've looked at it with material eyes rather than spiritual eyes. If we look at the problems of our lives with a new spiritual vision, we begin to see that we have help. We have angelic help, but it's optional.

That means if we open our souls to the level where we can receive what the angels are willing to give us, they will give it to us. So now the question arises, how do we open our souls to that point? It is my belief that there is no other way to really connect with the angels than through service. One can experience a greater connection with one's guardian angel by feeling gratitude and acceptance and a sense of wonder and reverence for truth and beauty. But to really work with one's guardian angel requires the desire to be of service to fellow humanity.

Q Can you explore the concept of channeling?

KMK People are exploring their spirituality through many routes. One of them is to channel, to channel their higher self, or perhaps their guardian angel. But I feel that there is a higher way, and I feel it has been successful for me, and I know it has for many others. That way is to expand the consciousness by developing a much more holy form of imagination, a type of inspiration that allows one to interact with the heavens. Inspiration comes from the word *inspirare*, "to breathe in."

But there is still another level where we are able to interact with the heavens. The third level is the most powerful of all. And I think that's where we're headed. That is the development of pure intuition. When we have that pure intuition, we become that which we are intuiting. So if we are intuiting God, we at some point have to become connected to the Divine. It's a difference between looking upward and saying something is descending and coming through me, or saying I am going to rise to that level of consciousness. I prefer to rise to that level of consciousness—and hopefully I do.

Q   What is our responsibility to angels?

KMK   I think the real message today is for humanity to take

Raphael, *The Three Theological Virtues*, 1507.

responsibility for their inner life, to become more spiritually mature. To lift the soul and the spirit up higher, to create a very chalice out of one's inner nature and to lift that.

For ages humanity has asked, "Well, how do you perceive the spiritual world, how do you get into it?" There have been a thousand books written in our time about this. How do you enter those realms? We have the path of the saints, the path of the philosophers. We've had experiences portrayed in art. We've had great genius in music. Who could say Mozart did not work with angels? And Beethoven, and his "Ode to Joy"—there was the glory of God in his works. So we have had the gifts and working opportunities to expand ourselves with the angels all the time.

But we're being called now to go about it a little bit differently. We're being called to do it in a responsible way. No longer [are we] just recipients, receiving from the angels. Instead, we are to form ourselves, to take responsibility, and to say, "Okay, I am going to formulate myself into a better human being. I am going to do something that is going to be more than my day-to-day life. I'm going to do something that will help the civilization in which I live."

It may be as simple a thing as getting a plan of action to spend an hour a day just doing specific things you haven't done before. That hour a day might really have an effect on all civilizations; why not? We do not realize the power of pure imagination—it's what started this whole universe. God had an imagination. From that imagination, all that exists has been created. He then had inspiration; He infused it with breath and it became alive. It became part of Him. I use the word He, but of course, God is not sexist. I use that word because it's more used in our language; I'm more familiar with it. But you could say God, or Goddess, or Creator.

Q What about the angels themselves? What is *their* responsibility?

KMK Service is what the angels are all about. They do nothing but serve the Divine out of love. And the more love that they have, each rank of the angels, the more responsibility they're given. So a guardian angel has less responsibility than an archangel, all the way on up to the Thrones, Cherubim, and Seraphim. The Seraphim have the responsibility of holding in faith the thoughts of God. That's really incredible when you think of it.

Unfortunately, people think of angels as those cute cherubs with little wings. Those are a far cry from the greatness of these beings, who have the responsibility to make sure the sun stays in its place, and that the moon rotates, and that the planets stay in position, and that the stars don't collide.

When you think of the magnitude of that consciousness that can do this, you must be humbled. It is time for us to prepare for a turn in our path away from self-absorption and self-gratification in the realm of matter. We must begin to look at heaven once again, to raise our eyes to the sky.

Q Is our current world situation unique—either uniquely dire or uniquely promising?

KMK Today on Earth we have a great deal of suffering. We have wars. We have diseases that are killing in huge numbers. Whether it's AIDS or tuberculosis, it does not matter; it still has the same effect. This is not the first time. Way back, prior to the time of Saint Francis of Assisi, plagues were rampant on the earth. And what happened at that time was that there were initiatives that came down from the heavens, individualities who consciously said, "I, through my will, will focus so much on the Divine that it will create a substance that can transform the moral fiber of the earth."

We have a moral situation on the earth now that is frightening. There is a lot of fear, and fear breeds more fear. We have illnesses. We have homelessness. But if you look at it from a larger perspective, the homeless represent the part of us that is not at home spiritually. And if we are not at home spiritually, what will happen is that eventually the inner will be carried out to the outer. Eventually the inner image will manifest itself.

The way to cure the homeless condition isn't only to build shelters. We must do this; we must help at an economic level. But the greater solution is for every individual to take responsibility for their own inner self and to feel at home in their spiritual nature. It's not the razzmatazz of the quick trip to heaven, or how to get an angel in ten easy lessons. That's not what it's about. It's about looking to the Boss of the angels. The angels have their eyes only on God. And we have a choice as a civilization coming up: Are we going to continue to look at ourselves as God or are we going to begin to look at the most Divine source?

Q Do you see some greater or higher purpose behind the problems that are besetting us—the illnesses, the wars, the hurricanes?

KMK My answer is that the angels are seeking to awaken us in a new way. Often, suffering is to help release us from the obstacles of our moral development. We need to release ourselves from the addictions that we have that distract us from the Divine. It can be an addiction to believe that this world works on money and money alone. That denies the Source in its fullest.

Q How do we find our way back to "the Source in its fullest"?

KMK If we could get to a place of inner stillness of soul, we would be able to experience a bliss, a moment of the Divine. We would be able to experience the truth of who we are, aside from what we like, and aside from what we dislike. You must realize the angels do not respond to what we like and what we dislike. They respond to light. The more we can radiate light from our soul, the more the angels will interact with us. The question then arises, "Well, how do you overcome these likes and dislikes that are rampaging and interfering with the moral development of our life and the planet?" We do this through the practice of equanimity. And the way to have equanimity is by accepting *everything* and recognizing the presence of the Divine *everywhere*. The first step is to remember that we have a guardian angel with us, standing right by us at *all* times, witnessing our life, and loving us. And if we feel that presence of love—even only in our thoughts—it will eventually expand into other areas of our life and we will be able to overcome the difficult times.

There's an image I have about what happens when you really work with an angel through these difficult moments. The road will still be there; there will be rocks upon the road perhaps, but what happens is that you are given a pair of quilted shoes, so you can walk on that same road but you don't feel the stones. You have the same experiences, but you do not feel them the same way. So the more we center in on the presence of the Divine in our life, the more we center in on the home within us, the more we center in on the practice of balance, the more we will be able to meet eye-to-eye with the heavens.

Q How have the depictions of angels in art changed through the centuries?

KMK There are many Renaissance paintings of angels, and in almost all of them the angels are shown in profile. In the portrayal of Gabriel making the Annunciation to Mary, it's usually a side view. Only a few of the old paintings of angels have a front view. We could only experience the angel side view [then]; we couldn't take the full experience. But now humanity is beginning to be able to experience the full direct gaze. This has to do with the change of consciousness in humanity.

In history, many times people would be overwhelmed by the experience of an angel, or an Archai, or an archangel. They would express it as a god appearing in their life. They would view the angel as God because the power of the light was so enormous. But there is a difference between our God, or the Divine, and the angels. And what has happened is we're developing our consciousness throughout these many thousands of millions of years. We've always had the same angels, but we're beginning to perceive them differently. Now we know that an angel is *not* God. Now we know that they work *for* God. And we can connect with God through the angels. I do not recommend that anyone really pray directly to an angel, but if they choose to, that's okay, as long as they know that they are really praying to God. You address the letter to God, the Creator. But the angel is the one who delivers it.

Q   What is it like to be so involved with angels in your work—in your art?

KMK   In order to do that and do it well, I have to be at a level of consciousness where I'm interacting with angels all the time. I would say that the most profound impact of experiencing angels since my beginning days here as a little child is to learn to love God more. With each phase I've gone through, I feel more and more the compassion of the heavens. And I become more and more aware of the extremely limited number of opportunities for the heavens to work with a conscious humanity.

I've found in the growing years, I barely rest. I work almost all night and day. The angels, you see, don't sleep. So I find many times they wake me up in the middle of the night. Or if I'm doing a painting for somebody, I'm living with the guardian angel of that person for weeks on end. I'm carrying their soul deep within my heart for a long time.

It does have an impact on me. It makes me more determined than ever that I've got to learn to become a better servant every single day. I have to become more alert in discerning my tasks at each moment. I do miss a lot of opportunities. I've learned that the angels present so many, many, many opportunities to us that we can totally ignore [them]. The way to offset that, I think, is to dedicate your life to service. This doesn't mean that we have to become greater than everyone else. We need to become *ourselves*. If we become who we are in its fullness, then we will glorify the heavens and the angels will sing. *That* is our purpose. For me, I have a task of trying to reveal that heaven exists.

Q How does this contact with angels and with heaven change people?

KMK The Divine exists, and if you walk through these veils and consciousness, you will become a changed person. You will care more about what you can do for the world than what the world will do for you. You will forgive those who have harmed you. And you will begin to expand your creativity to a level you never thought possible. But you don't expand that creativity for *yourself* or to make a great career or to become powerful in the world of matter. You expand that career only as a way of possibly serving the Divine. It's a hard balance to keep because sometimes you have to expand your creativity, and the world will be there. Other times the world may not want to receive what you have to offer. But the true worker has to accept that it's not important whether the world accepts it.

I have learned in my development to become very committed to the service of the Divine. Everything flows out of that. And every moment I reestablish that commitment, I find I have greater freedom. And I find that I begin to have more responsibility given to me from the heavens. It's as if I'm allowed to fly with the Great Ones. When I paint, when I do guardian-angel paintings, or life paintings for someone, I would describe my studio as being very much like an airport. It's a meeting time, a change in dimensions. And it's my responsibility to be very precise and very exact—to be there at the right moment and to develop all my creative skills as a painter to their highest form. If I believe that I can really achieve *nothing* without the Divine, then perhaps a miracle on canvas will happen. I have to face each piece of paper or each canvas with prayer. I must realize that I may have already painted my last painting.

It's always a fact in my life, too, that gifts come out of suffering. I'm mostly blind in one eye, and I have problems with the other eye. Yet I paint. For you see, what appears to be a hardship, isn't. I see on so many other levels.

Q Can you describe your work process, and the role that angels play in your artistic creativity?

KMK When I walk into my studio to paint, I begin doing the humblest of things: I scrape the paint of my prior painting off the easel. And with each scraping, I give thanks for the piece that has been there before. And I begin to check over the brushes, and I begin preparing the canvas I'm working on. And that's a very humbling thing, to stretch the canvas yourself, and to prepare with gesso, and to see this white canvas which has to be prepared carefully.

As I put the staples in, or the nails, I do each act with blessings, and I ask that mercy may be granted to me that I might possibly be able to create something of worth. And then I begin to go to the colors. And I let the colors speak, because the colors are directly connected to the angels. By that time, the veils are opening from heaven and there is a gathering of angelic beings around, depending on the piece I'm doing. And we begin to do the work together. I, the painter, am lifted into that realm. And so the paintings are done at the same time, as the images are experienced.

It's very hard for me actually, because I become quite spacey, yet I have to be very grounded at the same time. There's one painting that I did, which I still haven't completed, of the face of Christ. I could only do five or ten brushstrokes at a time; then I would have to lie down. So I only go there and add a few brush-strokes to it every once in a while. But if I'm doing a painting of Buddha, or if I'm doing a painting of a great angel, or a painting for the future of America, the same process is always there. I must literally give from the very cells of my body. It is a form of agony, going through these various dimensions, expanding through these different dimensions [while] at the same time I'm here. And I always have to rest. But I always feel, at the same time, a moment of glory. For I've been permitted to see, to work with, the realms of heaven.

Q Are we living in an age of breakthroughs in art— breakthroughs that are influenced by the Divine?

KMK One of the things happening on this planet this cen-tury is a development of a new art form. I think the heavens are asking us to create out of a new place. I call this "sacred creativ-ity." We have an opportunity to create out of the nonpersonal, out of the part of us that is greater than the greatest within us. We have the possibility of merging with the veils of heaven and al-lowing the glory of God to flow into our works. To create music that has not been created before. To create colors not seen before.

Agostino di Duccio, detail of portal of the Church of San Andrea and Bernardino, ca. 15th c.

We still don't have enough sacred creativity now. We have a lot of creativity related to self-expression, a lot related to the financial development of our culture. We need much more creativity that is originating from the sacred within. The question will arise, "How do you get to that level of the sacred within in order to create?" There is no other way but through prayer and by experience; by inner commitment. We need to approach our creative acts, our creative deeds, on this level of inner stillness where we remember that the very word *creativity* is strongly connected to the reason we exist.

We are the finest paintings of the Divine. The angelic hierarchies are the sculptures of the heaven. Humanity, in our development, is the finest art project that has ever been. And perhaps through our humility, we can remember that there is a greater architect than us, a greater painter, a greater musician. Everything that we can do from that space will contribute to the betterment of our planet, not to its deadening.

Q How does the new interest in angels relate to this sacred creativity?

KMK The interest in angels is not something put out by book publishers, or mass-marketers; it is not orchestrated by the newspaper, or articles that appear in magazines. It's much more powerful than that. It's happening on the inner plane; it's happening through our sleep, it's happening through our inner life. You realize that the angels are all connected. All the angels of light know each other on some level. They're all connected through the archangels. So it's easy for the Divine Source of all that to issue orders, or thoughts, if you will, that will descend through the various hierarchies down through the archangels, finally down to our guardian angel. The angels tell us in this way, "It's time for humanity to remember the heavens." It's not just some individual who is suddenly gifted with the ability to work with angels. That's not what it's about.

What's really happening on a planetary level has been orchestrated by the great archangel Michael, and many of the great spiritual leaders of all the religions. It started in 1879 with the impulse of Michael. He is one that divides the light and the dark and says, "Choose, commit yourself to the light, and if you commit yourself to the light, you will have greater freedom, but it must arise out of your own will, not by the force of anyone." The Age of Michael, which began in 1879 and will endure for many hundreds of years to come, is an age when we will become spiritually strong. When we will also be able to work out a new level of integrity. When we will begin to see the results of our needs. When we will begin to automatically work from a level of compassion—not just compassion for someone who has no coat on the street, but compassion for the impact of our deeds on the lives of others.

We will be able to automatically sense what is truth, what is beauty, and what is goodness—and be repelled by that which is not. No matter how one would market something of ugliness, and of violence, it will not be long lasting. The choice is coming; you have to choose if you are going to endorse the workings of the Creator, and that means working *only* with the angels of light. You can't compromise or continue to work with the opposition.

The way it works in the heavens is that you can have as long as you want to work with the opposition, but the suffering gets greater and greater and greater with each delay. As we prepare for the turn of the century, we now have an act of grace happening. We are getting conscious reminders that we would not normally have. People are having experiences of overt rescues and many different things that prove that there must be something beyond this life. There's a phenomenal amount of these events happening on a global level.

We even have the manifestations of the being known as Mary. A lot of visionary experiences are occurring to remind us that there is something greater and that it is time for us to put away our toys and begin to become responsible spiritual citizens of our universe. Our universe starts in our own home, with our family and friends, and expands out. We can't go and focus on environmental pollution without having an awareness of how our own thoughts pollute the world around us.

The real threat is not toxic waste from our auto emissions, although they do have impact on the environment. That's not the greatest threat. The greatest threat is our power of negativity. It pollutes everything we do. But through the impulse of Michael we can free ourselves from that influence. We can also free ourselves if we serve others. I'm not talking about going out to feed the hungry on Thanksgiving Day. I'm talking about living in a way where you're aware of the impact of your life on all of civilization. Not only do we have an impact on our immediate fellows, our compatriots on this earth, we have an impact on our environment, and on the spiritual body of the earth as a whole. Are we contributing to a finer spiritual body of light for our planet, or are we contributing to a body of darkness? It is our choice. There is no more margin. This is the reason for the interest in angels, particularly in these last thirty years.

Q Are there specific ways that people can use to get in touch with their guardian angel?

KMK Actually we have an 800 line. It's 1-800-28-ANGEL, and people call that for information on angels at all different hours. It has led me to see how many people in our country are interested in this question, and it's phenomenal.

The answer I give to, "How do you connect," is really very simple. You don't have to connect, you already *are* connected to your angel every moment, every second of your life. We are continuously in contact with our angel. It's a question of whether we are aware of it. So I recommend certain things to do to remember our guardian angel.

Be grateful for everything that is difficult. And be grateful for what is easy, too, for what is good, for all the blessings in life—this is like a child saying, "thank you" for a present. What I mean by gratitude is that we'll be grateful for the loss of a limb, because that may mean we'll learn to walk in a different way. Grateful for financial strife because we'll learn to work in a different way. Grateful for all the hardships, for an illness that may bring out more qualities of a soul that would not have been brought out any other way. Grateful for the difficult things.

When this attitude of soul is attained, a remarkable thing happens. The guardian angel that is so filled with love becomes overwhelmed with compassion and cannot hold back. If you become grateful for all the difficulties you've had to endure and your angel has been with you throughout all your experiences, it's very moving to the heavens.

The second most important quality is compassion. I don't define compassion in the usual way. I think compassion means to have *passion with* another. It means to connect with the life of a friend or associate, and to feel the passion of *their* life. What's the mystery of that soul? As soon as you wonder about this mystery, your guardian angel is connecting with the guardian angel of the other person. And pretty soon you're beginning to work one guardian angel with another.

And then I think we can go on further and begin to work with faith. There's an age ahead of us now when we are going to experience faith with a new meaning. The faith that I'm talking about is the faith to know that even if we can't understand the circumstances, there is a Divine presence; there is a guiding influence. No matter how difficult, there is a way through that set of circumstances.

And there's still another quality that I think is particularly important to us at this time. And that is to have the willingness to serve. Most of us don't know about service. You can't really serve without that very, very hot word: *sacrifice.* Nobody wants to hear about giving up something and they run from that word, but I have a different definition of sacrifice. I say it means using your sacred face—coming from a place of sacredness within. How can one serve without doing that? The two are united. If you serve, you must come from the best from within. And if you do that, then you will automatically work toward the three sister qualities: truth, beauty, and goodness. If you have truth, then goodness will show up; if you have beauty, then truth and goodness will be there; and if you have goodness, truth and beauty will be there. Usually, the three are together.

Q Is there some greater purpose to life that we have lost sight of?

KMK A great man named Rudolph Steiner said a wonderful thing that had a great impact on my life: "We are all thoughts of God." God thought each one of us into creation. The purpose of our life is very much to reconnect with that original thought, to remember. We have glimpses of this memory when there's an act of grace, or when we have an experience in a vision or a dream. But humanity as a whole has forgotten the thought behind our whole purpose. And this is one of the reasons there is an intervention happening right now.

The call has gone forth from the angels to humanity to begin to remember the greater picture.

Q What will happen to humanity as we begin to remember?

KMK As we begin to remember who we are, who created us, then we must act out the highest within us. We will begin to become light. We will begin to radiate out the Divine force, each one of us. And the light we will radiate out will be nothing other than love. It will not be the kind of love that says, "I love you, I want you." It will be the kind of love that does nothing but heal, by its essence.

It's the kind of love that does nothing but fulfill. It's the kind of love that we are not experiencing right now. This love is an expansion. It's there, but we've been given free will so we cannot receive it unless we *decide* to reach for it.

And if we reach for it, it's there. There is a new time ahead of us. There will be those that understand that the love we need to attain is not the gushy type of love, nor is it the type of love that is connected to a result. It's a kind of love that only thinks of honor and of giving.

You may say, "This is fine and good, but how can you be loving when people are battering each other in an area of the country or the world? How can love overcome that?" But, you see, the angels respond to the greatest amount of light you can release, so the more light and the more love one releases, the more angelic help there will be, the more intervention help there will be. So the more that we actually allow for this quality of selfless giving in our day-to-day work lives, the more resolution to problems will come about.

Q How can the angels help us find the type of spiritual love you're describing?

KMK   You can't possibly work with angels without having the love of which they are composed brush upon your soul. I tell people that one of the most lovely things about working with angels is to have time to be with your own guardian angel first thing in the morning. And if you do that, you will begin to feel—I swear you will—the brush of your guardian angel's wing on your cheek upon rising. It may not be a physical brush, but you will begin to feel the love that the heavens have for you, the individual.

Most of us are absolutely terrified of all the struggling we do in life. And yet there is a God that loves us. We want everything to be easy. But love does not mean that things should be easy. . . . What love means is that it awakens us to a higher and higher and higher level where we can become more in tune with God.

Q   Given the state of the world today, do you think we're approaching the Apocalypse described in Revelation?

KMK   I would rather say that each person is approaching the end of an old way of being on this earth, and that we must create tools to exist in the new world ahead of us.

We've always had suffering as long as there has been life, but at present, we're more exposed to the pain than we used to be. However, we can choose to live with the consciousness of heaven, or we can reject it as impossible. The world can be a cold, hard place, or it can be filled with love and softness and warmth; the choice is ours. And we must make that choice in all areas of our lives.

Q   Is there something the angels want from us?

KMK   Angels do not desire anything other than to fulfill God's will. This means that they don't seek anything from us. The angels do, however, hope we will all do one thing, in all the many ways it can be expressed: to love God above everything else. And to the extent we are able, the limited extent we are able, then we have made the world a little warmer, a little kinder, than it would be otherwise. Would this not create a new song of joy among all the angels of heaven?

Pieter Brueghel the
Elder, *The Fall of the
Rebel Angels*, ca.
16th c.

FATHER
JAMES J. LEBAR

The Reverend James J. LeBar is the Catholic Chaplain at the Hudson River Psychiatric Center in Poughkeepsie, N.Y., and the Consultant on Cults for the Archdiocese of New York. A founding member of the Interfaith Coalition of Concern About Cults, Father LeBar is the co-author of Cults, Sects, and the New Age.

QUESTION The first thing I want to ask you, Father LeBar, is about the origin of the word *exorcist*.

FATHER JAMES J. LEBAR The words *exorcist* and *exorcism* both come from the same root—a Greek word which means "to bind or command in an authoritative way." It has to do with the use of the command of Christ to tell the devil to get out of a person and go back to hell where he belongs.

Q I have heard Jesus Christ described as the first exorcist. Do you think that's accurate?

JJL   Well, I suppose that would be accurate, because certainly in the New Testament we read several times where Jesus came upon people who were possessed by the devil and He chased them out. The only inaccuracy would be that there were rabbis prior to the time of Christ who could do the same thing.

Q   So exorcism is also a part of Judaism?

JJL   Exorcism has been around since the very beginning of things. In many places in the Old Testament we read of people who have had encounters with the devil, and rabbis have been able to chase the devil out. So it is a part of the Judaic tradition. It really came to the forefront, however, at the time of Jesus' life on Earth. The instance of His visibly and immediately chasing the devil out became apparent.

Q   How did this rite of exorcism evolve into a formal formula within the church?

JJL   In the beginning Jesus did exorcisms and the Apostles did them after Him, and later on the successors of the Apostles—the bishops and the priests down through the centuries—did them whenever they came across cases of demonic possession. As things grew more formalized and more expansive during the subsequent centuries of history, the church formalized many of its liturgical and ceremonial practices. In the thirteenth and fourteenth centuries, they began to develop a prayer ceremony for exorcism, and in 1583 and 1584 we had a very definite one; and then finally in 1614 the church codified and authorized the use of the ritual which is still in use today.

Q   Can you describe what the formula consists of and how it works?

JJL   In order to perform an exorcism a priest must be duly appointed by the bishop of the diocese in which the person afflicted is located in order for it to be considered legitimate. The ritual of exorcism is basically a series of prayers directed to praise

Hieronymus Bosch, *The Expulsion of Adam and Eve from Paradise*. Detail from the Haywain triptych, ca. 1500–1502.

and give honor to God and then to command the devil to leave. It's as simple as that. It can take a few hours, it can take a few days; some take years because the devil is a very stubborn creature and sometimes refuses to leave. But the essence of the exorcism ritual is to command the devil to leave in the name of Jesus Christ.

Q Can you take us through the actual process of an exorcism?

JJL The best place to do an exorcism is a church or a chapel. Second would be the place where the person has experienced the most difficulties. But for the most part we try to do it in the church, where we have the ambience of holiness, and where we have the Blessed Sacrament, which we believe to be the true Body and Blood of Jesus. Now, oftentimes a truly possessed person won't go near that room with the Blessed Sacrament present, so the ritual has to occur in the room next to it.

When a person is going to receive exorcism, the priest is deputized by the bishop to do so, and he finds an assistant along with seven or eight other people who perform various tasks. They may be asked to pray. They may be asked to hold the person down, and also to watch the exorcist to make sure that he doesn't suffer from fatigue.

The ceremony of exorcism itself usually begins with the celebration of Mass. Following the Mass, the Rite of Exorcism itself begins with a series of prayers—prayers first of all giving all glory to God, and secondly getting down to business, trying to determine which devil is there, trying to find out the devil's name, and trying in the name of Jesus to expel the devil forthwith here, now, and immediately. Now, because the devil is a very stubborn and very proud person, when an exorcism begins the devil sometimes will refuse to go, even though ultimately it must leave the person. It exercises its pride and its stubbornness oftentimes over a long period of time, and it will cause a person to resist. That's why we have people there to help hold the person down—so they don't fly to the ceiling or something of the sort. The ritual basically is very short, but then additional prayers are used and additional commands are used, and during the ritual itself, the person is often sprinkled with holy water. For most people, if the holy water hits them, it doesn't evoke a very violent reaction. But in one exorcism I was placing the holy water on the person, and each time that I did it they screamed, "You're burning me with oil, stop that!" Of course, the cold water was not the problem; the problem was that the water was blessed by the Church for this particular ceremony and it had spiritual power behind it.

Q Can you describe to me the biblical version of how Lucifer was cast out from heaven? Why did it happen to him and how did it transpire?

JJL It's very difficult to know what happened up in heaven before people were created or even what goes on there now. But in the book of Revelation, the twelfth chapter, there is a section in which the writer John describes a war going on in heaven; one third of the angels ultimately were cast out of heaven for refusal to do what God commanded. These angels then became what we know as the devils. They were under the leadership of Satan or Lucifer, and they refused to listen to God.

Q Do we know what the reason for that was?

JJL If we go back to the first book of the Bible and we read about Adam and Eve and their encounter with the slimy serpent, which is identified as the devil, we find pride and disobedience as the two main causes. So I would put forth, as do most theologians, that the same problem was at hand for the devils. Saint Thomas Aquinas, for example, states in his great theological work, *Summa Theologica*, that he thinks that the angels were given a test: they were shown a vision of God becoming man, the Incarnation—Christmas, in other words—and they were told to fall down and adore the Christ child. Most of the angels who loved God and did whatever God said, they said, "Fine." But some of them said, "I'm not going to do that, God. You're too powerful. I'm not going to worship this baby." God said, "Do it anyway," and they refused. And so, therefore, since they were full of pride—meaning they thought they knew more than God did— and disobedience, God put them out. That's the opinion of Thomas Aquinas, the great theologian of the Middle Ages.

Q Most people think of the devil in singular terms; we

think of God on one side, the devil on the other. Is the devil a singular concept, or are there many devils?

JJL   In the same twelfth chapter of the book of Revelation where it tells of how the angels fell from favor, it also tells us that one third of the angels followed Lucifer or Satan in the same path. So there are certainly many, many devils, not just a single one. Lucifer or Satan is the head of the devils, but there are many.

Q   In this day and age, many people consider evil as an abstract interpretation of bad things that happen in their lives. Do you agree with that?

JJL   Well, there is always that question of what is evil. Philosophically, we would define evil as the absence of good, so that in a sense evil does not exist; evil is a total absence of good. But we have to personify things or we can't talk about them too well, and so what's happened is that in the modern day and age, evil has taken on its own reality. Evil is certainly a reality in its effects, but evil does not exist by itself.

Q   Now, this brings up an interesting thought. In older times, people saw evil as a malevolent force at work in the world, but nowadays people see it almost as a necessary power that helps us realize what's good; it helps us strengthen our spiritual muscle by testing us. Do you think that the Church would agree with that view?

JJL   In the plan that God has, according to Christian theology, there is this constant battle between the forces of good and the forces of evil. So those things that do come up that are difficult, hard, evil, are an opportunity for people of faith to rise above them. They become a better person because they encountered that particular evil force.

Q   But what about the concept that evil is a force outside of people, outside of their control? That evil has its own agenda? Is that recognized by the Church?

JJL We've got to add one thing here, and that is evil is the result of the action of the real person, the devil. The devil is the person that is real and outside of the individual: the devil is causing the evil actions to happen.

Q Most people don't think of the devil as a person. They might think of it as an entity or spirit or something.

JJL Right, and this is part of the difficulty of things today. Some people want to see evil—let's say a natural disaster—as the real force. But according to Christian theology, God created angels and some of them fell, and those who fell are the bad angels and they are real. When they fell, their orientation changed 180 degrees from serving God to hating God. The mistake that's made sometimes, I think, is that people equate God and the devil, and that's not right. God is on top of everything, and the angels who are faithful and the angels who are not faithful are on a level below that.

Q Does the Church see that certain things that happen in the world are the result of the meddling of those bad angels?

JJL When you begin to talk about the things that happen in the world, it's easy to say the devil did this or God did this. But God made the world and it runs according to the plan that He has. Now, in the case of natural disasters—the earthquake in California, the floods in the midwest, and our wonderful snowstorms in the east—these are all natural phenomena and that's not the problem. The problem is when these things happen to certain people or when people are unexplainably put in the middle of them; *this* is the work of the devil, not the natural disasters.

Q The recent example that leaps to mind is that church in Alabama where the people were all praying. A tornado hit and

Limbourg Brothers, *Fall of the Rebel Angels*, ca. 15th c.

just flattened the whole thing. These were people in some sort of discourse with God, and yet a natural force provoked a huge tragedy. How would that fit in that regard?

JJL   I don't think we have a real answer for that. Certainly, from one point of view, you could say, well, this was the time for God to call certain people to heaven, and what better way to do it than while they are in church? That's an easy answer and I wouldn't push that too much. Was God punishing people because the tornado hit? No; that would mean God is vindictive, and that's not the kind of God that we have. We come down to the basic answer: we don't know why it happens. It's just one of those mysteries of the universe. We don't know why it should happen at that time and that place.

Q   Given that an individual has free will, what happens to someone who consciously chooses the path of evil as a directive in their life?

JJL   When a person consciously chooses the way of evil instead of good, then they are making a determination not to follow God. In Christian theology, if that happens unto death, then that person would be condemned to hell.

Q   Do you believe that hell exists?

JJL   Absolutely! Yes! Because it is part of God's justice. If a person is good, they go to heaven; if a person consciously chooses to be bad, God in His justice cannot say, "Come on to heaven anyway." Hell is the place of torment for those who have chosen to follow the other path instead of the path of goodness.

Q   And is hell inhabited by devils and demons?

JJL   Hell is the place in the next life where those fallen angels who disobeyed God have been consigned, and also those people who decided not to follow the path of goodness in this life.

Q   Why then would any rational person, believing in these ultimate realities or destinations, choose Satanism?

JJL   In my experience with these people, God hasn't provided them what they wanted, and somehow or other the devil manifests himself, either by thought or word or actual appearance, and promises great things to the individual. In this way, the person feels the devil is going to be more powerful than God and chooses to follow him.

Q   Why do you think there is a rise in Satanism in the world today?

JJL   I'm not so sure there is more Satanism in the world today than there was twenty years ago. I think that people today are just beginning to be aware of what was going on in the early fifties and through the sixties. There was an awful lot of serious devil worship going on, but nobody heard about it. It was kept very secret. What we're seeing today are people who were victims of that in the fifties who are now forty years older and starting to remember awful things which happened to them in Satanic-worship ceremonies.

Today we have a different aspect of Satanism, where people are actually going to Satan, trying to conjure him up through Ouija boards or tarot cards or Satanic rituals. These people are looking for an experience and that's far different than seriously worshiping Satan.

Q   When you look back through history, you have pictures of Lucifer as this handsome, wonderful, winged creature that has fallen. And then there are other, more contemporary images where he's become totally bestial. Has our culture's image of Satan changed over time?

JJL   Well, the devil—being an angel—has no real appearance and can take on the form of anything or anyone that he wants to. Oftentimes the deception is needed to lure somebody into following the devil. He uses an image of a handsome young man or handsome young woman to seduce the person. Later on, as someone gets into Satanic rituals, the true nature of the devil comes out and he appears as an ugly creature.

A lot of this is reflected in art as well. In the very earliest

Hans Memling, *Last Judgment*. Right panel of Hell triptych, ca. 1466–1473.

days of the church, angels were never represented, and only later on did they come to take on beautiful features. They were young usually and they had wings to signify that they were special creatures. Similarly, the devil was given certain accoutrements, too. The devil had horns, had a tail, and was always carrying a pitchfork; that's one image of the devil. The Bible speaks of the devil as a beast, and so this became another image—this horrible beast. People have told me that they have really seen the devil or some creature in these guises.

Q Do you think that the devil appears to them in a certain guise because of their upbringing or because of his choice?

JJL Well, you have asked me to read the mind of the devil, and of course I can't really do that. But from talking to exorcists and others who have been involved in things, I know that the devil takes on whatever he needs in a particular place. So if a person is looking for a horrible creature, he is going to find a horrible creature, and if the devil is trying to seduce somebody and the person is not going to react to a horrible thing, then they see something very nice. I think allied to this is something we find in the rite of exorcism itself. I can testify personally that in several exorcisms I have witnessed, the devil speaks in the language that needs to be understood, either by the exorcist or by the person himself. For example, I came into a situation where the devil was being exorcised by an Italian priest and the language was Italian. A Frenchman came in and it immediately switched to French, but words about me were spoken in English so that I would hear them. So the devil can use all of those trappings either to identify himself or to warn people. This is one of the ways that the devil operates, and it proves that we're dealing here with a highly intelligent creature, a fallen angel.

Q How do you determine whether someone is suitable for an exorcism? What are the signs that you look for?

JJL Today we have developed a pastoral practice that takes into account medical science and psychological advances. Before an exorcism would take place, we ask for a medical evaluation to make sure there is no physical impairment causing a hallucination or a particular problem. We ask for a psychiatric evaluation, too, because people who hear voices often are called schizophrenic and we have to determine what's going on.

When we get a report back from all disciplines that there really is nothing wrong, then we move into the spiritual area. The person generally has been complaining that the devil's bothering him or something awful is going on, unlike a mental illness problem, where the voices may be just about anything.

To determine whether someone needs an exorcism, we do what we call a provocation, in which the priest seeks to find out if the devil is there. Sometimes it could be as simple as a conversation. In one instance, I said to a priest working with me, "Well, I wonder what we should do now?" and all of a sudden the voice came out and said in a very gruff and deep tone, "You know what to do, stupid; stop wasting time!" Well, that was a little surprising, to say the least. As I questioned this voice I was able to determine that there was knowledge of events known only to me. This is another sign. We call that clairvoyant knowledge.

Other times we will take the cross and show it to the person, and if the person recoils from it, really, in an awful way, this is another sign—not the only sign, but one of the signs. Sometimes we will take a glass of holy water and a glass of ordinary water, and unbeknownst to the priest doing the testing or to the individual, one of those glasses of water would be given to the possessed person. A person can drink down the ordinary water fine, but if the devil is present, the holy water will make them gag and choke, and they'll throw it up along with a whole lot of other stuff.

But perhaps the most meaningful thing is we take either a relic of the Holy Cross or a Holy Communion and place it in a container. Now, the container could contain one of three things—the relic of the cross, the host, or nothing—and only the assistant would know which. Again unbeknownst to the person, we would touch them at the back of the neck with this container. Now, when the container holds a holy object and there is a devil present, the person will recoil and really need to be restrained and complain, "Oh, you're burning me, you're hurting me." But if an empty container touched them, nothing happens.

Q   What about levitation? Has anybody ever witnessed that?

JJL   Levitation—the unexplainable rising up of the person off the ground—is one of the signs that diabolical possession is present. I haven't seen that myself, but I do remember talking to a bishop who told me that he went to visit a hospital one time, and as he was going to see a sick priest, he walked by a room in the hospital and suddenly heard a loud noise. He looked in the room and here was a woman up on the ceiling. He said to his secretary, "Let's get out of here," and the secretary was very happy to leave quickly. But later on, the bishop came back and heard a noise the second time; there she was, up on the top again. And he then went into the room—being a bishop, he could perform an exorcism anyplace—assessed the situation, and in a few short sentences commanded the devil to leave and the woman came down.

Q   Was she cured?

JJL   She was cured, yes, and she had no idea why she was there, and she was most embarrassed to find the bishop and the priest and a few other people in her hospital room. When told what happened to her, she was absolutely chagrined over the whole thing.

One other sign of devil possession is extraordinary strength. In one case that I was working on, the person involved just reached behind and picked a large picture off the wall with one hand, ready to throw it at me. The picture weighed probably twenty-five to fifty pounds and could not usually be lifted with one hand.

Q How many inquiries do you receive each year from people who require your screening or investigation?

JJL From 1960 until 1989, chancery officials in our office in New York said they never had a single case to deal with it. In 1989 we had two, and since the publicity beginning in 1990, we now have a backlog of cases numbering about 250, of which probably less than ten percent will actually need help in the exorcism area.

Q Twenty-five cases. That's still a lot of exorcisms, isn't it?

JJL I would think the number twenty-five would be significant in that in a thirty-year period we had none and in another period we had only two. But, you know, different cultures do things in different ways. In Italy, for example, the head exorcist of the city of Rome is Father Gabrielle Amorth, and he told me himself that he does about two thousand exorcisms a year, so he certainly has a different way of approaching it than we do here in America. Such a large number doesn't necessarily mean the society is very bad. Father Amorth doesn't do any of the psychological or other evaluations that we do. He feels that if somebody confesses that he needs an exorcism, the best course is to give it to him right away.

But here in the United States and certain other countries, who is going to do all these exorcisms? It was a requirement of the Church for a long time that each diocese have a duly appointed exorcist to whom people could turn and to whom the bishop could turn for help in these matters. Now, because so few exorcisms took place between 1960 and recent time, most of the exorcists have retired, moved on, or perhaps even died, and were never replaced. So right now we have a shortage of exorcists. However, this is only a temporary situation. Many countries are training priests for this important work. It is my expectation that here in the United States many dioceses will soon have their own exorcists, and the larger archdioceses, such as New York and Boston, might even have more than one.

GUY MARTIN

Guy V. Martin, M.A., B.D., is the Director of Financial Aid and a member of the faculty at Harvard Divinity School. A graduate of Colgate University and the University of Chicago–Chicago Theological School, Martin is an ordained minister in the United Methodist Church. He has researched and written in the areas of religion and literature, and his most recent work has been on the religious correspondence of poet T. S. Eliot.

QUESTION   You teach a course at Harvard about angels, ghosts, and incarnations. How did you develop this idea? What was your inspiration?

GUY MARTIN   It was the summer of '88. I thought to myself then that you could be at a cocktail party or in a discussion with people outside the divinity school, and talk about ghosts and spirits would make people a little uneasy to begin with per-

On facing page:
Caravaggio, St.
Matthew and the Angel,
1602.

169

haps, but they would have a way to talk about it. On the other hand, if you mentioned angels, you were liable to be left on your own very shortly. You didn't hear much about angels then, and who would know what to say about them?

The other thing I thought of at the time was a line from one of the theology professors at Chicago: "If you really want to know where a theologian stands, just find out what he or she has

Gian Battista Tiepolo, *Jacob's Ladder*, ca. 1726–1728.

to say about angels." It just sort of struck me. I forgot all the other wonderful things he said, but that one stayed with me. The more I started getting involved in it in my reading, the more I thought this might be an interesting topic to look into. And so I developed a course.

Q   So in the course of the semester, your students study literature and look at angels as metaphor?

GM   It's primarily devoted to looking at the appearance of angels in literature and particularly modern literature. But to give some background to that, we look at Dante because Dante's *Paradiso* is probably the preeminent presentation of angels in Western culture's fictional literature. We do some sections of Dante mainly to get people familiar with the ideas of the heavens and different beings.

Then we take a look at some short stories—a Malamud short story, a Tolstoy short story—and in the process we see how angels function in literature: How and where do they come in? What's the interest of the author? Why have an angel?

I usually spend a lot of time on Wallace Stevens's poetry because Stevens is certainly a modernist and Stevens is not a person who is interested in promoting religion. In fact, he comes out of religious tradition in order to focus more on what's going on in this world with our imagination, with what is human, with what we human beings are endowed with. Having said that, Stevens somehow can't stay away from angels. They keep appearing in his poetry and often have very much the same role that an angel might have in a theologically orthodox context. Angels serve to bring a message, to change a direction in someone's perception. In fact, in the poem that we look at very closely, "Angels Surrounded by Paysans," Stevens says something to the effect that I'm not one of the old angels or one with "a tepid aureole" and things of that sort, but I am an angel of the earth and it's only through me that you come to understand or see what the earth is all about. That sense of revelation, that sense of bringing a new vision, a new direction, is very much the role that the angel Gabriel plays with Mary.

Q   What is your opinion of the recent popular surge of interest in angels? Why are angels suddenly everywhere?

GM   The reason I started preparing my course on angels in the summer of '88 was because nobody was talking about angels. And then lo and behold, by the time the course began, the Wenders film *Wings of Desire* had come out, and although it wasn't a popular success, it certainly was a noteworthy achievement. Subsequently people have taken to talking about angels. I think when people talk about angels, they are looking at the future, and when people talk about ghosts, they are talking about the past. Certainly up to '88 the American culture was very much looking at its past. There were a lot of ghosts, whether they were ghosts of Vietnam, ghosts of racism, or whatever. The positive aspect of this current interest in angels is perhaps a willingness to look into the future.

What worries me most about the popular-cult aspect of angels is the emphasis on angels simply as human projections. They have become sort of wish fulfillments of things we would like, things we think we deserve. This is an overstatement to some extent, but the popularization of angels may not lead us into new directions but instead lead us down the same old paths again, and that would be unfortunate.

Q   Do you think the new interest in angels is a symptom of our culture's shift from the material world to a more spiritual focus?

GM   Angels gave folks who felt the need for it some sort

of faith and the means for talking about it, a way of dealing with it, a way of exploring that faith. In the *Wings of Desire* film precisely the opposite thing is happening: the angels are being seduced by this sensual world we have. The seduction is not that we should be like angels but, rather, that angels may well want to be like us.

Q   Do you have a theory about what the message of angels might be? Is there some way in which the message relates to human responsibility and human growth?

GM   One of the things that religion has always fallen into is that it's served as an answer for people. It gave people a sense that somehow something magical could appear in our lives that would solve our problems. To the extent that we project angels in our own image, that's another one of those idolatries that we fall into. But the truth is, angels surprise us. They are not what we expect. They tap you on the shoulder when you're not ready. If you are open to that possibility, to a new direction, to hearing a new voice, a new message, you can make a turn in your life that opens up, challenges, and elicits an energy and a willingness and a joy that hasn't been there before.

Interestingly, the Malamud story "Angel Levine" precisely deals with that issue—that one prays to God for respite from the pain and suffering one is going through. And yet, what the angel does in that story is to shock Manischevitz the tailor in a conception of angels that he never thought of before: he's never seen a black Jewish angel, and it was hard for him to conceive of and for him to give his faith to that. Once he makes a decision and starts to do that, he has dealt with something that's important for him to deal with in his life.

I think the function of angels theologically is to keep people open to the future so they can find something that allows them to grow and move in a new direction, that enhances their responsibility and allows them to take charge of their lives.

Q   Do you see literature or art in general as a way for people to touch that other world?

GM   One of the wonderful things about art is that it is often associated with new perceptions, with new sounds, with new voices, with new ways of looking at things. And in fact that helps the theologian be open to new possibilities and new connections. And so as the artist mediates between a vision and an audience, in a similar way the theologian is a mediator as well. The theologian stands in between an audience and a transcendent God that he or she understands to be a creator. And so the roles of the theologian and the artist are often in some respect parallel roles. Both open up new images, new metaphors, new rhythms, and enable us to see things new for the first time.

Q   What are your thoughts on the parallel between science and theology? Are they more in tune than we would like to think, or do you see essential conflicts between them?

GM   I don't think anything in the phenomenal world is contradictory to my own religious faith. First of all, I am a body. I have to live in this world, I have to function in the laws of this world. Nonetheless, this world doesn't tell me the direction I'm going, where I give my energy, what is meaningful in life, if it's more important to love or if it is more important to protect my backside. There is always a need for human beings to find a source of meaning—the important angel in my life is the one who opens up a new possibility—and in that respect, I don't see any conflict between science and religion.

Q   Where does the concept of dark angels fit into your view of the spiritual realm?

GM   Darkness in and of itself is not bad. One can't stand in the light all the time. You need the rest, you need the resuscitation of light and of darkness, that part of the rhythm that we all live in. Too many people, as Flannery O'Connor pointed out rather graphically, want to divide the world into good and bad, light and dark, and evil and positive, and the world just doesn't divide up that way. True, it makes the world easier to live in because you can always tell who your enemy is. The difficulty is, the enemy often turns out to be us, and we've spent a lot of time and energy messing things up for other people when we should have been looking at ourselves.

Q   Do you think the angels described by Wallace Stevens and by Rilke are more powerful, more compelling than the angel descriptions we're seeing published today?

GM   Yes. Angels came with terror. When angels speak to Mary, she's not bright-eyed and [saying], "Oh, it's nice to hear your voice." She's terrified. Any representation from a divine realm is not a happy experience. There is a sense of fear connected with the newness that it [the angel] brings. I think that's what Stevens forces us to consider in his poetry, for it's not easy poetry to deal with. One doesn't pick it up and go, "That's nice" and then go on to the next page. You stumble over lines, you stumble over language, and the irony is that Stevens is trying to make angels much more a part of this world. It is not in a simple easy way, but in a way to get people to see things freshly and with new eyes.

That is frightening for most of us. We are either spending most of our time doing everything new, so we can't settle on one particular thing, or we're so committed to one thing that any change is a threat. To domesticate angels is to emasculate any theological sense or actually any human sense that they may have.

Angels are precisely *other* beings, whatever metaphysics are behind them, and it takes that presence to get us to consider something new, to be open to a new direction the older we grow.

Q   Do you conceive of angels strictly metaphorically or do you see them as actual beings playing a divine role?

GM   There have been a number of recent reports of people who have had experiences of angels and I certainly would never try to argue someone out of their experience. The critical thing is what happens next as a result of that experience: What does this lead me to do? Does this lead me in a productive way for my life? Does this lead me in a direction that's going to be helpful and open up new avenues of thought and expression? That's what's important. I think it's a mistake to try to debate the wrongness or rightness of these experiences—did they or did they not happen. If a person has them, they have them. The issue is what now, where do I go, what was the message the angel brought?

Q   Is there a divine world where angels are beings?

GM   I believe that's a possibility. I really don't want to spend a lot of time trying to figure out how it works or what sort of physical laws are necessary with it. I do think that in all our lives the function of revelation is critical and that revelation is not something we manufacture but is given as a gift. If the gift comes in a Technicolor form of an angel, that's fine; if the gift comes as a process remembered from my earlier life and understood for the first time, that's important as well. That's the sort of thing that artists help us to do: artists help us to remember and to see and to hear new things.

Q   Are we into something new with these angelic encounters, or does it somehow relate to the end of the millennium?

GM   The end of any millennium is always going to bring with it a great deal of excitement, predictions, a sense of unease. So I don't think it's unusual that these things are coming up once again. It's the need to try to find some control over a world that's very much out of control.

As the world we live in becomes much more complex— complex in terms of different people, different languages, different technologies, different information—it's very hard to get some sense of stability. So in this age it is not unusual to see people grasping tenaciously on to a variety of things. We all need something to hold on to, and the kind of world we are living in frustrates that at almost every turn. It's important to have some center in your life that doesn't shift every time the world shifts.

Q   Is there some larger theme or concept that links the view of angels presented in Western literature—especially recent literature?

GM   Artists like Toni Morrison or Flannery O'Connor or Bernard Malamud or Leo Tolstoy or Wallace Stevens present a vision of otherworldly realities that doesn't allow us to escape from being human but forces us into a responsible look at what it means to be a whole person who can live and meet the challenges of the kind of pluralistic technological world we live in. The angels (or ghosts, in Morrison's case) presented by these artists open up these options in a different way than much of the popular reference to angels. The popular way leaves us with a good taste tonight, but it is not going to solve our problems tomorrow.

Q   Is there some sense in which reading a literary text is like encountering an angel—some way in which reading transfixes and transforms the reader?

GM In any piece of literature, there's a beginning and there's an ending and there's something that happens in between; the question is, how does the author bring about that shift in between the opening and the closing that catches your attention? That ability of the artist both to bring us into a world and then show us something in that world that we weren't prepared to see—*that's* the important thing that writers and artists do. Trying to be open enough for that recognition and for that sense is something that we all need to train ourselves to do. As T. S. Eliot said a number of times, when you confront a new piece of work, you literally have to be knocked down by it; you have to let it wash over you, you have to offer no resistance. But once that's happened, then you've got to get up, recover yourself, and have something to say. One would think the easiest part of that would be to be knocked down, but that's *not* the case. Most of us already have a man-locked set—to use a phrase that Wallace Stevens uses in his poem. Most of us have the man-locked ideas when we go into a film, when we confront a picture, when we read a text; it takes discipline to remove our presuppositions and allow the text or the piece to speak.

Reading this way helps me hear voices I would not otherwise hear. There are a lot of voices in this world that haven't been heard before; there are a lot of voices that we need to hear in order to make the world a place that we can live in comfortably, reasonably again. That's the ability that good art and good literature provides: it opens us to hear new voices, and new voices bring new options. That is something we all need.

Q Can you describe your personal attitude to living life in these confusing days?

GM The attitude that I bring to the day is very much the

fact that God created the earth and all that's in it and God saw that it was a good creation. It's important that we love our neighbors as ourselves, and the source of that loving comes from the God who is the creator of this world. What I would look to is a day open with possibilities. I don't mean that to sound as if happiness is a goal, because even in a world in which we look at possibilities and at human beings with potential, there is still tragedy, pain, suffering, and injustice. Try as we may, we are not going to avoid these. But within the context of this life, one needs the angels to offer options and hope and possibilities for our future, and I think that only comes from a kind of commitment that this ultimately is a good world that is worth loving.

Q   How would you describe your daily experience of God?

GM   I don't have a day-to-day experience of God. I celebrate the being of God in liturgy, and that is important. It's important for me to worship and to celebrate the presence of God in worship rather than expect that God is going to be with me day to day. My concern as far as religion is concerned is to practice that faith with respect to other human beings and to worship God and not be so much concerned with whether God is paying attention to me.

Q   What are your thoughts about death and the possibility of life after death?

GM   From my point of view, the difficulty with death is the fear of death—that, in fact, the apprehension about dying so inhibits the way I live now that it takes life out of this day. What happens after death for me is a matter of faith: it's not something I'm going to speculate about, it's not something I think I'm going to be heroic about. What *is* critical is how one lives one's life now. One establishes how one feels about death and then one makes sure that one takes advantage of living this day rather than being concerned with what's going to happen after death. The presence of death often brings a sense of reality into our lives and catches our attention the way other things don't. That's important. It's also important not to be cowed, so that you're always just trying to keep death at a distance. That would take away the joy of this world.

$\mathcal{T}ara's\ \mathcal{A}ngels$

SANDY MOORE AND KIRK MOORE

SANDY MOORE   We always knew that our daughter Tara would make a difference in the world. From the time she was little, she had that aura about her that she was going to make a difference, and she grew up to be a very beautiful girl who was very intelligent. She was going to affect a lot of people's lives, although we didn't realize it was going to be in this way. From day one, she was very unconditionally loving. She was not always an easy child—always busy, always into things—but she was always unconditionally loving. She never left the house or ended a phone call without saying, "Mom, I love you." Never.

KIRK MOORE   We said that from the time she was born, she never had her feet firmly planted on the ground. She just always was ten feet off the ground. And she would see somebody on the street, a homeless person, or somebody needing money, and she would say,

"Let's stop and give them something." She always wanted to help people; that was the way she was.

QUESTION   Can you tell us about the accident that happened?

SM   Well, it was Tara's fifteenth summer. The night that Tara was killed, we'd had a girls' night in our home, and Tara made dinner. And she looked at me, in the midst of burritos and lettuce and cheese, and said, "Mom, do you believe that when you're finished with your work on this plane of existence, you can go at any time to do your work on a higher plane?" We talk spiritually often, so it wasn't like this was a strange question. Tara was very spiritual and a deep thinker. I said, "Well, Tara, you know my beliefs. I absolutely think there's important work to be done elsewhere, and you go when you're needed." And I remember she locked into my gaze at that time for a few seconds longer than normal and then we went on laughing and having a good time. Now I realize it was her connection with the angelic side and her way of saying, "It is my time. I have something more important to do."

Well, the rest of the night all of us girls sat there watching a movie, laughing and having fun, and I just remember thinking, "Life couldn't be any more perfect than this." And that was my last thought.

Two hours later Kirk came home. Tara had left with two other girls to take another girl home, and they were late, but I had thought, "Gosh, they must have gone in to talk to the girl's parents or something." But when Kirk walked in, he said, "I'm sorry I'm late, but there was a very bad accident down from our house." I knew instantly what had happened; there was no question. I said, "Kirk, it is Tara. And we have to go." My mind put everything together, and that was it.

Q   Can you tell us about "Tara's angels"?

SM   Two days before the accident, Tara handed her sister Deanna a book which she carried with her all the time; it was her bible. It was about angels and was called Messengers of Light. It was all tattered and dog-eared with notes to her angels. And she said to

Deanna, "I will always be your guardian angel." I remember the joy in Deanna's eyes when she told me this later: "Mom, Tara gave me her favorite book and told me she'll always be my guardian angel."

KM   The morning after the accident, we found on Tara's bedroom floor a song sheet titled, "You're an Angel." It was right in the middle of her room. And then, in our kitchen, there was an angel-shaped cookie lying on our counter.

SM   Tara had made one angel cookie. I don't know where she got the dough; I don't know where she got the cookie cutter, or any of it. But we knew that these were her little ways of saying, "I love you and I have gone to do other things and I will be with the angels." It was a gift that she gave us. As hard and as sad as the accident was, Tara left a lot of joy behind.

KM   Then there was a teen camp that Tara went to with Sandy and her sister Deanna.

SM   Tara spent a lot of time there making little ceramic angels: hand-painted angels with bare bottoms, cute as a button. This wasn't like Tara, because she liked art but preferred being with people. It was different for her to spend quite so much time doing that.

KM   She made three of them: one for Deanna, Sandy, and me. One of them had a tear coming from its eye, which I think was really interesting. Tara had given one of the girls in the car one of the three angels. And the girl was holding it during the accident; she was right behind Tara. She could easily have been killed also. But she was okay, and she was holding the angel that Tara had made.

And we found that in Tara's notebook from school, she would ask questions of her angels. We would find math problems and on the next page, "Angels, what do you think I should do about this? Help me with this." We found this after her accident.

Q   Do you feel the angels, then, were really instrumental in helping you get through the grief?

SM   After the accident, we were so touched by all of the angel *signs that Tara had left us that that really became our focus. Angels kept us together. Our whole life was pretty much based on our family, and to lose an integral part of it was absolutely devastating. But now we don't feel we've lost her: she's in a different realm, working in a different way with a different group of people.*

Since we talked about Tara's angels after the accident quite a bit, people started giving us angel gifts and books and ceramics. Angels started filling our lives. It was just amazing, because people picked up on that part of our life. We started feeling comforted by the angels and much more in touch with the spirit world.

KM *Well, we wanted to keep Tara's love and spirit and memory alive somehow. To go through a tragic death seems so senseless unless you can turn it around and create a positive out of it. So we created our store that sells all kinds of angel items, and we feel that through it we're reaching out to people. It's [the store's] been such a positive. Tara wouldn't want us grieving the rest of our lives over the loss, so we tried to create a positive out of it. People come in and tell us they feel good being in there, that it's inspirational; it's doing what we want it to do.*

Q *Do you find that Tara's still with you? Are you visited by her specifically?*

SM *Absolutely, but I know she's very busy. I connect with her often and I've heard her say "Mom," as she did here on Earth, "I'm with you a lot, but I'm very busy. I have important things to do." So yes, I feel her often, and I always feel angelic presences, but it's not always Tara that's there; I know she's doing other things.*

Q *Do you think Tara was conscious of what was about to happen?*

SM *She didn't know consciously. I don't believe that is something that you know consciously.*

KM *No. But there was just something that tells me that this was what was supposed to happen.*

SM   *And, as I said, she loved us all so much. Teenagers can be so difficult, and it is a very hard time to lose a child because oftentimes there is disharmony and conflict in the family. But she made sure that is not the way she left, that she left with everything mended and healed and lots of love. And I feel very, very thankful for that.*

Hieronymus Bosch, *Paradise and Ascension into the Empyrean*. Left panel of diptych, ca. 1500–1504.

RAYMOND MOODY,
M.D., PH.D.

Raymond Moody, M.D., Ph.D., is an award-winning scholar and re-searcher, and a leading authority on the near-death experience. He is the bestselling author of, among others, Life After Life, The Light Beyond, *and* Reunions: Visionary Encounters with Departed Loved Ones. *The Director of Special Programs for the Parapsychological Services Institute, Inc., he has worked as a psychiatrist and as a professor of psychology and philosophy.*

QUESTION   Can you describe your religious background and how you first learned of near-death experiences?

RAYMOND MOODY   I started out as a person who wasn't particularly religious; as a matter of fact, in my early childhood I was antireligious. The few times I got dragged to church, my re-action was they were fooling themselves. So I grew up assuming that when you die it is like a wipeout of your consciousness and that you go into an impenetrable blackness from which you never recover. Then when I was an undergraduate student in philosophy at the University of Virginia in about 1965, I met a man, a Dr. George Ritchie, who had a very amazing experience when he was on the verge of death. He had actually been pronounced dead on two occasions about nine minutes apart some years before, and when I listened to Dr. Ritchie, who was a psychiatrist, talk about his experience, I really didn't know what to make of it. It was an extraordinary experience that obviously a very sane and sincere man had had—it obviously wasn't fabricated. But since I had heard of only one story like that I really confess I didn't think much else about it.

Then in about 1969, after I had gotten my Ph.D. in philosophy and was a philosophy professor, one of my students came up after class one day and said, "Dr. Moody, I wish we could talk about life after death in this philosophy class," and I remember him emphasizing the word *philosophy* as though I had been slack in my duties by not talking about this issue. So I asked him why he wanted to talk about that because I thought that life after death was something antique, like the notion of how many angels can dance on the head of a pin. So he said, "Because about a year ago I was in a bad accident and the doctors said I died, and I had an experience that has totally changed my life and I haven't had anybody to talk about it with." I took him into my office and listened to his experience, and it was identical to what I had heard from Dr. Ritchie four years before.

At that point I realized that if I had run into two of these things just by coincidence over a four-year period, there had to be more. So when I then went on to medical school just a few years after that, I interviewed patients who came back from the point of death and I found out very quickly that there was indeed a marked tendency of people on the verge of death to report this kind of experience.

Q   Can you describe a complete version of the near-death experience?

RM   People who return from the verge of death after a cardiac arrest tell us that at the point when their heart stops beating, they come to leave their physical bodies and to go up above to witness the events of the resuscitation from a point of view—for instance, right below the ceiling of the emergency room or up in the corner of the hospital room. Then, after a time in this situation, they realize that although they are acutely aware of what's going on, no one seems to be able to see or to hear them. And so they realize that this is what we call death, whereupon they become aware of a passageway of some sort—they may describe it as a tunnel or a hallway. They go through this tunnel and come out at the other end into an incredibly brilliant light. And they say as they go into this light, they are enveloped in a sense of love and peace. They may meet, in this context, relatives or friends of theirs who've already died and who seem to be there to help them through this transition. They undergo what we call "panoramic memory," in which they see all of the events of their lives displayed around them in a full-color, three-dimensional panorama; they get to witness this from a third-person point of view— along with all of the feelings that they have engendered in the lives of others through their actions, both loving and unloving.

At some point, they have to come back. Some of them tell us that they were told they had to go back because there were things that they had left to do; they are not told what they have to do, but just that it's not their time to die yet, their mission is not complete. Others tell us that they're given a choice either to go on with the experience that they are then having, or to return to their life that they had been leading. All of those whom I have talked with who've made the choice to come back have told me that they've come back for someone else. The typical reason is that they had children left to raise. They said that from their own personal perspective, they would rather have stayed with this wonderful light and love, but they knew they had an obligation to the kids they'd left behind—so they went back for that reason.

Q Does the divine being, or an angel, direct those involved in life after death?

RM Very often, in these experiences, the person encounters a divine or angelic being. This may be described as Christ, an angel, even God. Typically they don't report these beings as having the wings we see in the paintings, but rather as luminescent beings that seem to emanate love and saintliness. Quite a few of the people who have ND and report a being of light in connection with the experience will use the word *angel* if they are asked for synonyms for these beings of light. I think the idea is of a helper, a person who is there to assist them through this experience, and to help them understand so that they won't be left alone at this moment of transition.

It really gets interesting from the point of view of human psychology because what we find are very powerful effects of this experience on the people to whom it happens. The most common positive aftereffect is that thereafter they feel that the most important thing we can be doing while we're alive is to learn how to love each other. Second, they have no more fear of death whatsoever because their experience was personally assuring to them that what we call death is simply a transition into another kind of reality.

Human beings have always had mystical experiences and visions and near-death experiences. And they have always seen angels. Since this has been such a big part of our past, it is quite obvious to me that the more we know about experiences like these—and therefore, the more we know about our nature as human beings—that the more likely we are to get ourselves out of the monumental difficulties we have.

Q How prevalent are these near-death experiences? What percent of the population has undergone them?

RM Near-death experiences are really remarkably common. George Gallup got interested in this in the late seventies and used the entire resources of his polling organization to try to determine how many Americans might have been through such an experience. In a survey that was limited entirely to the adult population, he found that over eight million people had had a near-death experience. Subsequent to Dr. Gallup's survey, we've learned that kids have this experience very commonly, too.

Physicians and cardiologists and psychiatrists all over the world have replicated the results that we have achieved in the U.S. with near-death experiences, so that we know that worldwide this is a phenomenon that involves literally tens of millions of people.

Q Are these experiences more common today, or are we simply more aware of them?

RM The reason why we are so acutely aware of near-death experiences today is that we have the technology that enables us to bring a lot of people back from the state of near-death. But historically there's evidence that the ND goes back many thousands of years. Plato wrote about a classic ND, and medieval accounts are full of these. The Venerable Bede, who was an early writer in Britain, and Gregory of Tours, in France, wrote of ND, and these have been reported from cultures all over the world literally. They also occur sometimes as themes of paintings. Hieronymus Bosch in the 1500s did a painting which fairly clearly depicts a typical near-death experience.

Q Do you see a shift in the way that we as a culture view death?

RM I believe that there have been cultures in the past in which death was far more integrated as a concept than in our contemporary society. Of course, there have been societies that are even more fearful of death perhaps than we are. I'm not so sure that it has to do with the historical time line, but perhaps more with the structure of the culture and the ideals and norms of the culture and also with the temper of the times, with the stresses of the external events that the society is faced with. We're living in an age in which the threat of destruction is very real, whether from environmental calamity or, heaven forbid, nuclear calamity or the meltdown of reactors—this sort of thing. My speculation from thinking a lot about this is that given all of these horrendous specters that loom over us, people tend to deny it; they don't want to face this. They would rather watch football or the cartoons instead. But at some level it must be registering in the minds of even the most denial-prone among us that things are pretty hazardous right now. Perhaps this is why we have this renewed interest in our society with death: we realize that it is coming to all of us and that potentially now it could happen to many, many millions of people at once, in a way that in previous times in history was unimaginable.

One reason why our society is focused on events like NDs is because we do sense, even if it is on a preconscious or unconscious level, that we are in rather scary times.

Q Do you think part of our denial of death stems from the fact that people don't die at home, but rather in hospitals?

RM One reason why we're so fearful about death in contemporary American society is that we have essentially isolated it. We've removed it to the hospital and surrounded people who are dying with these incomprehensible machines and tend to exclude

the family from the room at the point of death. In earlier eras, it's
not that death was ever regarded as a friend, but it was regarded
as something that people did at home. In medieval times, there
was a tradition that the person on his or her deathbed would go
through a certain ritual of requesting that all of the people in the
family come to the bedside and then the dying person would dis-
pense wisdom. But now what we've done is to mechanize death
in a way . . . almost hiding the dying person from the family
members on the pretense that this would be too overwhelming
for them. Of course, this is entirely a subterfuge. It probably
comes from the anxiety of helping professionals rather than from
any real facts or evidence about the reactions of family members
at the bedside of dying people.

Q   Do you have a sense of many spiritual changes happening now?

RM   One thing that's obvious to me is that the world is in
great trouble right now, and there will be monumental changes
over the next few decades. I'm not talking here about the biblical
end of the world or whatever. One thing that strikes me is that
the world has come to an end many times. It came to an end for
the ancient Romans and for the ancient Greeks; the Victorian
world came to an end, and so on. All of history is littered with
things that came to an end. But I really do have a sense that what
we're on the verge of now is something quite different than the
kinds of changes that have transpired in cultures past. I think it
might have something to do with expansion of consciousness in
new directions and also in some old directions. There's a dawning
of a kind of consciousness that I have seen come about in my
own life which has to do with the electronic media.

When I was a kid in Porterdale, Georgia, back in the late
forties, we listened to the radio. And then television came in, and
at first there were just two or three channels of black and white

from 7:00 A.M. to 11:00 P.M., with fifteen minutes of national and world news. And if something big had happened in Japan that day, they could show you a map and a photograph of the correspondent. And you would hear a kind of scratchy telephone-line description from Japan of what was going on. But it was three days before the film could get through. But now we're on the verge of five hundred channels of full color stereo around the clock, with two channels that do nothing but bring us the news all the time. You can see the wall come down as it collapses and you can actually be there and feel the immediacy. And this has a profound impact on people. I've seen it in my own kids—how they have been raised in this. They see the world in a different way than I did—much more globally, I think.

How this is all going to sort out and what's going to happen, I just haven't the faintest idea. But one thing I do know is that something dramatic has to happen because when you sum up all of these things that are upon us now, whether the AIDS epidemic, or the ozone hole, or the threat of nuclear destruction—either by warfare or even the peacetime uses through reactors—the vast environmental pollution, the overpopulation, the horrible situation in the Eastern Bloc and in Russia, something has to give over the next few decades. Who among us can predict what these changes are going to be? But I do think it's going to be something quantitatively and qualitatively different from the kinds of changes that we have seen in the world before.

Q Do you see any possible positive outcome in the current world situation?

RM Vaclav Havel, the president of the Czech Republic, some years ago gave a speech to Congress in which he said that if we are to be saved, or to save ourselves, the only thing that can do it now is what he called "a worldwide revolution in consciousness." And basically I completely agree. It seems to me that the only way out of the dilemmas that we currently face in the world is to find some way of bringing about a situation in which we genuinely love one another all over the world. To me, it's not out of the question that this could be. And the only way that I could picture pulling this off is through studies in altered states of consciousness and this sort of thing. If we did have some way reliably to bring about in people in good health experiences such as the great saints of history have had—mystical visions and experiences like near-death experiences, yet without any danger—to open people up to love and to inner departments of themselves that we have so systematically excluded, that potentially might be able to bring this about.

Trinity of Uglic. Russian icon.

Q   Could you comment on *Life After Life* and its backlash?

RM   Prior to the publication of *Life After Life*, friends of mine had sort of warned me that I was in for trouble from the medical and scientific community, and more particularly from the fundamentalist wing, who would say that this was "in with the devil" and so on. It makes a very nice story to say that I was persecuted, but it's not true. To the contrary, I was impressed with the positive responses that I got from physicians all over the world, who had said that they had heard of these experiences from their patients and were very happy to see that someone was investigating them. And a lot of ministers came to me with the same sort of tone and said that they'd heard these same kinds of stories from their parishioners and were happy to see that this was being faced now.

But I have gotten some static from the fundamentalists, who say, of course, that this is "of the devil." I say this with all due respect, but to me, that kind of thing is just amusing. I mean that that frame of reference or point of view is always raised against anything that's new. I remember my grandmother telling me that airplanes were an invention of the devil and that God had never meant men to fly. When Galileo first looked through his telescope and reported that the planets were not crystalline spheres as the church propounded, but rather were worlds with uneven surfaces and worlds at great distances in space, the theologians responded by saying that the devils were creating those visions. They refused to look through Galileo's telescope because they were afraid that the devils might distort their perception in that way, too. There are going to be people with that kind of attitude with whatever new comes along.

I'm not saying I have any bitterness about this. As a matter of fact, I understand and sympathize with the fundamentalists because where they're coming from is fear. Fear of the unknown is something that's particularly troublesome for people who come from that particular kind of mentality. For some reason, I've never had a fear of the unknown. I've been a very curious person since the time I was a very young child. And so I always take great delight in finding out new things. But I can understand where the fundamentalists come from, because there are plenty of things that I do fear. I hate driving, for instance; literally, I would rather walk barefoot across a trench of hot coals than take a car for a spin around the block. Everybody has their own sets of fears and the people who come from the fundamentalist perspective are basically afraid of novel information.

Q Can science adequately define or measure angels or near-death experiences?

RM One thing that is very important for people to realize is that these studies of near-death experiences and angels and so on are not scientific studies about the possibility of life after death. I think the notion that we could prove there's a life after death scientifically is really like barking up the wrong tree. That's not to say that near-death experiences aren't very, very important. I think it is important to investigate these very ancient human phenomena for the simple reason that these kinds of events, when they happen to people, transform them very powerfully. Think of how many of the great literary works have dealt with the near-death experiences, or with reports of angels, or of apparitions of the departed. Whatever the nature of these phenomena is, and I'm not sure that science is able to tell us this, we now know that it is a tremendously important part of being human.

I think we also need to be aware that the fact that we can't prove that near-death experiences imply life after death scientifically doesn't mean that we can't systematically study near-death experiences and angel reports. I think we've gotten into a situation in our society where we identify scientific inquiry and systematic inquiry as the same thing. That's not true at all. Science is one form of systematic inquiry, but thank God, there are a lot of other forms of systematic inquiry, too—history, for instance, or the study of literature. The work that goes on in a courtroom, for instance, is not scientific inquiry, and yet it's a kind of inquiry that humans have concluded over their centuries of experience that is very important to do.

Q From your experience in talking to all kinds of people and from your research, do you think that angels exist?

RM The question of whether angels exist is probably too complicated a question even to ask. What is existence? You know, philosophers still debate about that—and I keep going back to Immanuel Kant's old idea that existence is not a predicate, as we often assume it is. Maybe by exploring the question not of whether angels exist, but rather of what kind of reality they have, we might learn some interesting things about human nature.

I'm beginning to think more and more that there are all

Michelangelo, *The Creation of Adam*, 1510.

kinds of realities, and all kinds of layers, and all kinds of dimensions—and that it's too early for us to get stuck on one conception of existence or one level of reality. Electronically, pretty soon, we're going to be entering other realities with what we call virtual realities. If things continue to go as they're going and people in the media don't come up with some even better technique, our children's children are going to be going to school in virtual-reality tanks. History will be a pretty neat subject then, not boring at all. One thing that we're going to be learning more and more about, I think, is how to make transitions among and between these different layers of realities in ways that hopefully will be beneficial to us.

Q   Where do you stand personally in your relationship with God?

RM   I started out in life thinking that God was a fictional being made up by religious people for whatever reason they had to do it—whether insecurity or a desire to control other people. But I must say I've come around in my life to quite a different perspective. Now, I think of God primarily as a loving parent—a lot more loving parent than I am even, even though I know I love my kids very much, and I can't imagine anything they could do that would make me not love them, no matter what it was.

I also think of Him as almost like a producer and director of this show that we're all in. I mean that seriously—not literally, but nonetheless seriously.

Q What is your opinion about what happens at the time of death?

RM I'm convinced that it's impossible to put into literal language what happens to us at death. People who come back from close calls with death relate that in their near-death experiences they entered into a world that wasn't temporal or spatial, as we are experiencing it. One woman told me that "you could say that my experience took place in one second, or that it took place in ten thousand years, and it wouldn't make any difference which way you said it." And since we can't describe this event in terms of time and space, then we can't put it into language—because our language is temporal and spatial. So the most we can do is to resort to metaphors.

I think of death in terms of transition; in the sense of expansion of consciousness; in the sense of entering into love; and in the sense of going into a reality that is incomprehensible from our current point of view. Everything I have learned in the course of my studies has left me with the sense that death is nothing to fear. I can honestly say—and I am certainly not a macho person—I'm full of all kinds of fears, but death is not one of them. I regard death as simply a transition into another kind of reality, one that is more interesting than the reality that we're in because I think it includes this one. I was born in the radio age, and now we're on the verge of five hundred channels, full color stereo around the clock with video-playback capacity and a channel changer. I kind of think of dying as like going immediately from the radio age to five hundred channels.

THOMAS MOORE

Thomas Moore is the critically acclaimed author of Care of the Soul *and* Soul Mates. *He has written extensively on the subjects of archetypal and Jungian psychology, mythology, and the arts. Moore holds a doctoral degree in religious studies from Syracuse University and lived in a Catholic religious order for twelve years. He has also worked as a musician, college professor, and psychotherapist.*

QUESTION Why do you think there has been such a strong surge of interest in angels at this point in time?

THOMAS MOORE I think the current interest in angels reflects our desire, our hunger for something. I think the hunger is for something that is beyond the mechanical world that we believe in so ardently. The trouble with twentieth-century life, es-

On facing page:
William Blake, *Angels Hovering Above Jesus,* ca. 18–19th c.

pecially in America, is that we really have bought into the idea that not only is nature a machine, in a sense, but the human being and our experiences are also understood and imagined as being mechanical.

Now this could go back to maybe two or three hundred years ago, when the dominant philosophies described the human being as a clock or the universe as a clock. Before that time people didn't use these mechanical images for human life. If you asked someone about a thousand years ago what human life is, they would say it's like the night sky; it's something vast and mysterious. So I'm interested, in my own work, in refocusing our attention on the mystery, going back to images like the night sky or something that is infinite in scope rather than something that is mechanical. I suspect that the interest in angels has to do with transcending the limits to this mechanical world.

Angels don't preach brimstone and fire and hell and damnation. They don't do that. For the most part, they're beautiful and they do things that are inspiring to us, so I think that angels give us a way of imagining our spirituality in ways that are beautiful. They guide us to become spiritual people for the pleasure of it, not for its moralism, because the spiritual life itself has a great deal of beauty and real satisfaction, even pleasure. And this is what the soul needs. The soul doesn't need to be informed at all, though it does need pleasure; it needs deep pleasures.

Q   We speak of angels, but what do we really mean? How can we define these heavenly beings?

TM   In the fifteenth century Marsilio Ficino gave a sermon on the magic of Christmastime and about the three kings who came to give gifts to the infant Jesus in the crib. He said that angels are actually stars. The light of stars condenses into this incredibly intense, small sphere of light, and that is what an angel really is—all this light coming into this small space. That's a pretty nice poetic image. It reminds me of Blake's angels, which are so fiery and seem so full of spirit and flame and activity and energy.

I'm not defining angels, but I'm trying to find images that say something about what they are. Even Aquinas's idea that an angel is a separated substance is an interesting one. He says that they are a substance, they're real, and yet they're apart from the real that we know, the world that can be measured and quantified and touched. Love is very real but you can't measure it. Or I hope not anyway. You can't put it through an oscilloscope or some kind of instrument, and yet it's very real and it's felt and it's an important thing in the lives of people. In that sense, angels are very real. They're substances, but they're separate from the usual way we think of the world of substances.

Q Where did the great painters get their image of angels from? Why do angels' wings receive such emphasis in art?

TM I think first of all we have to say that these painters were painting a reality of some kind that was experienced in the community in which they lived. We can look at the paintings of angels and take those paintings seriously, but it doesn't mean that this was a literal presentation. It's not like finding UFOs some-where, and wondering what they're made of. Rather we can trust that artists have an intuition about something that is real and can-not be defined or cannot be placed in our usual physical way of understanding things. And we can learn from the artist what an angel is.

The wings we see in paintings of angels suggest a rising, a capacity to fly, to be in the air, to be off the level ground that we live on. So there's a kind of transcending of ordinary life in the angel. You know, the Greeks describe love very much as an an-gel. One of the beings they pictured in their art was Eros . . . and

Eros often had wonderful big wings just like an angel. And in fact, some of the modern books on angels often reproduce pictures of Eros, calling him an angel. Doesn't love sometimes sweep us off our feet and take us into the air, give us a high, take our feelings and emotions—even the way we live—and lift it? I also think it connects to dreams of flying. You might even say in our dreams of flying we become angels. A lot of people have dreams of flying. I think that the flying dreams suggest we can raise our awareness, our emotions, and our feeling up and away from mundane life. That's a hint as to the nature of angels and what those wings are for.

Now, some pictures show angel wings crossed, covering things around them; they're big and sometimes they shield almost an entire painting. So I suspect that one of the purposes of the wings is to hide the mystery, to keep divinity mysterious, to prevent us from trying to explain all of this. I'm afraid we're close to trying to explain love as a chemical reaction. If we do that, I think we have invaded the sphere of mystery that is so important to us. We have effectively pulled back the wings of the angel because the purpose of the angel's wings is to hide certain mysteries from profane human gaze.

Q How is angelic time different from ordinary human time?

TM The time in which the angels exist is more a kind of eternal time than it is the chronological time that we live in day by day. For example, when we remember something from childhood, or just from a year or two ago, that memory may seem very vivid and may still seem to have a great deal of influence in our life today. In that sense memories often seem to be the work of angels. Angels lead our imaginations out of this flat ongoing chronological time toward a more vertical sense of time—

vertical in a sense that it has to do with the depth and the heights of our experience, as opposed to what happened before and what's going to happen in the future. So in that sense, too, angels are living in a different kind of time than we are.

Q   Angels seem so remote from the problems and the horrors of our day-to-day lives. What relevance can they possibly have to current events?

TM   When we look at the terrible things going on in the world—the wars, the division, the natural disasters, the illnesses—all of these things can be overwhelmingly depressing. We try to react by using our ingenuity, getting experts, assigning commissions, putting as much money into these things as we can. And things keep getting worse. I think the reason is that these responses are purely human; they're at the level of secular life. I think we need to realize that the realm of angels is appropriate here. Angels can resolve these things for us.

The sixteenth-century physician Paracelsus said that there is no disease that doesn't have a cure. There's an incredibly mysterious optimism in that because when we look around us we say, "Well, there are no cures for these problems we have." We don't see them, we can't find them. I think that suggests that we're not looking at the right level and in the right places. What it calls for is an appreciation for the angelic order or the angelic level. Now, what does that mean? It means that we have to be able to imagine ourselves living in a world that has a deeper dimension than just the human level, without making this other angelic dimension a carbon copy of the world we live in. I think that's what we do too much. We say angels must be formed from some kind of gases. That if we had the right telescope we'd see them. Or the right microscope we'd see them. We just keep thinking at that level of physics. But it's beyond that. Angels are not material.

That's what Thomas Aquinas said. They are of another order altogether.

And in order to appreciate and live in that order, we need an imagination very different from the one we live in right now. That's why I think the beginning of a cure for our ills is a revitalized imagination, one that truly recognizes that there is a sacred dimension to the everyday life that we live. That's where angels are, in that sacred dimension. William Blake said that Newton's world, this one-dimensional world that we live in, is death to us. We need fourfold vision, he said, a vision that will get beyond this Newtonian place. And I think that's exactly where we are today; we're desperately in need of a vision that goes beyond that. I do think we could solve these problems. I believe with Paracelsus that there's no problem and no disease that can't be cured. But in order to do it, we have to change our way of thinking, so radically that it's hard even to begin to imagine what that would be. I do think it's possible, but I don't see too many signs of it happening in the next week or two.

Q What is it about the Annunciation that continues to grip our imaginations?

TM One of the great stories in Christianity is the Annunciation, where the angel appeared to Mary. We have seen hundreds of paintings of this event. I call it an event. It's an archetypal image, it's an image of something that happens eternally to us all the time.

In these paintings Mary is always sitting by herself. She is sitting, often reading a book, or if she is not actually reading, the book has fallen down. She has been reading a book. That's a very interesting thing, too, because it suggests there is a kind of learning going on, or meditation. In a way she's prepared for the angel. She's prepared in two ways—she's waiting quietly by herself and she's reading.

Now, the other thing you see in the Annunciations is a pillar or a wall placed between Mary and the angel. That pillar is not just architecture; it also suggests a difference between reality in human life and angelic life. There is a boundary line between the eternal and the human, and the angel is able to transcend or penetrate through that boundary and make an Annunciation, announce something to Mary. What the angel is doing is just telling her something is happening to her—that somehow you are going to conceive in yourself something that is divinely created, divinely seeded.

Fra Angelico, *Annunciation*, ca. 1430–1432.

In these paintings we sometimes see this golden ray coming down toward Mary, not from the angel, but from either a dove or apparently from divinity, from God Himself; [it's] almost as though the whole scene is a scene of divine sexuality in some way. She is conceiving a child, a divine child. That's an incredible mystery, and I think the important response to this is not the question of what you believe. The point is not to dwell on what you think happened or what it all means exactly, but rather to reflect on it as an image of what angels do—that even for us, the angels make annunciations; they tell us that something eternal is beginning to develop within us. Like Mary, we have to be ready and prepared in order to catch the angel when the angel appears. And that means we have to be alone sometimes. Solitude is an important part of the experience and certainly a big part of the spiritual life. And secondly, a special kind of reading is important—a reflective kind of reading, a reading of a sacred text of some kind. I don't mean it has to be a Bible or something of that sort. It might be a reading of some book that really is very, very sacred to you for some reason—a book of poetry, a book of your dreams, a book of fiction or nonfiction that has been significant to you. There is a way of reading that invites the angel's presence.

In a certain sense we need to be very careful what we read, because reading prepares us for these annunciations, which are the most important things in life. These revelations really can shape our lives and shape our reflection and the meaningfulness of what we experience. So I think we have to be very careful what we read. If we read carefully, if we give ourselves opportunities for contemplation of some kind, the angel appears.

Q   What about fallen angels—the dark side? Have we tried to exclude them from our consciousness?

TM There's something dark about this whole process. There has to be. If we don't talk about the darkness, we haven't got the whole thing. The dark angels certainly have a place—the fallen angels, the angels who live in hell, Lucifer (whose name means the bearer of light). [Lucifer is] someone who can carry light, yet he's down in the darkness of hell.

It's a very interesting paradox. I think there are dark angels, black angels, deep red angels, all kinds of angels that suggest darkness and fear. [There's] the angel of cancer, the angel of ignorance, the angel of failure; I think angels bring these things as well.

Fate, karma, something is happening there which is the work of angels to interfere with health, interfere with sanity, interfere with a good marriage. There's a lot of stuff going on that doesn't appear to be good. And yet it has its necessity. Now, that's an interesting word we don't use these days very much. Necessity. The Greeks used it a lot. An illness or a failure may have its place within one's life, as painful as it is, as literally destructive as it is. It may have its place in the destiny of the soul. An illness may bring a person in touch with his or her soul in a way that nothing else has been able to, and as horrible as it is and the more life-threatening it is, the more it might evoke soul.

Q How much does imagination enter into your contact with the spiritual realm?

TM One way of talking about imagination is to say what it isn't. Imagination, as we use the word anyway, is not about being clever, coming up with new ideas. I don't mean being imaginative in that sense. A lot of people hear the word *imagination* and they think of something rather superficial, not exactly at the heart of matters, not terribly important.

Imagination has to do with the way we picture ourselves,

our own lives in relationship to the world around us. It's about the stories that we live that might be quite unconscious to us. Almost every situation that we're in is a drama. Wherever you go, you're in a drama. You drop your child off at school and there's a little drama there. You feel the tension. Maybe you're worried about leaving the child, and you see the child go off to school and here is this institution that has all kinds of associations for you. There are a lot of very poignant emotions involved in this little drama. And that's true of every single situation in our life. You could see that every single day. To focus on those dramas is to look at the imagination of what it is we are experiencing.

And I think we are in a kind of rut of imagination in our culture, where we only imagine our world through the eyes of extremely technological scientific values. Again, this mechanical view of life isn't the only imagination we have, but it's very, very strong, and we're so dedicated to it that other possibilities of imagination are excluded. They're set off to the side. And so this applies also to our talk about angels. Our imagination of our lives is so strong in a certain direction that angels don't really fit. Angels seem to come from outside of that. They may be ushering in a new imagination, if we could entertain the idea of angels seriously. That means we must leave this very hard-core, scientific rationalistic way of looking at life, and that means a new imagination. We all live in a mythic world, a mythological world of characters and scenes and events and memories. And the appearance of angels is from another mythic world altogether.

In a sense, what we're experiencing now is like a melting. [It's] a clash of two fundamental ways of imagining human experience. One has to do with this ordinary secular view. And the other has much more spirituality wrapped up in it.

It's going to be very interesting to see what happens if this meeting of worlds is sustained. We have the opportunity to make a big step in dealing with our own individual lives, and these things that occupy us so much: our health, our relationships, our families, and also our social lives, which have to do with the way our cities operate and the way international relations are conducted. All that has to do with the imagination.

MELVIN MORSE, M.D.

Melvin Morse, M.D., is a recognized authority in the field of near-death studies and coauthored the bestselling Transformed by the Light *and* Closer to the Light. *A graduate of George Washington University School of Medicine, he is Clinical Assistant Professor of Pediatrics at the University of Washington.*

QUESTION   How has the medical community reacted to the recent breakthroughs in the spiritual realm?

MELVIN MORSE   The most irritating thing that medical science does with regard to spiritual experiences is to trivialize them and make them into some sort of pathology instead of acknowledging that these experiences happen to normal people. The medical literature on near-death experiences describes them as temporal-lobe seizures, or products of a lack of oxygen to the brain, or reactive fantasy to the stresses of dying, or grief-induced

On facing page: Hugo van der Goes, *Kneeling Angel.* Detail from Portinari triptych, 1476.

hallucinations. Words such as *hallucination* and *seizure* and *pathology* come up again and again.

Q How have you responded to this sort of scientific skepticism?

MM We have taken the same research that these skeptical neuroscientists have offered, but simply reinterpreted it to suggest that near-death experiences and spiritual experiences in general are nothing more and nothing less than the normal functioning of a certain area of our brain that reacts in times of stress, at the point of dying, during childbirth, or sometimes, for some lucky people, during religious meditation or prayer. What angers me about medical science is there's absolutely not a shred of data to support the rationalistic, materialistic, skeptical viewpoint. In fact, all of the scientific evidence indicates that near-death experiences are real. There is not a published study which shows that near-death experiences, for example, are a reactive fantasy of the mind to grief, whereas there are well over half a dozen excellent studies which say that near-death experiences are quite the opposite. They are not pathology, they are not drug-induced. They are the normal functioning of the brain at death.

Q Can you describe some recently researched cases?

MM At Seattle Children's Hospital we did a very simple and yet very convincing study in which we used proper control groups and systematically showed that patients who survived clinical death, cardiac arrest, often report spiritual experiences, whereas control patients who had the same lack of oxygen to the brain, who were treated with the same medications, who had the same psychological stresses of thinking that they died, do not report spiritual experiences. This kind of study needs to be replicated by other institutions, and I'm pleased to tell you that it has been. The University of Ultrecht has done a very similar study in adults. There have been studies from Boston Children's Hospital showing again that children report near-death experiences by and large at the point of nearly dying. This is the most exciting research that compels me.

Sometimes an individual case is even more compelling than all the research. We have documented a case in California in which a woman who had a heart transplant earlier in the evening had her heart stop beating at 2:15 A.M. She says that she floated out of her body and attempted to contact her daughter, whom she felt she just couldn't communicate with. So she traveled out of her body well over a hundred miles and instead was able to somehow communicate with her sleeping son-in-law. Her sleeping son-in-law then woke up and said, "Wow, I just had an amazing dream that my mother-in-law came to me and said, 'I nearly died but don't worry, I'm going to be okay.'" And this dream meant so much to him that he actually wrote down the time of his dream. This case has been thoroughly authenticated and clearly shows in my mind that the dying brain at the very least has remarkable paranormal abilities. Instead of death being the cessation of brain activity, at the very least the process of dying involves the activation of areas of the brain that we never use during our typical day-in-and-day-out life. And if we accept that the dying brain has paranormal abilities such as the ability to travel at great distances and communicate, then we need to accept that human beings possibly have some sort of soul that exists outside the human body.

_Q_   These days you see angels everywhere—in our cars, jewelry, and _Angels in America_ on Broadway. What is this? Where are we going with this? What does this say about us as a people, and as a culture?

_MM_   When I started near-death research, it was only a

small part of my life as a busy critical-care physician. But I have found that there is intense public interest, not only from the media, but from the thousands and thousands and thousands of people who write me letters, and this has sustained me in the whole field of near-death research.

It's obvious that near-death research is just the tip of the iceberg, that there's a tremendous spiritual longing and craving in our society. When you read the works of men like Joseph Campbell, you can put it in perspective, because Joseph Campbell said that our society has lost its collective myths. We've lost our religious structures. Joseph Campbell said that death is the beginning of myth, and I believe that that's what we're seeing in our society today. We're learning about death, a subject that we have conveniently forgotten about for the last hundred years. Learning what death is like has taught us something about what the process of living is like. It's just as simple as a child who told me that she learned from her experience of nearly dying that life is for living, and that light is for later.

So by removing this fear of death, coupled with the reawakening of the spiritual side of man, we're going to see a reintegration of man's technological genius and his spiritual self. When I started in near-death research ten years ago there was some skepticism from my colleagues. People would whistle the theme from "The Twilight Zone" when I walked down the hallways. But by and large I have published my research in American Medical Association pediatric journals—mainstream medical journals—and I don't think that that would have happened twenty years ago. I think that has only happened in the context of our society's spiritual reawakening on all levels.

What do we learn from the near-death experience? That all of life is meaningful. What are these people painted with after their encounter with light? The indelible belief that their life is filled with meaning. That whatever they do is important. They don't just run out and bungee-jump with that information, they don't try to kill themselves. No. They do things like trying to help other people.

Q   Is there also a practical side to this spiritual awakening? Are we going to see an impact on the way medicine is practiced in this country?

MM   I believe that if we listen up to the near-death experience, we can cut health-care costs in this country by 10 to 15 percent. Listening up to children's stories of angels could actually lead to a decrease in health-care costs. How could that be? It seems ridiculous until you realize that we spend 10 to 15 percent of our health-care dollar on futile and irrational medical care in the last few hours and days of life. Medical care that doesn't even have a one-in-a-thousand, or one-in-a-million chance of working. Why do we do this? Why are most patients subjected to the humiliation and the indignities of having tubes put into their lungs in this kind of expensive, intensive-care-unit medicine? It's because of our own fear of death. We believe that since we have these kinds of interventions and medical technology available, we must do it. We have not had the courage to make these tough decisions, to say, "No, this person doesn't need thirty thousand dollars' worth of intensive-care-unit medicine before he or she dies."

Why don't we have that courage? Because we're afraid of death and we have an irrational belief that medical technology can keep us alive forever. And yet we learn from children that it's not scary to die. One girl patted me on the wrist and said, "You'll see, Dr. Morse, heaven is fun." If only we could institutionalize the lessons that we can learn from these children who have experienced death and who can tell us what it's like, you bet we'd see a withering away of this irrational medical technology and we'd see health-care savings. So it's not just silly stories about angels. It's dollars and cents, it's billions of dollars a year that can be saved from listening to these children's stories.

Q   Why is it that children have so many more experiences with angels than adults do?

Peter Paul Rubens,
*Madonna and Child and
Angels,* ca. 16–17th c.

MM   Children have very pure and simple and direct spiritual experiences. They don't filter them, they don't add in lots of stuff from their own life, they don't delete stuff that they think they shouldn't be experiencing. Since the heart of the experience is the spiritual experience of light, then of course they have angel experiences more than adults do. There are no filters on their brain; they see the real thing.

Q   Could you tell us the story of Jamie? How did that case first come to your attention? What was unique about this child?

MM   Jamie's story is unique and interesting because she had no idea that she had a near-death experience and she was able to come to me in a completely unsophisticated way. In fact, she herself misunderstood her experience and was quite terrified by it for years. Her mother happened to work as one of my receptionists in my office, and she was familiar with my research at Seattle Children's Hospital, and she knew that her child had had terrible nightmares for years after nearly dying of bacterial meningitis.

When she was five, Jamie had come as close to dying as you can come and still be revived, given today's medical technology. My partner told me that if it had been another ten minutes, she would not have lived. She [fell into a] coma from a severe infection of her brain and spinal cord. She was immediately taken to our trauma room. Of course, an IV was started. She was given oxygen, and then her heart stopped beating. And so she received a full cardiopulmonary resuscitation. In other words, she was clinically dead and they had to restart her heart. They had to do chest compressions, put a tube in her lungs and breathe for her, and give her powerful antibiotics. And she was airlifted to Seattle Children's Hospital.

Q   How did you get Jamie to share with you her experiences of that time?

MM When I interviewed Jamie after she had recovered, she was intensely shy and very fearful and very frightened, and I could tell that whatever experience she had had meant something to her emotionally. It was so powerful and personal that she was afraid to tell anyone about it. I had to spend hours playing video games with her. It took many, many patient hours of working with her. Finally I got her to draw a picture, and I asked her if she could draw a picture of what she'd experienced. She drew a striking picture of herself on a hospital gurney. Then she very accurately drew my partner, Dr. Christopher, resuscitating her. She even had his fingers properly interdigitated and properly positioned on her chest. I told him I gave him an "A" for cardiac resuscitation after I saw her drawing. She had every detail of her own resuscitation accurate in her drawing. She had a nurse at the head of the bed wearing a hat. She had the cardioversion machine. Clearly these are details which I don't think she could have invented from watching too much TV, or anything like that.

Then in the picture, she had herself floating up in the air, and as she drew I could ask her about each detail. I said to her, "Who is that man sitting on the log?" And she said to me, "Oh, that's Jesus. He's very nice." And then she showed me the angels which she drew in the picture. Then she drew a rainbow, and I said to her, "Well, tell me about the rainbow," and she said, "Well, that's the light." I said, "Oh, the light?" and she said, "Yes, a light that told me who I was and where I was to go." She was very clear that this light was separate from Jesus and the angels.

Once she had shared this experience with me, it was amazing how profoundly she transformed herself. She stopped having her nightmares. She started doing much better in school. She had gained a lot of weight since her infection and she started to lose that weight. Even more interesting, verbalizing the experience has given her a sense of validation. She now believes that what happened to her was real. She's now sharing that with other children who are seriously ill or who are dying of cancer or other fatal diseases. In fact, she goes to Seattle Children's Hospital, Marybridge Hospital, and Valley General Hospital, and talks with children in these situations, and helps to comfort them about the process of dying.

Q   From all your years of research, how do you define a near-death experience? What are the characteristics that commonly define that experience?

MM   Near-death experiences happen to people who have survived clinical death, meaning that their hearts have stopped beating, or that they are in profound comas in which we would expect irreversible brain damage to occur. They also occur in situations of impending death, such as mountain climbers falling from great heights who are saved, for example, by falling into a snowbank, or miners who are trapped in mines underground for many hours or days, in a near-fatal situation. In fact, in this second category is where we see most angel experiences. Miners who are trapped in mines by landslides or cave-ins frequently describe guardian angels or other spiritual miners who assist them in finding safety. This has been recorded in medical literature for well over thirty years.

Q   From all the stories you've heard, is there a pattern that emerges—a kind of archetypal near-death experience?

MM   The near-death experience, first of all, begins with the sensation that you're either physically dead or going to die. Then there's a sense of being drawn up out of the body; the person actually feels they're floating out of their body. They can see hair on the top of their head. They can see what's going on around them. They can see resuscitative techniques, or hear people commenting, "Oh, we've lost them." They then enter into complete darkness. Often this transition is accompanied by hearing whooshing or roaring sounds, or interestingly enough, heavenly music. They're then plunged into total darkness, and this darkness is scary. Many children say that they are frightened by it, because they have a sense that they're alive. They have a sense that they have left their body, and they're in a total nothingness.

It's in this nothingness that they usually encounter a spiritual light. It could be a dead relative. Sometimes for children the spiritual light takes the form of a living teacher. Usually it's perceived as being some sort of religious figure—God or Jesus, or Buddha in the case of Buddhists, Muhammad in the case of Muslims. This light is very comforting to them. It's not just some sort of reflex spasm of the optic nerve, or persistence of light on the retinal vessels at the point of death. It's a sense of love, and peace, and serenity, and an unconditional love that many of us have never felt during our lives.

In this light, often something gives them some sense of choice to return to the body. You can stay, or you can go back; it's up to you. Sometimes it's not a choice. In the case of Jamie, she says, "I was told it wasn't my time to die. I have to help my mother with my brother." Invariably, when there is a choice, this choice is for a sense of love, or for a sense of meaning or of purpose to life. I never hear people say, "I came back because I didn't spend enough time at my job," or "I came back because I hadn't made a killing on the stock market yet."

As one boy said to me, he floated out of his body and was climbing the staircase to heaven, but he didn't think it would be fair if he continued up that staircase, because his younger brother had been killed. He meant it wouldn't be fair to his parents if he died as well. This boy prefaced all this by saying to me, "Dr. Morse, I have a wonderful secret to tell you. I've been climbing a staircase to heaven." That's why I love the child's near-death experience, because that's exactly how simple it is. They don't have a lot of elaborate embellishments or endless detail in the experience. They just see what they see, and tell you just the way it happened to them.

Q   In the cases you've studied with children and others, how often do angels play a part in the near-death experience?

MM   In childhood near-death experiences, angels are seen in the great majority of cases. In my own research, between 60 and 70 percent of cases. In the research of the handful of other childhood reports, they're seen at least 50 percent of the time.

Interestingly enough, that is not seen in adult near-death experiences. Angel experiences are perhaps part of only 10 to 15 percent, or as high as 20 percent, of adult near-death experiences. It's almost as if children have some sort of special relationship with angels, and you hear these kinds of angel experiences coming again and again and again. Often they're very simple. One boy nearly died of complications from routine surgery, and had three cardiac arrests. He told me that an angel was at his side and he was zooming down a long tunnel that seemed to be lined with airplane landing lights. That was his entire experience. He did not know what that angel was doing, or where he was going, or why.

Sometimes the angels aren't identified as angels. One girl who nearly died of complications of diabetes told me that three doctors were dressed in white and gave her a choice to live or die. I said, "How did you know that they were doctors?", and she said, "Well, they were really tall, and they were all white, and white was coming out of them, and I was afraid to look at them."

Interestingly enough, she comes from a very atheistic family, a family which gave her no formal religious training. So when she was faced with the image, she simply assumed they were doctors, and yet the elements of the experience are the same. They gave her a choice. They said, "If you come with us, you will never see your family again." So here again is that choice involving love of family members.

Sometimes the angel experiences are quite complex. One boy told me that he fell from a great height—a fort that he had built—when he was a young boy. He told me this when he was fifteen. He was five at the time, and he said he fell a great distance to the ground, well over twenty feet, and on the way down he said that an angel appeared at his side. It was a woman whom he just felt great love for. He had never felt such love for a human being. This woman said to him, "You must hold your head in a very particular way. If you hold your head just like this, then you'll be all right." His mother said that after he fell and was taken to the hospital, that in fact doctors had told her that he very narrowly missed breaking his neck and that it was only the circumstances of how his body was positioned when he fell that saved his life. He has a very intricate angel story about how that came to be.

Q What is the reaction of the medical community to these stories, to this phenomenon?

MM The medical community doesn't take these experiences seriously. I think that it is relatively rare to find a doctor who believes that an angel story is real. Most physicians are not even in a mind-set to acknowledge that near-death experiences are real. Most doctors, quite frankly, believe that near-death experiences are simply the mind's effort to fill a large memory gap, which occurs when we nearly die. According to this line of

Raphael, *Madonna del Baldacchino*. Detail of angel, ca. 1507–1508.

thought, after you are resuscitated from nearly dying, you might be waxing and waning in and out of consciousness, [and thus] you hear scraps and pieces of emergency-room conversation. Perhaps you hear a doctor saying, "Oh my God, we're losing him," and then this is coupled with religious beliefs, and the fear of dying itself, and then the mind invents a pleasing story to fill in the time when one was nearly dead.

Now, we did our own scientific study of precisely that issue. We looked at whether near-death experiences are secondary fantasies after the fact, or real experiences that occur at the point of dying. We found to our great surprise that near-death experiences are real; they do occur at the point of near-death. They are not reactive fantasies after the fact. Furthermore, they are mediated by a specific area in our brain. Fascinatingly enough, when the rest of our brain is dying, there's an area in our brain which starts to function and allows us to have these kinds of near-death experiences.

These recent advances in the scientific study of near-death experiences simply aren't widely known. However, just in the last three to five years, there have been three major reviews of near-death experiences in major scientific and medical journals, all of which have reached the same conclusion that I just shared with you. This tells me that this cultural logjam surrounding our complete ignorance of the spirit of man is starting to break up now. This is the role that I see near-death experiences are playing. It is the role of a cultural icebreaker.

We have gotten to a point in our society—not only just in medicine, but in our society as a whole—in which we don't believe that spiritual things are real. Nowadays, when people say that they talk to God, we think that means they're crazy. We believe that people who are regularly speaking to God or regularly seeing angels should be treated with medication, not listened to. But that is starting to change. I believe that it's been changing over the past five years. Interestingly enough, it's beginning to change because of the scientific research on near-death experiences, and that research comes out of our technological genius. We have the ability now to resuscitate people who are close to death, and for the first time we're learning from them what the process of dying is all about, and we're learning that it's not just ending into darkness, but it's actually wonderful and frequently joyous and spiritual. In my mind, then, this research validates a whole host of research on spiritual experiences, from angel sightings to predeath premonitions, to the afterdeath visitations that the parents of children or infants who die of sudden infant death syndrome, or widows or widowers often experience.

This is what I've tried to explore in my new book, *Parting Visions*. Instead of just narrowly focusing on the near-death experiences, I've tried to look at a whole range of spiritual encounters which are all cut from the same cloth. They're all mediated by the same huge hunk of our brain which allows us to have near-death experiences, and they're all part of the normal human experience.

People always say to me, "Well, are they real? Are angels real? Are near-death experiences real?" You bet they're real. They are as real as any other human experience. It's just the same as everything about reality. Some people have the ability to see angels all the time. Some people have that ability during a dying experience. Some people have that experience during severe trauma. Some people have it during childbirth. One of the most common times that people have near-death experiences is in childbirth, when they are not near death at all. Sometimes it happens during typing class, and yet it's all the same experience.

Q   What are the common consequences of having a near-death experience or seeing an angel? Do people come back changed?

MM   Yes. People who encounter spiritual beings of light, angels, are remarkably transformed by the experience. They are truly changed by their encounter with this being of light, and that to me is one of the proofs that these experiences are real. After all, very few things change human beings, and I don't believe an encounter with an active, grief-induced fantasy would profoundly change your spiritual outlook. They're spiritually changed in that they feel life has a purpose and meaning, in that all of life is interconnected.

A common thing for people to tell me after having a near-death experience is that they don't mind waiting in line at the supermarket, that they understand that that's part of life and there's something to be learned there. They don't let the small things in life irritate them as much. One man told me that he had been sent back from his near-death experience to do a job. So I thought, all right, what's he thinking of? Some messianic vision of a new church or a cure for cancer? Absolutely not. I asked him what job he was sent back for. He said, "I already told you my job. I run a construction firm. I have thirteen employees." So that's his big secret of the near-death experience: he was sent back to run a construction firm, and yet he believes that that experience is the most important contribution he can make—returning for his family and his job and the people around him.

They're not just changed, though, in terms of their attitudes. They're actually physically changed by the experience. We find that people who've had near-death experiences or people who have had visions of angels are people who eat more fresh fruit and vegetables than the typical population. They take fewer over-the-counter medications. It's kind of like, see an angel and never take aspirin again. They spend more time with their families. They volunteer more time, more hours per week to the community. They give more of their income to charity, as documented by their tax returns. They spend more time in meditation, or taking a walk alone at night, and they have a unique zest for living. When we give them sophisticated profiles of adaptation to life, and what kind of life they're living, they score right off the top of these charts. They score comparable to people who have been in therapy for years and years and years, and yet the only common element that these people have is that at some point in their lives, they had a spiritual encounter with a being of light, or an angel, or someone they thought was God.

The Beating of Wings

STEVEN MAXWELL

The very first time that I saw angels I was four years old. I had double pneumonia, to the point where I could not be moved from our house to the hospital. I was too ill. And even though I was very young, I can remember my mother had moved me into her bedroom and she had brought me in some hot ginger ale and I think that's why I remember it so well; I remember being so surprised that the ginger ale was hot. And I said, "Mommy, can you see them?" And she said, "What?" I said, "The angels." And they were all over the ceiling—not just one, but lots of them. And I remember not so much their wings but the sense of light and the sense of movement. Of course my mother thought that I was dying then, and she became very concerned. But I recovered and was fine. I don't remember them talking to me; I just remember seeing them.

The second time I remember being very aware of a presence outside of the physical world was when I was eight years old. I was a physically abused child, and at that particular instance, my stepfather was beating me unconscious. But before I became unconscious, I clearly heard—and still today, forty years later, I can hear the voice in my head—someone who spoke into my ear and said, "Don't worry, he can't really hurt you." And I wasn't afraid after that.

Recently I had some significant angel visitations which probably were related to my illness. In October of 1991, I was having some physical problems—symptoms that didn't seem to make sense—and I went to my doctor and was told that I was HIV positive. Through some extensive testing, he concluded that I had three years to survive, even with intensive therapy. My first reaction was an acceptance, because there were a great many of my friends who had already died. I was always surprised that I had seemingly not been touched yet, and in a way I was kind of glad that I wouldn't have to grow old.

I started not being comfortable with the fact that I was dying when the physical symptoms became very difficult. I was having headaches, and whenever I would try to move, the pain was very intense. It seemed that I was being tortured physically. So I started becoming very angry. I didn't feel that I had to suffer; it seemed that I already suffered enough. I contemplated suicide because I was so uncomfortable and I could not seem to find any relief. That's when I started appealing to something outside of myself.

Up to this point, I had survived many of the problems in my life by being very much in control—by building my life to a point where I was in charge. And I had to release that, because I couldn't control what was happening to me physically. I had to go outside of myself if I was going to get any help; there wasn't any physical person who could give it, there wasn't any physical help available. The medications help, but they don't fix anything.

Well, it was in July of 1992 that I became so ill that I could no longer work. I couldn't even walk, I was having a lot of ongoing infections and problems, and I started preparing to die. I gave away all of my things, and moved in with two old friends of mine who also were expecting me to die. Friends came over and closed up my old apartment. And while I was in bed and preparing to die, I was communicating in my mind to the God image that I have and trying to escape from the pain. And during that time, something started happening.

First of all, I started feeling that I wasn't alone in the room, that there was energy around me. And then, every morning around four o'clock, I would get awakened, and an entity would appear at the foot of my bed. He—I just knew it was male—was holding a ball of light, which he handed to me. It was the size, maybe, of a large grapefruit.

He stretched out his hands and I knew that he wanted me to take the light, and so I did. And as I was holding it and focusing on the light, it kept growing larger and larger and it reached a point where I couldn't hold it anymore; the light became that huge. And then it encompassed me, it fell over me. From that point on, I started focusing on the light whenever I was trying to achieve this sense of connection with the world outside of here.

That second type of visitation also occurred when I couldn't walk. An angel appeared at the side of my bed and this was very clear. He appeared as a light, but the thing that I remember the most is his wings. In the first entity, I wasn't aware of the wings, just the light. With the second angel, who was also male, his wings were very apparent and I could hear them. I still can't get that sound out of my head; it was that intense.

And he took my hands and lifted me up and we flew out of my bed, up through the ceiling. I don't know where we went; I just remember the sense of leaving. And although I didn't think of this at the time, it was as if I were dying and being lifted up.

When he took hold of my hands and we rose up, it was such a release. It was a true freedom, and I started being able to walk after that. The nerves on the right side of my body that had totally died, it seemed, recovered, and I was able to walk without pain. Because of it,

I became functional in the world again. I'm expecting the same to happen as I make the transition out of this life: I'm expecting to be free, to be able to function on a different level. And I tend to feel that at the actual time that I die, I will hear the wings again.

The next active visitation was two angels. Two female angels, and again, although I don't know why, I knew that they were women. I was not frightened, for I felt that they knew me; I felt safe. These two angels basically communicated to me that the process that I was going through—the process of dying—was a comfortable process to experience.

As you can tell, my relationship with the fact that I'm dying changed completely after these visitations; it's what they brought to me. Before them, I didn't know how to surrender the body and how to accept the transition out of the living experience. But they made it very clear to me that it would be a comfortable experience.

After the visitation from these angels, my symptoms started disappearing—some of them immediately, some of them slowly. I continue to give the appearance of being more and more well. It's difficult for some of my friends, who saw me last year, to even understand what's happening. It's difficult for my doctors to understand what's happening. They don't want to necessarily give credit to the angel experience. But something happened. I wouldn't say that I'm cured— all of my blood tests, all of my laboratory tests continue to show evidence of my deteriorating physical condition, and I still have both good and bad days—but I continue to be much more functional than I was a year ago. My mental, my spiritual, my whole relationship with living has really been impacted by the angel visitations.

What I find now is that instead of spending my time dying, which is what was happening, I spend my time living. My focus now is to take my life and fill it with life during the time that I'm here, and in that sense, the angels are definitely helping me do that. And they're excited about it because what they communicate to me is that not only do they have nothing else to do but they live through us; they don't have a body. And I won't have a body for long, but I do have one that's open to their being able to experience the living force through me. There are times where I ask them even to do simple things, like drive my car. My office is forty-five minutes away, so I have to drive a great deal, and in the beginning, it was very difficult for me to drive. It was a risk because I am very medicated, and so I surrendered and said you're going to have to drive this for me; I don't feel safe doing it. And next thing I knew, I was home. And you know, they did it.

Anything that is difficult or something that seems like it is not going to work, I ask the angels to help me. I personally have a particular way of starting that communication, and I don't know where I got it. It's kind of a chant, either in my mind or sometimes verbally. Verbally is much more effective; it seems to clear everything out. What I say is, "Circle of circles, angels in flight, come to me and bring your light." And then I ask them for what I need help with.

Earlier, I used to go around obstacles, just escape from them. Now I've learned that I can challenge them, and I've been doing that. Currently I have several situations where I'm being harassed because of who I am and what's happening in my life. My first reaction was to just escape from it, but then I meditated and communicated with the angels, and now I'm doing what it takes to stop it in the physical realm. I'm experiencing what's here and now, and I no longer feel like I have to escape from it, and that's a gift.

So I ask for help whenever I'm confused or whenever I have a problem, and I do think that they intercede for me. The communication or the information that they seem to make very clear to me is that I shouldn't hesitate to ask because that's their job; their job is to come to our aid and support, and they do that without us knowing it. At the times that we do consciously need them, however, you can actively ask them, and so I do.

However, you must be careful, for in my own experience it seems that the more that you call the angels, especially the good angels, the more the dark angels try to interfere and create a situation that confuses that flow of communication and energy. As soon as I opened my life force to that entity outside of the physical, I started being tricked by angels that were just enjoying being able to use my body and my mind and to take me places that I didn't want to be. I expel them by recognizing that that's what they're doing.

A close friend of mine, whom I had not seen in a while, died recently. And I didn't know until I saw his obituary, and it impacted me more than all of the other deaths that I'd experienced; there's a lot of them, and I thought I'd become numb to them. But it bothered me that he died alone. Well, an angel came to me and told me that he was not alone, that he was there with him.

SHERWIN B. NULAND, M.D.

Sherwin B. Nuland, M.D., is a Clinical professor of surgery and also teaches medical humanities and history at Yale University School of Medicine. Nuland received his medical degree at Yale. He is the author of How We Die: Reflections on Life's Final Chapter *and* Doctors: The Biography of Medicine.

QUESTION   What, in general, is the response of the medical world to the idea of angelic visions?

SHERWIN B. NULAND   Well, different people have explained it in different ways. My favorite way, and the way that makes the most sense to me based on what we know of these episodes, is that they are due to certain chemicals that are produced within the body, specifically, internally generated morphinelike compounds—things we call endorphins. It's been demonstrated over and over again that under situations of acute stress, most specif-

On facing page:
Victory of Samothrace,
ca. 3rd–2nd c. B.C.

ically blood loss, the brain produces these morphinelike compounds, which have receptors within the brain. This has the effect of a very large dose of a narcotic such as morphine.

Now, what is the effect of a narcotic? It produces not just an increased pain threshold, but for many people, a certain serenity, and for other people, even certain kinds of hallucinatory phenomena.

That's my guess about what happens in the situation of seeing angels. The question really is, *why* does it happen? What value does it have for our species? Now, the answer, I believe, has to do with evolution. If you stop to consider, ten million years ago our ancestors were fighting saber-toothed tigers or whatever; those who survived to have children were the ones who could maintain some kind of serenity in the face of being close to death. Because they survived, their children were more likely to be able to produce endorphins. And that's the way evolution, in general, works. So our species is gifted with the ability to create large doses of endorphins at times of enormous stress.

Q As a surgeon, have any of your patients had near-death experiences?

SBN I have to admit that patients are not likely to tell a hardheaded surgeon like me that they have had a near-death experience. Only once in my career have I known about this: a young woman of twenty-two with severe peritonitis, diabetes, actually in shock, was being taken to the operating room. As she was on the gurney about to be wheeled in, she saw her father, who had died ten years earlier, and her uncle, who had died about eight years earlier, and two brothers, all standing near her gurney. Her father took a step forward, put his hand up, and said, "It's not time yet. Everything will be all right." And then he stepped back and she was taken into the operating room.

That's the kind of near-death experience we sometimes hear

about: someone who has been dead—usually a very close relative—who is thought to have some contact with God or an angel reassures the person, [who is] apparently on the point of death, that everything will be all right. It's exactly the kind of fantasy a very sick person would like to have.

Q   If it is a fantasy, what is the medical explanation for how it could happen?

SBN   Well, how does any hallucinogenic agent produce its effect? We're not really sure about that, just as we're really not sure why a narcotic reduces the amount of pain someone has.

The exact pathways, the exact neurological connections, haven't been worked out, but we know that certain drugs produce certain—we might even say hysterical—phenomena. There are a group of drugs that act in similar ways to improve mood, and some of them even have chemical structures that are like each other. So this is why I think we're not dealing with supernatural phenomena. What we are dealing with is an inherent ability of the body to produce certain kinds of drugs that make us feel good, just as Prozac makes us feel good.

Q   Could it be that if the body thinks it's about to die, it will deliberately release these things to make death easier?

SBN   I think not only could it be, but it is. In my book *How We Die*, I tell this famous story of David Livingstone, the explorer of Stanley and Livingstone fame, who in the middle of the nineteenth century was attacked by a tiger. The tiger had him by the shoulder, and was shaking him back and forth like a wet puppy. He experienced no worry, no discomfort, no fear, no panic, and someone shot the tiger, and he was released from its jaws. It took him months to recover from the shattered shoulder, from broken ribs. He attributes [his response] to an act of God. Interestingly, he was a medical missionary with medical training.

A hundred years later he might have said, "My God, it's endorphins. It's not my God, but endorphins." There have been descriptions of mountain climbers who fell off a precipice and, as they were free-falling, felt completely calm. Later, if they survive because they've hit a bank of snow or whatever, and people try to figure out what it was, the explanation is thought to be those endorphins. And I think that is what produces the angelic phenomena that we're talking about.

Q   But what are we to make of the similarity of these visions across time and culture—the bright light, the angels, the deceased family members?

SBN   When I was a little boy, it was commonly said that when you die, you go to heaven and there are bright lights and you see your deceased family members. There may be God with a big long beard. In other words, we have been conditioned, at least in Western society, to believe that is what heaven is like. The type of visual fantasy we will have will be the type we hope for. Just as Prozac increases serotonin and gives us these good feelings, I would say that the endorphins live up to our expectations of what heaven will be.

Q   What about so-called miracle cures, as in the case of the young woman patient that you mentioned earlier? How do you explain these cures for people who have been diagnosed as terminally ill?

SBN   I have never been able to document a true miracle cure. What I have seen from the descriptions that I've read is that these people have been treated properly. They get a blood transfusion if they are having a major bleed, and they recover.

Sometimes, when someone has had a major bleed, the blood vessels clamp down and the bleeding stops. In fact, in the nineteenth century, upper-intestinal and lower-intestinal bleeding was treated by sucking blood out of a vein; people would stop bleeding because they went into shock. Betty Eadie, author of *Embraced by the Light*, may have stopped on her own because she spontaneously went into shock and then later could recover. She may have been transfused; we're really not quite sure about this.

Q   Are there any connections between what we're talking about and acupuncture?

SBN   I've been very interested in acupuncture in China, specifically acupuncture used for surgical operations. I have seen several operations, one in Beijing and one in the central city of Changsha—thyroid surgery, done under acupuncture. During the seventies, many groups of American physicians saw cardiac surgery, brain surgery, and abdominal surgery being done with nothing but acupuncture and minimal sedation—sometimes no sedation. All caesarean sections at the Beijing maternity hospital are done with acupuncture.

Why does it work to take some needles, put them under the skin into some muscle groups, put a little electricity into it, and just go buzz or twiddle them with your fingers? If you go and watch the research at the Shanghai Medical University and their acupuncture institute, the research is being done by people with doctorates in neurobiology and computer science. You find out, [through] working with animals, that the minimal trauma of acupuncture produces a massive increase in endorphins in these animals just as it does in human subjects. Some of these acupuncture patients do experience a kind of euphoria—the same euphoria induced by morphine or Demerol, or whatever. I think what we're dealing with here is a kind of a euphoric hallucination.

Q   What about people who say, "Well, yes, there's always going to be a physical explanation for something otherworldly, but this doesn't prove for a minute that angels don't exist." How would you respond to them?

SBN I'd say they are absolutely correct. Nothing I have said should be construed to rule out God, angels, or anything else. I'm simply saying there's a good medical or physiological or clinical explanation. I am not saying that God doesn't do it or angels don't do it. I'm saying that it's pretty unlikely that God does it or angels do it or that people are really seeing angels. For all we know, there are no angels but there is a God. And God created endorphins and wants us to have them. In the process, He makes it easy or She makes it easier for us by showing us angels.

I always say that the essence of being a skeptic is not just to question everything and anything, but to believe that anything and everything can be possible. That's the way I feel about angels, that's the way I feel about God, that's the way I feel about an afterlife. Anything is possible, but right now I have an explanation that suits the observed phenomena, that fits well with scientific theory, and so I don't go any further. Others obviously wish to.

Q Do you have colleagues in the medical profession who believe that there might be divine intervention on the operating table?

SBN I have not met anyone who has been willing to say that, to me at least. I know that there are physicians who believe it. Several have written about it. But I personally don't and I haven't met anybody who does.

Q To your knowledge, have there been any attempts by science to actually prove or disprove these angelic visions?

SBN You know, there is a school of science—I will call it science because these are honest and good scientists—known as psychoneuroimmunology. Psychoneuroimmunology began in the early 1960s when people began to do very well-organized, well-thought-out experiments to determine whether conscious thought could have any effect on the immune system, for example. Over the years there has been an increasing body of evidence that under some circumstances, with some subjects, the immune system and the endocrine glandular system can be affected by conscious thoughts. So when we begin to prove some of these things, we start finding linkages to different hallucinatory phenomena and different visions that we may have. Within our bodies, there are probably all kinds of mechanisms meant to preserve serenity, and the secondary function of preserving serenity is to preserve life.

I'll tell you my own experience of drowning. One dark night in south-central China, [when] leaving a banquet, I took a misstep and walked into what I thought was a reflecting pool. It turned out to be a very deep pit of water. It must have been at least fifteen feet deep, and I'm terrified by deep water. I never learned to swim until I was thirty-nine years old and I've never gotten over my fear. I was wearing one of those airport carry-on bags over my shoulder because I had cameras and things inside. Ordinarily I would have panicked, as I always do when I find myself in water over my head. But instead of panicking, I went deeper and deeper and could feel the water closing over my head; all I could think about was, "I ruined everything. These Chinese professors I am with will think I'm an idiot. I've fallen into water, I'm going to drown, I'm not going to be able to carry out my mission. If for some reason I survive, they'll never take me seriously."

I reached the bottom of that pit and I kicked off like an expert swimmer, which I am not. I rose to the top and there they were shouting and screaming and trying to pull me out. Then I noticed that about six inches from my head were jagged rocks that were along the pathway. Had I panicked, I would have been killed: my head would have dashed against the rocks, I would have sucked in eight quarts of dirty water, and I would have been dead. I think that what happened was, the sudden stress released my endorphins and I remained very calm. I did the right thing, and survived.

Q   There are those who say, "Science always has a pat explanation for everything, but science hasn't even begun to scratch the secrets of the universe. We could be living in a universe that is totally beyond even the thought process of modern science." How do you respond to those people?

SBN   Anyone who says that he or she has a pat response is no scientist. Real scientists never talk in terms of things they know. They speak only of theories. They don't speak of facts. Even evolution we call the *theory* of evolution. I'm fond of referring to the germ theory: no scientist is ever satisfied with the explanation he or she comes up with. Certainly I'm prepared to believe that in coming generations things will be discovered about human thought processes that we have never dreamed of— including, perhaps, the ability to have some contact with the supernatural. I don't think it will happen, but I am prepared to believe that. I love to quote Goethe, who once said that there are no miracles, there are only mysteries waiting to be solved. And you know, in the sixteenth and seventeenth centuries, there were all kinds of things that people thought were supernatural. Well, you stick 'em in the test tube, you look through a telescope, and you find out there are perfectly good explanations. But again, maybe the backup is God, maybe the backup is an angel. We're not prepared to say.

Q   Could it be that there's also a realm outside of the physically provable? For example, none of us would argue with the existence of love and hate, yet you couldn't prove them.

SBN   Love and hate are abstract phenomena. They are subjective phenomena. They mean totally different things to differ-

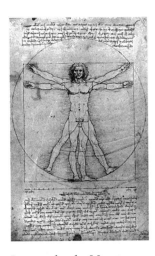

Leonardo da Vinci, *Vitruvian Man*, ca. 1492.

ent people. But I will say that there can be things that can never be subjected to the rules of scientific proof. Otto Loewia, who won the Nobel Prize in medicine in 1936 for discovering neurotransmission, the thing that makes Prozac work, once went to a concert and watched the pianist and said, "There are things that this man can do that will never be explainable on the basis of neurotransmitters." That's the romance of life. I like to think that there will always be romance in life, and part of romance, of course, is mystery.

Q   In the end, medically speaking, is there any help or any harm in someone believing in angels when their critical time comes?

SBN   That's a difficult question to answer. It's like asking whether it helped devout Christians in the nineteenth century to believe in an afterlife. Did it help them to die? It certainly did help [them] to die. It will always help devout people who believe in an afterlife to die. Whether believing in angels helps people or not, I'm not prepared to say, because obviously I don't know enough about what it is they really believe. There are people who believe in supernatural things because they are psychotic. And there are people who believe in supernatural things who are perfectly healthy, normal individuals, whose way of looking at evidence makes it appropriate for them to believe that.

In my own experience of life, nothing works if it's not true. I love to talk about the fall of communism, which I predicted forty years ago when I was twenty years old. I said it can't work; it's based on a phony economic theory. That's the way it is with phenomena like this. If they are not true at some level, eventually the whole thread of it comes apart.

Q   And that's the case even though it has an apparent history of about six thousand years?

SBN   You are talking about biblical times, you're talking

about times that we cannot verify at all. That's interesting that you should bring that up, because I keep thinking about Raphael's great painting, the *Transfiguration*. And remembering what

Raphael,
Transfiguration, ca.
1518–1520.

Raphael's name means in Hebrew. *Rapha*, Doctor, *El*, God, Healer of God, *Raphael*, Healer of God. And here we have this perfect supernatural scene, the *Transfiguration*. His last and greatest painting. Healer of God. There are hospitals all over this country called Saint Raphael's Hospital, where the most modern, scientific, nonsuperstitious, nonfaith medicine is being practiced.

FATHER JEFFREY
G. SOBOSAN

Jeffrey G. Sobosan, Th.D., is an associate professor of theology at the University of Portland in Oregon. He is the author of six books, including Christian Commitment and Prophetic Living *and* Bless the Beasts: A Spirituality of Animal Care. *Father Sobosan, whose theological research interests are Christology and contemporary spirituality, is a graduate of the University of Notre Dame and the Graduate Theological Union at Berkeley.*

QUESTION Could you begin by describing the place of angels and demons within the Roman Catholic Church?

FATHER JEFFREY G. SOBOSAN To begin with, you must understand that Scripture tends to think of creation in increments of complexity or perfection—there are intermittent stages representing more complex forms of existence than humanity, and we typically call these the angels or the demons. They're the inter-

On facing page:
Peter Paul Rubens, *The Damned*, ca. 1614–1618.

mediate states of being between God and humanity. Like all of creation, they are endowed with a certain ethical dimension. Now, this dimension varies with how animate and complex the being is. We don't hold the tectonic plate accountable for how its will is exercised, for its freedom. Its freedom is very, very minimal. It's there, but it's very, very minimal. We don't hold the virus accountable ethically for how it behaves, but it's free. The virus chooses to infect you. But at a certain level of complexity, self-consciousness begins to develop: there's an awareness of self and particularly an awareness of the relationship with God that becomes important.

This is the origin for what we would call an ethics or a morality. So you must keep in mind the fact that creation occurs in increments of complexity and freedom, so that you go from the dead and only slightly free matter that composes the universe up through more complex types of matter until you achieve life, and then the more complex types of life until you get to human beings. You have further stages beyond that before you would get to God.

Q It sounds as if you're integrating evolution and a very sociological approach to the development of morality.

JGS Right. It's evolutionary in the sense that there are different things and that they show differences of freedom and differences of complexity. The Bible doesn't know anything about evolutionary process the way contemporary science does, so you can use that word as long as you understand that in the biblical view, there are these increments and they were created that way by God. Now, the beings we typically call the angels or the demons have varieties and degrees of freedom and complexity amongst themselves. There are hierarchies within most traditions, certainly within the Judeo-Christian tradition of angels.

Q This brings up an interesting point. I have read that

fallen angels were not tempted. They chose evil out of free will, that it was an exercise of free will. How can something like that occur?

JGS Well, they're tempted. They have to be tempted. The presupposition is that there's a choice, there are options, and the options are what formulate the temptation. You just don't fall. You just don't commit evil. You just don't commit sin as kind of a natural process. It involves the posing of options and the choosing of one over the other. So, for example, in our own tradition, the fall is always going to be the result of a free choice. Options were available, and Lucifer chose one.

Q Why would he choose evil?

JGS The typical approach here, and I think it has some worth, is that there's a tremendous seductiveness and power in control. We see that in our own behavior all the time. I would rather be in control and be powerful over a small group that is my own than be less in control over a larger group that isn't. So, you have the kind of classical interpretation that the fall from heaven was a type of power play, that there was a profound interest in control over a group on the part of the figure who is typically called Lucifer and that the choice was one of rebellion, an exercise of freedom against the will of God.

Q You speak of an independent being exercising his free will, but it seems that in contemporary society Satan has become an abstraction.

JGS That's right.

Q He's gone from being an entity to being a concept.

JGS That's right.

Q Do you think that that's really all he is—a concept to designate the evil we experience?

JGS No. I think that's handy and I think it's been quite useful, particularly in psychological investigations of evil. But there's a problem here. We have developed what I like to think of as a type of sophisticated conceit; we employ interpretive jargon or interpretative conceptualities to get ourselves out of very ancient, very definite, and very insistent beliefs. We've even done this with the words of Jesus. For example, at the end of the Our Father, the actual request is not "deliver us from evil." We've abstracted that, because we believe that that's the more sophisticated, perhaps the more intense understanding of that prayer. What Jesus actually taught as the request was, "deliver us from the evil one." It's a *person*. It's a personal being that he is seeking delivery from at the end of that prayer. We tampered with that. We altered that. As you were saying, we abstracted the evil away from its personality. We don't like the idea of the personality of evil. We like the personality of good.

Q   Does Satan truly exist?

JGS   Yes, of course. You can trace this back all the way to the beginnings of human consciousness. When you have an idea that goes all the way back like that—this idea of unseen, independent, personal evil that can exercise its will in the world—you have to be very, very careful before you get rid of that. It is always there. It is probably not the path of wisdom to defeat that idea or to ridicule it or to ignore it or to reinterpret it out of existence. It's probably the path of wisdom to confront it directly.

Q   What you're saying is, it's not just an idea, it's a force to be reckoned with?

JGS   I would think so, yes. I think that would be the better thing than to ignore it or, as I say, to interpret it into a convenient conceptuality or a convenient jargon. This rejection of personal evil dates only from the beginning of the last century. There was a rather sudden conclusion, particularly with the development of scientific psychiatric study and psychological study, that we had the key to interpret more accurately what previous generations had described directly and somewhat grossly and sometimes crudely in personal terms as a demon.

Q Does the Catholic Church still teach the rites of exorcism?

JGS No. In the Catholic Church it's not taught anymore and there's no ordination to the office of exorcist anymore. That stopped . . . I think it was in 1973. Again, I believe that one of the reasons was that the Catholic Church didn't want to be identified with what educated segments of cultures had in general defined as an archaic idea whose time was over. We had developed other ways, other techniques of analysis that were more productive, that didn't raise the awkward questions of an ancient mythology. These techniques in effect dismissed the reality of personal beings, certainly not God, but personal beings of evil.

Q So even at the top levels of the church, the concept of evil has been depersonalized?

JGS That's right. The standard teaching of most American and of most European Catholicism is to look at evil as a proclivity, as a tendency, as a temptation that we sometimes fall into. Any personalization of evil nowadays is understood to be confined exclusively to human persons. That's where evil gets personalized. There's an avoidance of the idea that personality extends beyond humanity, that there can be persons who are not human and who are evil, just as there can be persons who are not human and who are good. There's an oddity here. People speak of God very, very comfortably and God is good. But the converse possibility—that there are persons who are evil, but who are not God and who are not human—that doesn't exist.

Q Are we in some state of denial?

JGS Yes. I suspect so. Or it might be a desire to get evil under control, to get it entirely within the human being and to control it within the human being through laws and through injunctions and through punishments. The idea of an evil roaming the world that is not subject to human control is very unpleasant for most people. It is not something that we wish to entertain. We don't mind the idea of good roaming the world freely and entering our lives independently; we like that idea. We encourage that idea and we speak very positively of the good presence of God or the good presence of angels, but obviously there's a certain natural revulsion against that idea being applied to personalities or to presences of evil. We hold this view even though you can count up the narratives and the examples and the illustrations of people who claim that this evil roams the world freely, independently, autonomously, and largely unseen. It is there. It is actual. It has been in my life and in such a way, in such a persuasive way, that I am not going to deny it even if it makes me look like I'm quite primitive or archaic or uneducated, that I'm prone to superstition, to hallucinations.

Not everything that we do is an act of the will, of our own will; some of the things that we do—not all of us, but some of us, perhaps not frequently, maybe just once or twice in our life— are the result of the will of someone else. For most people, when that will has been identified as evil, it cannot be the will of God. People cannot tolerate the idea of one god who is both good and evil. If you have many gods, some can be good and some evil. But that is not true of one god; that god must be good all the time.

So, what do we do with experiences of evil that come into our lives, that appear to be independent and powerful and influential? We can keep our mouths shut, because we find it an embarrassment and we don't wish people to think badly of us. Or we can interpret it out of existence, typically through psychiatric, psychological jargon. Or we can ridicule it. We can demean the whole idea. We can poke fun at it.

Well, people who have had these experiences don't really want any one of those three things to occur, because all three of them appear to be dishonest to the experience they've had. I'm talking about people who are highly and thoroughly and critically and analytically educated.

Q So these people keep it to themselves?

JGS They keep it to themselves or they will express it to someone else in a situation of absolute confidence.

Q These are incredibly profound experiences, perhaps the most devastating things that could happen to them, and yet they don't want to talk about them.

JGS No, not in the ambience of our culture. Would you talk about such things if you were going to be greeted with raised eyebrows, with questions of your seriousness or questions of your sanity?

Q What about you personally? Have you had people come to you who have said that they feel they have been affected by outside forces?

JGS Oh yes.

Q What is that like? Is there any consistency or is it all different each time?

JGS It's all consistent to the extent that what has been experienced is power. The power is malevolent and largely not controllable. It is exercising itself with large degrees of freedom and autonomy in a person's life.

Q What's it doing in their lives?

JGS If it's demonic power, it's damaging them. It's damaging them physically in their own personal selves or in the situations and the events around them—the dwelling in which they live, the material objects that are associated with their home or with their life. Sometimes the demonic presence is identified as some other human being or some other life-form in their lives.

You'll get designations of the presence as having the visage of a distorted one—usually a corrupt one of a human being or animals. Certain animals are typically understood as familiars of demons, or as being the demons themselves.

Q   What animals?

JGS   It depends on the culture. It varies. Some cultures will look at goats. Some cultures, as we all know, look at cats. Other cultures look at dogs. They are all animals that you run into quite frequently in your life. You never hear of a possessed butterfly. You never hear of a possessed whale, or a porpoise. You hear of the animals that are all around us because we do like to familiarize evil. The more familiar it becomes to us, the more we think it becomes controllable. You can control a goat. You can control a dog, or a cat.

Q   What about visions of Satan? Where does the consistency of these images come from?

JGS   The consistency in the pictoriography of Satan is that the images are always frightening: the wicked look on the face; the way the eyes are slanted; the fanged teeth; the ears; the horns. You find all of them repeated constantly in cultures that had nothing to do with each other. These are not transcultural depictions; they are autonomous. They emerge independently.

The depictions of evil are like the smile. In all cultures the smile has a meaning that is very definite. It has a meaning of pleasure, of greeting, of comfort and relaxation and happiness, and that's always been the case. It seems there is built within us a kind of natural proclivity to express certain things in certain ways that everybody recognizes.

Part of our human impulse in drawing or painting images of the unseen and the untouchable is to familiarize ourselves with it. Our thinking is that if we can only picture it in the proper way, if we can only address it or speak to it in the proper way, we can get rid of it. As with the angel—if we can speak to it and address it in the proper way, we can bring it close, we can bring it near; it can protect us. The impulse is to make what is essentially

Mathias Gruenewald, *Temptation of St. Anthony.* Isenheim altarpiece, ca. 1512–1516.

nonvisualizable familiar. Because we do think that the more familiar something becomes to us, the more we can control it. The more we make it a part of our life, the more it is subject to our will.

Q Have you ever seen a demonic force? A demon?

JGS No, I have not myself.

Q But you think that demonic possession does happen?

JGS Yes.

Q What makes you think that?

JGS Well, I'll go back to what I said before: that it is not a wise thing for us to deny ideas, beliefs, insistencies that have been with us right from the beginning of human consciousness and that have never faded. It might be the professionally expedient thing to do. It might be the popular thing to do. But it's not the wise thing to do. I don't think it's any wiser to dismiss the notion of demonic influence than it is to dismiss the notion of divine influence. I can't believe that the whole of the history of these testimonies has been deluded or has been foolish or has been naive or childish. Socrates went to speak with and to seek the wisdom of his daímon, and no one would call him foolish, I shouldn't think. Anybody who says that is the foolish one.

One of the problems in studying Christ today is that there are not that many things we can say with a very high degree of accuracy about the person of Jesus. He is two thousand years away from us and is in a culture of first-century Palestine that has been dead for centuries upon centuries. But one of the things we can say about Him with certainty is that He was an exorcist. He cast out demons. This has been the bad boy of theology for quite a while; certainly through most of this century and probably well into the last century, you don't deal with this dimension. And yet He did it. He did it repeatedly.

When I was doing my studies in theology, it was bother-

Sandro Botticelli, *The Redeemer*, ca. 15th c.

some to me that I couldn't get any description of this very important part of His public ministry that seemed to take it seriously. If it was brought up at all in the analyses, it was brought up in order to be dismissed or to be interpreted in such a way as to make Jesus an extremely effective psychosomatic healer but nothing more. But it is my judgment that if we want to appraise the world from a Christian perspective, we have to try to appraise it as closely as we possibly can to the appraisal that Jesus gave it. And the simple undeniable truth is that Jesus was an exorcist.

Q   Now that we've brought up the concept of exorcism, what has been your experience with exorcism? Don't you have some background in that?

JGS   I've only been involved indirectly in two cases. I was not the exorcist, and was not present during the performance of the exorcism. I was consulted regarding them, particularly regarding the history of the practice of exorcism. Other than that, I myself haven't been involved.

Q   What were they? What were the two cases you were involved in?

JGS   Well, the one was a child who was born of Irish Catholic parents. They lived in a large city in this country. Now, people are going to find this very hard to believe, but the child was five years old and started jabbering. At least, that's what the parents and the people who experienced it *thought* it was: jabbering. It turned out to be ancient Hebrew, and the language that he was using was obscene. It was all in the nature of cursing— ferocious, tremendous cursing of people in the immediate environment. The child also developed inordinate strength, and the parents had to confine the child to their bed. It was a teakwood-frame bed—very, very heavy. The child could pick it up with one hand as high as the child went. (Preternatural strength is a common symptom in demon possession.)

The child would come in and out of these states with no

memory at all of what had occurred. He had been brought to physicians and had undergone batteries of physiological tests. They looked especially for chemical imbalance in the brain or in the muscular systems. Nothing showed up. Then he was taken for psychological and then for intense psychiatric examination. Nothing at all emerged out of that.

At that point, the parents had identified it in the traditional vocabulary of devil possession, or demon possession. They became more and more convinced. So there was an exorcism requested. It was performed. It lasted for several weeks. It was not successful. The child committed suicide by swallowing mothballs; before he could be attended to, the chemicals burned his body. He died just a few hours after that. So from the perspective of the exorcism, the exorcism was a failure. (An exorcism is judged a failure when the person dies possessed.)

Q   When the child swallowed mothballs, wouldn't it seem that it was the demon responding to this attack of the exorcist?

JGS   We don't know. Possibly. The swallowing of mothballs, of course, wasn't witnessed. It was thought that the child was asleep and in a state of temporary release from whatever it was that was afflicting him. He was already comatose before he was discovered as having taken these. The mothballs, of course, were in a drawer where sweaters were stored, and it never dawned on anybody that that might be the source of defeat, but it was.

Q   How did they try to perform this particular exorcism?

JGS   It's a set ritual of prayers addressed to God, [and] condemnations, injunctions, mandates addressed to the demon. The tradition is very thorough here that the exorcism stands a greater chance of success if you know the name of the demon and the demon can be addressed personally. When you read reports of

exorcisms, it sometimes takes considerable cleverness to try to seduce out the name of the demon.

Q So in this case you just described, they were not able to
get the name?

JGS No, they couldn't get the name.

Q Wasn't there another case of demonic possession in
which the child died of a heart attack?

JGS Yes. The girl was six and a half, and her familiar personality would seem to disappear, and she would either enter into
a kind of comatose situation where you couldn't rouse her at all,
or she would enter into a condition where she would make these
sounds, and roll her eyes and cross her eyes; then they would go
up into the head. The most alarming thing in that case was that
she became completely double-jointed—or at least it appeared
that way. She could turn her head 180 degrees. A lot of people,
of course, are reminded of that movie *The Exorcist*. Well, this girl
developed complete double-jointedness. They had a record of
her medically from the time she was born, including a complete
X-ray history. There was no double-jointedness in this child, so
she was in a physically dissociative state. [She also displayed] dissociative strength; strength that wouldn't be normal for a child
that age occurred.

Q Like what?

JGS Lifting objects. Hurling objects. If she came into body
contact with a member of her family, she twisted their arms or
legs with a power that was extraordinary. These are the sorts of
things that were reported about her.

Q What eventually happened?

JGS I don't know exactly. I had heard that the child had
suffered a coronary attack and died of that, but I had left that case
before there was a resolution.

Q Was an exorcism attempted?

JGS   Yes. In the history of exorcisms, if a certain amount of time goes by and the prayers and the rituals are not effective, the choice that begins to emerge is death: to get rid of the life of the possessed person, to defeat the demon that way. This, of course, is what underpinned so many of the witch trials in the Middle Ages. Witches were thought to be demon-possessed. The exorcisms didn't work, so we killed the host to drive the demon away. Sometimes in the history you read of transference; the demon leaves to enter the priest.

Q   Could you run through the real story on which the movie of *The Exorcist* was based?

JGS   Well, it was a boy—it wasn't a girl. And it wasn't Georgetown, it was Los Angeles. And the complete turning of the head was not true. In the movie, you remember, the head moves around completely; that did not occur. What you will typically find is an ability to turn 180 degrees, but you can't turn the head 360 degrees; it will come off. So that was a cinematic exaggeration. But the chronic vomiting, the obscene language, the manipulation of the crucifix in obscene ways, the ancient language, the identification of the demon as a great Persian demon—all of that is basically the case as it occurred.

Q   Are there any other recent cases of demonic possession or demonic appearances that you have heard of?

JGS   There is one going back a number of years that involved a young woman and her baby. This was a six-month-old baby boy. She was washing the baby in the bassinet and she claims that the face of Satan suddenly appeared on the boy, so she drowned him. She simply pushed his head underwater and drowned him. They put her directly into psychiatric investigation, and, of course, the typical result of that is temporary insanity—whatever that means, that's the final conclusion. She took leave of her senses. But she never has recanted her rendi-

Benedetto Bonfigli, *Madonna della Misericordia*. Detail of city of Perugia, ca. 15th c.

tion. She saw the face of Satan and she drowned her son for that reason.

Q   What's her psychological history?

JGS   She had no record of mental disturbance or illness up to this incident. After it ended, she went back to being the normal woman she was. There was another child, an older girl, and this woman was devoted to that child. She loved that boy, but to this day she will not recant or repent what she did. That's the power of the conviction that she had.

Now, what do you do with this? Everybody is shocked. They don't know how to talk about this because we don't use the sort of vocabulary anymore that previous generations would have—the vocabulary of sudden, assertive demon possession. If anybody starts using it, we get uncomfortable. We want to walk away. We want to shake our heads and say this is crazy—there must be some other reason; there was a glitch. All these euphe-misms are designed to say, "we don't know." We are reluctant to assert the most ancient of traditions to explain this.

Q   What do you think?

JGS   The demon was there, but the demon was in *her* momentarily—not in the child. She killed the child—that was the work of the demon.

I know of another case in which the mother took her two-and-a-half-year-old son out to the garage on Good Friday and crucified him because it was the day that the child of God was to die. The child survives because the child starts screaming and the garage door is left open; the neighbor hears and rushes over and the mother is sitting on the floor in a type of fugue state that she comes out of and doesn't know what has happened. The last memory she has is [of] being in the kitchen hearing Good Friday services over the radio.

Q   What's her background?

JGS   Normal woman who loved her child. Had a job, was a delight to her friends and her relatives. She doesn't remember the event happening. She comes out of this state, this dissociative state, and enters immediately, of course, into a second state of shock over what has transpired.

Q   And how is her behavior now? Has she ever exhibited any kind of aberrant behavior afterward?

JGS   Not to my knowledge. The husband left her and took the child, of course, so she has suffered because of an event she cannot even remember—an event that is so out of character. That woman now is suffering. She suffers the knowledge that she did this to her son. She's suffering now the absence of the child from her life, and, of course, if it was a demon, the demon is well pleased by the whole thing.

Q   These awful stories bring up the whole concept of Satanism as a choice. There's a segment in society that consciously decides to enter into Satanic practice.

JGS   That's right. There are covens all over this country. They keep themselves as unknown as possible because they understand what the response of the population at large would be. But they're all over. Some of them are mild black magic, some of them are violent black-magic practices.

Q   How does a person get involved in that?

JGS   I really don't know how you would do it. I suppose members of the coven walk around. They observe you. They probably have criteria for determining susceptibility to the influence of Satan, and in some fashion will coax or seduce you, in ever-increasing ways, into the life of the coven. Maybe at first it's just an invitation to come over for a drink or a cup of coffee, and then in the course of the conversation you deliberately bring up this idea and see how the person responds. And, of course, then, through gradual process of proselytization, you come to a type of judgment whether this person is fertile for Satanism. You bring the person into the coven.

So these people form a communion, and if they judge that the demonic presence is very, very powerful—more powerful than the angelic presence, more powerful than the presence of God—they league with it. You always league with the victor and this is where Satanic communities emerge. The fundamental judgment of people who get involved in this lifestyle and in these communities is that God will not prevail. Lucifer, Satan, Beelzebub—however you want to call the great demon—is the one that's going to prevail. You might think that God will eventually prevail, but not during your lifetime.

It's like the story of Faust. The demon will give me what I want, and all that really matters to me is this life that I know I've got. With Faust it's fame, with other people it's power, especially wealth and gratifications of the variety of forms that lust can take. The only life I know for certain I've got is this one, and it appears to me that evil is the most reliable way of securing me the pleasure I want. It is the lying, it's the cheating, it's the self-infatuation: all these things get the pleasure. And if I can somehow league myself with a spiritual force that I am presuming to be more powerful than I and that can manipulate situations and events, then my pleasure will be even greater.

What's going on here religiously is a very fundamental judgment that God does not prevail and that only the fool aligns himself or herself with the failure rather than with the victor. That's why people will come together in those communities.

Q Is devil worship an organized religion?

JGS No, each coven is independent. But within the coven, there are typically hierarchies. There is someone who is the master's disciple—the master, of course, is typically Satan, but need not be. It can be one of the other demons. Lilith is very popular. She's a very powerful demoness. She's the noonday devil of Psalm 100. When she comes up from the pit, she favors abandoned ruins. This is part of the origin of the haunted-house mythology. Many of the covens are gender exclusive. There are only females in them, and in those there is a tendency to center the ritual and the acts of submission on a female, a demoness.

Q How often are you personally contacted by people who feel they have a problem with demons, who feel they are being influenced by an outside force?

JGS A dozen times a year, I would say.

Q And how are you equipped to deal with that?

JGS Well, it very seldom gets beyond the stage of the person offering the initial descriptions of what is going on and my making the judgment that this is either an exaggerated interpretation of events that have natural causes, or it's a plotted experience. People have been thinking, it's been on their mind, they've seen shows on TV, they've read magazine articles, and it gets kind of unconsciously plotted to issue in an experience as preternatural or supernormal. This is true especially of descriptions of levitations, or of objects being knocked off shelves or knocked off tables for no apparent reason. I'm usually pretty suspicious of those. And so if I know, through an initial conversation, that somebody has consciously or unconsciously plotted an expectation for an event that's going to be interpreted as preternatural to occur, I generally will dismiss those as well.

Q   When do you sit up and take notice?

JGS   If the person is insistent that the sorts of descriptions that I'm giving do not apply to the situation that was experienced. If the person is insistent that full consciousness was being engaged. If they say, "I'm not falling in and out of a doze. I'm not on alcohol. I'm not on drugs." The person insists that he or she has experienced this with a full, waking, uninhibited consciousness.

Q   In your opinion, are there more angelic and demonic encounters happening these days?

JGS   That I don't know. There's certainly an increased amount of reportage of such experiences. People are very freely and sometimes very articulately and at great length describing such experiences. It's my position that in one way or another, the concerns of religion will have their say in a person's life. They will get out. And when institutional religions, especially, are not able to provide a proper focus or a proper understanding of experiences that people are having, then the religion gets privatized. But it will come out. It seems clear to me that the experience of angelic presence is a response to the need for tenderness and care and guardianship that institutional religions are failing to provide.

Q   Now, this brings up a very interesting sort of chicken-or-the-egg quandary. Which came first, the actual angelic encounter or the social need for this kind of experience?

JGS   What people are doing is adopting very traditional images, mythologies, and explanations, simply to be able to talk about the experiences. Everybody has a basic understanding of what an angel is and what an angel does—or what a demon is and what a demon does. There's a certain conceptual basis that everybody has for this.

Now, experiences come first. It is experiences that are supposed to control thought, not the other way around. If people are having experiences which in a comfortable vocabulary they are describing as angelic presence, or they're having experiences that in a comfortable vocabulary they are describing as demonic presence, this will emerge in a vocabulary that they share with others—a very basic vocabulary, perhaps a very ancient one, a very stylized mythological vocabulary. Why? Because no vocabulary is being provided in a formal way by the churches or by the formal theologies of the churches. People are having these experiences, they are thinking about them, they want to articulate them, and yet they never hear it preached. Until recently they never read about it. And when they did read about it, it was dismissed as superstitious, or primitive, or childish.

Q   Let me ask you this. Do you think all this has anything to do with the Apocalypse?

JGS   You mean as kind of a precursor for the end of days? The emergence of the beast, the prevalence of evil in the world? No. I don't think that. I don't think evil is any more prevalent now than it's ever been. It's just that in some segments of society there is a greater willingness in talking about it in very direct and sometimes very frightening language. You know, sin, evil, is one of the very, very few doctrines that is empirically verifiable in Christianity, and it strikes me as very odd that a formal theology in the Christian churches is not addressing this. We can't use scientific experiments to empirically verify life after death, or the existence of God, or the existence of demons and angels. But we can empirically verify the existence of evil itself. A personal evil. When a mother drowns her six-month-old child because she claims the face of Satan has appeared on it, that's empirically verifiable. She did it. She killed the baby. And by any type of even basic morality that we can generate, this is evil. The mother killed the child.

Q But the question is, did the evil come from within her or from without her?

JGS That's right. It is the evil that is empirically verifiable. We get into discussions and disagreements trying to articulate and identify the cause. I happen to think that most of the evil that is in our lives we generate. We are its cause—but not all of it. There is also evil that is just too consistent, too old, too cross-cultural, and this kind of evil emanates from personal sources other than humans. But the bottom line is, the evil is there, it's verifiable.

Q So the point is the devil is no less present today than in the past, but that organized religion has moved to deny or exclude this sense of personal evil?

JGS The concept is present in the common piety and common beliefs of a lot of people, but it is almost nonexistent in formal education, including theological education. You have a dichotomy in the culture, a dichotomy that has always existed in religions, especially in Christianity. It's between the common faith and the taught doctrine, or the taught theology. Certainly this is true within the Catholic Church and in a number of other Protestant Christian churches. A little less so in Judaism, and a lot less so when you get into Asia, or Africa, or South America.

The formal theology has dismissed as one of its concerns the idea of demonic presence, even though it seems to be very present in the common piety, in the common devotional life and belief systems of people. This, I think, is the heart of the failure of the institutional church on this issue. I don't mean just the Catholic Church, and I don't mean this as a colossal or an integral failure. It's more of a pastoral failure. People are not being cared for by the church officially or formally, so they are caring for themselves. They are finding kindred minds, kindred souls, people who have had similar experiences, and they are caring for themselves without the official church or without a formal theology being involved. I think that's wrong. I think the essence of the ministry is to serve the people as the people are experiencing their God and their spiritual life.

Q   What about eternal damnation? Has the Church also moved away from this concept?

JGS   There is no eternal damnation—at least not from my perspective.

Q   But I thought a basic tenet in the Catholic Church was that you'll be burned in hellfire forever if you align yourself with the devil?

JGS   Well, that is certainly in the popular understanding of Catholic education. But the more profound understanding comes from Saint Athanasius, who asserted in the second century that God redeems everything. All is blessed. There is a recapitulation in God of all that is good, and the evil is purified and purged out. So that hell is the dwelling place of demons until they are redeemed.

Q   So there is redemption even if you are cast into hell?

JGS   I think so. I don't want to represent my church in saying that I think so that directly. In the Catholic tradition, I would be representing more the line that comes from Athanasius than the dominant line that comes, of course, from Augustine.

The fundamental inquiry of theology is this: When you are presented with an experience or with a proposition, what does it require me to say about God? If it requires you to say something about God that you don't want to say, you get rid of it. Now, if somebody proposes to you the idea of the possibility of everlasting damnation in hell, damnation that will never end, that will be spiritually and physically agonizing, what does that require you to say about God? When you answer that, you have to ask yourself, "Is this something I don't want to say about God?" For it is always the God concept that must prevail—not the heaven concept, not the hell concept, not even the Earth concept. For the religious mind, the alert religious mind, it is always the God concept.

Q   And God has to be merciful.

JGS   If you're going to derive what you want to say about God from the teachings of people like Jesus or the Buddha or Saint Francis, it seems to me you have to get rid of the concept of hell as something that is possible by God's will as our destiny.

Q   So then why does God allow Satan to exist?

JGS   Freedom. All of creation is free. People make a mistake; they want to see God as either the only cause of everything or the cause of nothing. God is either the only factor or isn't a factor at all. But you don't want to look at it that way; all of creation is free, which means that while you might assert that God is a factor in what happens, God is never the only factor. There are always other factors. When the child comes down with leukemia, there's the genetic factor, there might be a viral factor, there might be some type of predisposition factor, maybe there's a dietary factor—we're not quite sure. And *then* there's the God factor. But if God is such that all of creation is free, God can never coerce events because there are always other free agents involved, and the most God can do then is persuade.

Q   Some people would say that the devil exists to test us.

JGS   That's the most ancient idea. The word *Satan* means adversary in a court of law. In the Book of Job, Satan is portrayed in heaven. He's not demonic. He's called the Satan. He's the one who tests and tries your faith. In the great prologue in the Book of Job, he's the one to say to God, "It is no wonder that Job is your servant and obeys you; his life has no pain. Everything has gone the way he wants. Let me put him to the test and he will deny you to your face." This is standard Old Testament piety. An untried faith is worthless because anybody can say anything that they want. It must be tested, and the satan is the adversary who tests or tries the legitimacy or the truthfulness of what a person says. Now, later he becomes the wicked one, the evil one, the perverse one, so that by the time of Jesus, that's the way that word *satan* is functioning. It has now become a proper name to identify the greatest of the demonic powers, Satan.

Q   We've been discussing Satan in the singular. Do you consider there to be many demons?

JGS   Oh yes. I should think so.

Q   Why do you think that?

JGS   Well, the tradition is unanimous here that they are many, they are legion, and that they are polymorphously perverse. There are demons of fury, demons of thirst, demons of lust, demons of greed, very powerful demons of indolence, acedia, laziness, and sloth. The tradition behind this is very old and very thorough.

Q   What about this concept of dark angels and the Antichrist? We hear a great deal about this in our culture right now.

JGS   Yes, it's the turn of the millennium. That's a big factor.

Q   How does that apply to the dark angels?

JGS   Well, the Antichrist is understood as a human being—very wicked, very malevolent, certainly very charismatic—whose attributes or qualities are the opposite of those of the Christ. So there is no healing. There is only the infliction of pain and illness. There is no enlightening of the mind. There is only a darkening of it, and so on. He would have access, and probably controllable access in this mythology, to the demons. They would see him as more useful for working their malice, because he is human and can work with his own kind. [He is] seductive in his appeal, and then eventually, of course, in all the mythologies, ultimately destructive.

Q   So the dark angels are his emissary, in a sense?

JGS   They kind of place themselves under his tutelage, just as the angels of heaven were told to place themselves under the tutelage of Jesus Christ.

Q   How did God come to be associated with light and the devil with darkness? How did this concept arise?

JGS   You have to remember that this hierarchy came from a time when the whole of the universe was supposed to be literally divisible into three parts. You had the sky above—it's dotted with little bits of white stars and the two great lights that move through the day and the night, the sun and the moon. The sky is a semipermeable membrane in this way of thinking. If you can get up high enough, you can get through it and you go to a locale called heaven, where God dwells. Then there's the earth which you and I walk on. But underneath the earth there's another locale. It's like a big subterranean bubble. If you can find the right cave that leads down, you can get to it.

The ancient obsession with flight, building towers, and structuring wings arose because they didn't think the sky was very high. They watched the hawk—the bird circled and it didn't have to go too high before it disappeared. Why did it disappear? Because it entered the heaven. If I can just get up high enough, I can enter that locale. It's the place of light, of course. The sun is there and the stars, and it's the dwelling place of God and it's wonderful.

Now, the other locale, the dwelling place of the demons, is a pit, an abyss. Again, they took this literally. There is an actual locale of darkness. Of course, it's the place of fear. We are frightened of the dark, especially if we're starting to structure our mythologies two, three, four thousand years ago. There are no electric lights. There are no automatic weapons. The dark is scary and it's dangerous, and it becomes a marvelous earthly experience for what hell must be like. The light is where there is joy. There is warmth and our food grows and it's wonderful and it's a blessing, and this, of course, is the dwelling of God. But the abyss is the worst kind of darkness—an utter darkness—and there is no way to protect yourself against it.

Q Why did the image of Lucifer degenerate over time from the suave prince of darkness to the beast?

JGS I suspect the evolution is due to pedagogy—the education of children. The more horrifying you can make Lucifer, the more effective he is in training children. If Lucifer is just like C. S. Lewis, you know, the cranky uncle who might smack you in the face a little bit if you don't behave, it's not going to be quite the powerful pedagogical device as the beast who won't just smack you in the face, but will chew your face off. He'll burn you. He'll poke at you. He'll kill your mother. It's very powerful, and it has an amazing talent for lingering on, even when you get very educated. It might not be the exclusive context, but I would bet it's one of the very powerful ones for the gradual monstrous satanizing of the demon.

Q Do you think we're living at a time when religious salvation is more difficult? That we have somehow excluded this concept from our public life, our public discourse?

JGS We're living in a culture that, of course, allows for religious freedom in private practice, but in public practice where most people live—in the business world, in the political, professional world—it doesn't. It's considered inappropriate. You go to a school of engineering or a school of business, and if you're going to function well and to function successfully, you're largely going to have to silence whatever values, desires, aesthetic appreciations that you have for eight, nine, ten hours a day.

This is not a good way to live. Salvation means wholeness. Salvation doesn't have anything to do with heaven as Jesus teaches it. It means achieving the whole life—the life that isn't divided against itself. The life that isn't bifurcated and fragmented. If you have to suppress values and serious interests of beauty for ten hours a day, this is not a saved life. You are fragmented. This is a Jekyll-Hyde existence.

A lot of people can live that way. They can chop themselves up into little pieces. I know a woman who works for the government. She spends her days plotting and planning theoretically the creation of weapons designed to destroy human life. When she gets home, if there's a spider on her floor, she picks that animal up and places it outside. She will not step on it, she will not damage it. There's a problem here. This woman is not of a whole. She's not coherent with herself.

Q Getting back to demonism, what is the worst example of demonic possession you've heard of in recent times?

JGS The closest you could come to a cultural consensus

that what is being done is demonic would be Nazism. It is the judgment of many people that clearly this was a demonic presence in the world. This was not just political perversion. This wasn't just megalomania on the part of one person and a coterie of other egomaniacs surrounding him. This was a true presence, an expression of satanic evil in the world. A lot of people take that description seriously. They're not using it just as a type of hyperbole to describe unutterable malice; they mean it literally.

TERRY LYNN TAYLOR

Terry Lynn Taylor is the internationally bestselling author of Messengers of Light, Guardians of Hope, Answers from the Angels, Creating with the Angels, *and* Angel Wisdom.

QUESTION Are children more attuned to angels than adults? Are they especially open to angelic encounters?

TERRY LYNN TAYLOR When we're discussing children and their experiences, it's probably a good idea to recognize that they go through different developmental stages. And at certain times they don't have all the vocabulary to describe certain experiences the way we would. And they don't think logically. So where we would put in logic and say, "Well, did this happen or didn't it?" to them it's just one big experience, where feelings, seeing, sensing are all one. For a child, seeing it in your mind may be the same as seeing it in person. They also like to say they know it in their hearts.

On facing page: Sandro Botticelli, *Four Angels*, ca. 1483–1485.

279

For adults, sometimes we have to see something to believe it. That's why when people ask me if I believe in angels, I say, "No, I *know* them." Because if I say I believe in them, they'll want me to prove it. And they'll want proof in a visible form. And I can't do that, I can't demand that an angel appear.

You know, the imagination is also a place of reality. That may sound ridiculous, but it is. I think the imagination is where we create the future. It's where we begin to know ourselves, and it's the place of creativity and knowledge.

Q   But at some level, don't you have to separate fact from fantasy? Otherwise, how do you know that a child isn't just making it all up when he says he has seen an angel?

TLT   Why would a child make this up? Sometimes there is a stage where children lie to entertain us, and usually a parent can say, "Oh well, that's a nice story." But when a child comes right out and says, "You know, an angel saved me," that is something different. I have a letter that somebody wrote to me about this little girl who was four and had many, many health problems. She was not expected to live to a very old age. She was at the top of a slide and she fell off, about ten feet. Her grandfather, who was watching her, ran over thinking, "Oh, the worst has happened," because this little girl just wasn't in good shape to begin with. The first thing she said is, "Grandpa, an angel set me down." Why in that very second, when there wasn't a scratch on her, would she make up a story that an angel set her down? In moments like that I don't know why a child would make up a story just to seem interesting. Another story that comes to mind is the twins who were playing in their yard on the swing; one was swinging very high and she fell off. And the other twin noticed that a boy angel and a girl angel on each side of her turned her so that she could be set down very carefully, and that all these pretty colors were around the twin that the angels were setting down. Again, not a mark on her. The twins waited for a while to tell their mother because they were really nervous they were going to get in trouble—the reason this happened was their little rabbit had run out in front of the swings and they were afraid they were going to knock the rabbit across the yard. This is why the little twin fell off. When they got over the fear of telling their mother, she started laughing actually, because she had been reading my book. And she thought, "Oh, this is really a coincidence."

There's just too many times that children come out spontaneously with this. Many times the parents have never even mentioned angels to the child, so where would they get the idea that this is an angel? There aren't a lot of cartoons with this kind of thing.

Q Are kids more susceptible to angelic encounters?

TLT I don't think they're more susceptible, but I think that they're more open. They don't have the logic to talk themselves out of it. So when these things happen, they think, "Okay, that's just part of life—an angel saved me. So? What else?"

Q Do you think all children are able to see angels?

TLT No, just as I don't think all people see angels. I think we're here to be human, so we want to pay attention to what's happening on Earth. And if we were seeing the angels all the time, we might not pay too close attention to what we're doing right now.

But I do think that children may see things that they don't say anything about or that might seem strange to adults but, to them, seem natural. Children are very in tune with nature. They'll talk to plants, they'll walk around trees and talk to the tree. I had one mother bring a little girl to one of my seminar workshops because she saw fairies. She'd be able to talk to them. It was just natural for her to tell me about that.

Q   Is there any prevailing pattern in the way children describe angels?

TLT   When children describe angels, probably the common denominator is light and feelings of comfort and protection. In the cases where children are set down on the ground, maybe they felt a floating feeling or some warm feeling. Adults will describe time expansion. I don't think children have the ability to do that, but they describe nice beautiful feelings. They like angels because they're pretty: pretty colors, nice wings. They love the wings.

Q   When adults see angels, they feel they're somehow changed afterward. Is this true for children, too?

TLT   I don't think it's necessary for children to have life-changing events like adults, because they're kind of on a natural path as it is. But angels do relieve children's fears. One letter in my book describes a childhood memory from a woman who remembers being in a very cold hospital room at age five and her parents weren't there; and the baby next to her was crying and then the baby had stopped crying, and she thought the baby had died, and she was very frightened. She described how a ball of light came in the room and it made her feel so much better and safer, and then she realized the baby hadn't died but that the parents came and got the baby. That was a moment of comfort, and I think it probably helped her; in any other future situation, she knew she wasn't totally alone.

Q   Have you ever heard of any stories in which angels have helped children to die?

TLT   I think with the near-death experiences, children see beings waiting for them to cross over. In the book *Closer to the Light*, children have drawn pictures, and definitely there are angels or angelic beings there to help the child.

Q   What about spirit guides? How have children described them?

TLT Some children have spirit friends. And parents are sometimes able to witness their child talking to the spirit friend, or they'll come to their mother and say, "My spirit friend says such and such." One woman asked her child, "Well, who is your spirit friend?" The child's spirit friend's name was Brenda. And the child said, "My mind talks to her mind, and her mind talks to mine; it's not the way you and I talk." This particular little spirit guide was giving information about the child's father, who was in the Gulf War. And the family was, of course, very concerned, but the spirit guide kept reaffirming, "Everything's going to be fine; your father will be home, and everything's in order." So actually, this particular relationship this child had with his spirit guide was a great comfort to this family.

Q How do parents know that their children aren't lying?

TLT I don't think there's any way we can prove that angels are with us. We have to trust. And children just do trust. They trust the process of life. To them it's an adventure; it's a way to have fun, play, be creative. Children are naturally going to be very in tune with angels. I think that if your child is worrying too much, it might be good to talk to them about angels—not overdo it, because I don't think we need to force children to believe in angels. But I think that it maybe helps them if you say, "Well, you know, there are angels that watch over you to make sure you're okay, and when I'm not with you, your angel will be watching you." It gives them a sense of comfort. Because the world's getting scary for some children. They can't help but see things at school or whatever that they don't understand or might be scary.

Q Is there a particular age when kids start to experience angels?

TLT I think it depends on how good someone's memory is. A one-year-old is not going to be able to describe an angel experience because he doesn't have the vocabulary. So I would say the most active period for angelic experiences is between the ages of four and eight. The child is still in that space where the world's a magical place, and they don't know how to doubt things yet or throw logic into it. After about age nine or ten, they're probably more interested in sports or their buddies, so they may not pay that close attention to it—although many children still do have experiences after that age.

Q Don't children also say that they're taken places with the angels?

TLT The little boy, Joshua, who had Brenda, the spirit friend, said that Brenda takes him to castles and places almost every night. And he draws pictures of them, paints them the next morning.

Q Is it as common with adults to be traveling with angels?

TLT Some people like to go on guided meditations where the angels are helping them go somewhere. But I want to get across that there's not any common experience because we're all so unique and different, and our lives are so different. So it just depends. Also, having an angel experience doesn't mean one child is any more special than the other. Some children may just never tell you about it. I don't want children to think that if one child is seeing angels and the next one's not, that they're not as special. It's just that the experience is a little different. It may happen in a different way.

Q How did you come to be involved with angels?

TLT I've always believed in angels, even as a child. It just never occurred to me that that wasn't a part of human life. It really never occurred to me to not believe in God either. I never had to go through a stage where I said, well, I don't believe in God. I always did. It was the way I was raised. This might sound kind of strange, but in high school I had a friend and we would get reckless and do something crazy and then we'd stop and go, "Oh, wow, our guardian angels have probably had it with us, you know; they're probably tired of working overtime." We just assumed we had guardian angels keeping us out of trouble. And believe me, they probably *were* working overtime because we sort of pushed the limit at times!

Then, in 1985, I was reading a lot of spiritual books, because I wanted to go on the spiritual path. I found I wasn't very happy, and I thought, this doesn't make any sense. I should be happy and joyful, yet I feel burdened by all this information. One day I came across the saying, "Angels can fly because they take themselves lightly." And I stopped and it was like a light went on in my head, and I went, okay, that's it. Number one, I've been taking myself way too seriously. And two, I realized the angels are our spiritual helpers on our path. They're not just there to save us from a car accident. They're not just there to comfort us when we're really down, but when we're on the path and we're trying to figure things out.

So I started playing with that idea. If the angels are my spiritual helpers, how can they help me? I would meditate on that, I would write in my journal. And I was looking everywhere for a book that might tell me about how angels help us. I couldn't find the book I was looking for. I continued keeping my own journal, discussing angels with people I'd meet, asking them whether they believed in angels and what they thought angels are. It just started growing in my life. I couldn't get enough information on angels.

In 1988, I was telling a friend kind of as a joke, "I can never find the angel book I want; I should go ahead and write one." And my friend said, "That's a great idea." I wasn't really serious, but I started to think about it. I'd been writing in my journal, I'd been doing these little practices. I knew that this was happening to other people; I just knew it. So I wrote up a proposal. I ended up running into people who could help me find a publisher. The publisher wasn't quite sure what he was going to do with the book. He thought, "Well, I like this; it's interesting," but he still wasn't so sure. And within two weeks, the first printing had sold out and everyone was amazed.

After the book appeared, I started to get letters from people who said, "The same thing has occurred to me, and thank you so much for writing this book, for I always thought I was crazy." I've always felt that angels have to be more than just rescuers. The whole thing blossomed into what I call angel consciousness. And it's really changing people's lives. It's giving people something totally positive to focus on, and actually a lot of help, too.

Q   You've talked about the role angels have always played in your life. But can you define exactly what an angel is?

TLT   First of all, angels are usually either seen or thought of as beings of light—beings separate from us. They're in constant praise of God. They do God's work. And they watch over us, they help us.

Angels' light is many different things to many different people, but it's always positive. It's always for the betterment of ourselves, of society, of the world we live in. There's always some improvement in morality, in consciousness. Angels of light edify us; they uplift our consciousness, give us something positive to focus on. They make us see where we can make choices to make the world a better place.

We can think of angels as light, and it helps us to understand them, because they have all the properties of light. Light is very fast; it can travel across very vast distances in just a blink of the eye. A light illuminates the darkness, and angels can illuminate the darkness in our lives and in our minds. So really you can think of angels with the properties of light. As beings of light.

Q   What about guardian angels? How do they differ?

TLT   A guardian angel is traditionally our particular angel, our guardian through life. If you believe in past lives, your guardian angel was with you in your past life. Our guardian is always with us. It's our personal guardian angel from God, unique to each person. But it's not an archangel.

Q   And everybody has one.

TLT   That's my opinion. Some people may not want to believe that, and that's fine. But in my opinion I believe everyone has a guardian angel.

Q   It seems that in times of crisis, whether it's an accident or a war, people seem to notice the angels more. Is it just that we

Gaudenzio Ferrari, *Musical Angels*, ca. 16th c.

notice angels then more, or do they come to our aid in those situations?

TLT   That's one of those questions that I think only God can answer. However, the angels are always around us; we don't have to attract them necessarily. I mean, there are certain things that we could do that probably would make them want to be around us more. But if we're in a frightening situation, life is more dear, and when life is more dear, we're going to find something to help us protect it. If there's one thing I've learned, it's that our bodies don't want to die. They're programmed to live. And they're going to do everything possible to keep us alive. And that's why a lot of miraculous healings come. So when we're in that moment where our bodies and our minds have focused on the dear aspects of life and keeping alive, certainly the angels may seem very much more real to us at that moment.

Q   Do you have an opinion about the healing aspect of angels?

TLT   I don't think of healing as curing an illness. I think sometimes an illness might be the greatest gift someone has in their life. I think healing is more making peace with life, making peace with the idea that life is really a mystery. We don't understand it always; we don't understand why good things happen to bad people and why bad things happen to good people. But if we can take whatever is given to us and make peace with it and figure out a way for it to uplift our consciousness and be better people, I don't think it really matters that you were cured of a disease. If that's in your life path or if that's what you're here to do or if that's what's meant to be happening at the time, then certainly there could be a miraculous healing. But if someone's ill, if someone's even dying and they do die, I don't think death is the punishment.

I'd like people to think differently about healing. I don't think the angels come in to cure us of something but maybe to help us accept it and look at it as what it is here for. How did we create it? Did we get sick because we weren't taking care of ourselves? Why? We're so focused on getting rid of it—let's rip it out, cut it out, take an aspirin and it will go away. Our society is very stuck on that. So if there have been miraculous healings and if the angels have helped that happen, then that's for that particular person. But it may not happen for everybody.

Q A lot of people would look at a situation in which a loved one has a terminal disease, and they expect an angel to perform the miracle of saving the person's life. But the real miracle can be healing the spirit or healing the soul, can't it?

TLT I think that life continues to go on, and that love continues to grow. If someone dies, that does not mean we stop loving them. It doesn't mean they stop loving us. Why would it? Love is an energy. It can go across the miles and through all the different dimensions. So it just doesn't stop. And it's silly to think, "Okay, I'm gonna grieve for a week and then I'll be over this person." How could that happen? I mean if you love someone, why cut it off just because they're not present in physical form?

Q Can other people serve as angels to people?

TLT In the Bible, Archangel Gabriel says, "With God, all things are possible." I am certainly not going to limit what God is going to do here on Earth. If God needs for someone to appear at that moment as an angel or as maybe a representative of heaven to get a message across, I certainly think God could do that, and definitely the angels could. Why should we put limits on this? You know, if God's will needs to be done, if the angels need to get a message across to someone at a certain time, another human may be the one delivering that message.

Q Do you have a feeling or opinion on dark angels?

TLT Number one, I think it's important when we're discussing dark forces or demons, to see that they vibrate to fear and a lowered will. For instance, if someone is doing drugs all the time, they aren't keeping their energy strong. They may be more susceptible to having experiences with a "dark force." If you wear yourself down, you create fatigue. And fatigue isn't just the need for rest; no, fatigue is a tired spirit. And a tired spirit is going to be susceptible to things that some people might think of as a dark force. But if we take care of ourselves, if we keep our spirits in good working order, in good condition just like a runner would do for a race, if we keep ourselves spiritually sound and focused on the divine, using courage to get through fears, facing fears, saying, "No, this isn't gonna stop me," then the dark forces are not going to really have that much of an effect.

I don't even like to talk about the dark angels because it brings up fear with people. Let's face it; if there are two forces in the universe—dark and light—which one do you think would be interested in fear? It's the dark force, because fear is very debilitating to people; it causes them to see things or go into terror. Whereas the angel of light would use love and comfort.

Q What about the age-old dilemma that you can't know good unless you've experienced evil?

TLT I think there are different forms of evil. I don't think that evil is just when something bad happens to us. However, when something bad happens to us, it certainly can make us understand the good better. Evil can teach us; it can teach us to grow. But we can't ever give up. When a person starts thinking that demons and dark forces are after them and that these dark forces are keeping them from doing the good, then they're cheating themselves. Light is so much more powerful that the dark can't keep us down unless we allow it to with our fears. One thing the dark forces don't understand is a sense of humor. If you're in a situation in which your fears are overwhelming you, stop and have a good laugh.

Q But if you look directly at the world around us, you see there is holocaust and horror everywhere. Isn't this an undeniable evil?

TLT It's evil, but each one of those acts is a decision someone made. It's a personal decision. We can call it evil, but within that evil, human decisions are being made. I think if we, as humanity, start to make a personal choice to make things better, to sacrifice instead of hurt, then the light will get so bright that the dark won't have a lot of room to exist.

Q Why is there so much interest in angels these days? What do you think is going on?

TLT This is interesting, because in the last fifty years we've had something positive happening and something not so positive happening. The positive thing is that people are figuring out how to do things themselves. They're figuring out self-help. People are learning how to make things happen for themselves. And that's good. But on the other hand, we've had this quick-fix stuff, where we've kind of skimmed over a lot of things. And there really isn't any shortcut or quick fix to life.

So I think we've reached a point where we've got the technology, the knowledge to help ourselves. But to create meaning in our lives, we have to go back to basics. It's the same basics that Benjamin Franklin was teaching. It's morality. It's doing the right thing. It's choosing the right way to be for the good of the whole. Well, when we realize that's missing, the angels can help us. And I think one reason that people find the angels a compatible part of their lives now is because they're willing to do the right thing. If it takes a little bit of sacrifice, they'll do it. [This is the case even] if it takes doing things maybe the long way instead of the short way. If it creates more meaning, if we're not compromising our values, that's important now. We've seen the other way just doesn't work. Maybe there are a lot of things that need repair, but I don't feel that the world is doomed. I think if anything, humans are becoming so incredibly magnificent now that angels want to be a part of that.

Q A lot of people look at the world now—at the crime, the poverty, the homelessness, and all the problems of the world—and say, "We're coming to the end." Other people say, "No, we actually are about to evolve into a different level of being." What do you think is going on?

TLT There's no strict answer yet for that. I think God's in process. One of the crucial things we're all realizing is that every moment is a choice in the universe. I don't feel that I can explain the wars or the evil. I don't understand that. It's part of the mystery to me. But I know that if we focus too much on destruction, we risk becoming part of that instead of part of the hope and the vision in the world that we know we can create. I don't mean to deny that there are horrible things happening on the planet; there certainly are things that are overwhelmingly horrible. However, I feel that we really have the chance to make it work. And the angels are really there to help us do that.

Q What can we do to contact angels? What can we do so that angels will know to be around us more?

TLT It's not so much how can we contact angels, or attract them, because the angels are always around us. But it helps if we practice certain things in our lives. Maybe this will sound funny to people, but we need to raise our vibration more in tune with the angels. If you look at light as a vibration, there are all sorts of things in the universe that vibrate to certain things. One of the most important things is gratitude. Some people are just so worn out by life that they forget this is a beautiful gift, and we need to be grateful for our life and take every moment with gratitude. What happens when you have a heart full of gratitude is you start noticing heaven everywhere. It's no longer this dismal world. You can see the most beautiful things in nature, in the sky. You can see a child walk by in the ghetto and just go, "Wow." Gratitude can just open you up to that realm. Then the angels can work with us. When we know where we're going, we don't mind taking our time getting there. But we have the help to get there in a glorious way.

Q Is creativity a key word in there?

TLT Creativity is a natural human trait. It's basic energy that we always have. Humans are creators. We love to create things. But some of us have talked ourselves out of it. We say, "Oh, I'm not creative; that's a creative person's thing." But I think we are all creative. Creative people are willing to *think* about things. They're willing to think something through on their own. We don't always have to stick with the answers that someone else has given us. Think beyond. Ask more questions; don't settle for answers. Answers will stop you from questioning and cut off your own creative energy—especially with the angels. If you want the angels to be in your life in your own way, then find your own questions to ask. Don't settle on just other people's experiences or answers. Be creative; think.

I will add that many times when the angels come into someone's life, they discover a talent that they never knew they had. A woman wrote to me one time that she wanted to give something special to someone and the angels encouraged her. She wanted to paint a little bookmark for someone. Well, then someone else saw it and said, "Oh, that's beautiful, would you paint one for me?" Then the next person wanted one; pretty soon she had a card line. She would never have done the first bookmark if she didn't have that joy inside her that she wanted to create something nice for someone and make a little angel bookmark. So that's an example of how the angels increase our willingness to use our creative energy. I had a man come up to me one time who was in the business world of graphic art—doing commercials and print work. And then he had this urge to paint angels all the time, to draw them. He thought the rest of the world was going to think he was crazy, but it kept coming to him. He couldn't not pay attention to it. So finally he quit his job in the real world and now he's doing angel art. So it happens. The angels encourage us to use our gifts, our art, our talents.

Q So the point is, we need not limit angels to the role of rescuers. If we think beyond, we can come up with our own questions and our own interpretation?

TLT Yes. Our relationship with the angels needs to be cooperative and cocreative. That means that we're part of this. We don't settle for saying, "Oh, an angel can take care of that thing." No, you think, "How can I do this? How can I get beyond this point? How can I take this project and go toward the end?" You have the answers. The angels aren't necessarily there to give you answers. And then if you have your answers, find more questions from the answers. *Don't limit yourself.* Because the angels want to help us go beyond. But we have to do our part and think for ourselves and think creatively. And think beyond just the basic answers.

Let's say that we all knew angels. That would probably mean we all would know ourselves better. And if we all knew ourselves better, we'd know the things that we were here to do. And I think the world would be a lot different. It may not even be the same world. It might be a whole new place. I don't see how the world could be the same if we were more in tune with what we came here to be.

Q Why do you think people resist believing in angels?

TLT   That's a good question. I wish I knew why. I think it might be again fear of the unknown.

As far as resisting the angels, it's almost like resisting yourself or your true meaning, the true reason you're here. If you resist the angels and they've come to you, then you're really resisting your purpose. I don't want to scare anyone into thinking, "Well, if I don't believe in angels that means that I'm not doing this." No, that's not the point. Some people can go through life and don't need to know that the angels are there. They don't need to be actively involved with them. And I think that's just fine. There are a lot of wonderful people living great lives. They don't even have a clue that there are angels out there. That's really not the point. The point is the angels are pointing us toward God. The angels are pointing upward. They're saying, "Look at the divine, look at what you can do as a human. Look at the magnificent gift you've been given by being born here as a human." So I don't know if people really even have the chance to resist that.

Q   How do guardian angels give hope to people? Is hope important?

TLT   I ask people who think that hope isn't important, "When was the last time a hopeless person inspired you?" If you don't think hope is important, try living without it forever. I think hope is very important. It's not a means to an end, though. It's not a goal.

Guardian angels are not exactly what gives hope, but the knowledge that we do have a guardian angel that protects us and gives praises to God all day and keeps us on the divine track gives us hope. But hope, again, is a catalyst. It's not something that you give and take so much. It's an energy or a feeling that keeps us going. And so I think the idea that we have a guardian angel can give us hope, but I don't think the angels themselves give us hope. It's part of the human spirit. I think that's why it was left in Pandora's box for us; we had all these awful things fly out, but what's left in the box once you put the lid back on is hope. There's a good reason for that.

Q   Do you believe that the angels can come to bad people and people doing bad things, like taking drugs?

TLT   First of all, I don't think we can rightly judge someone as bad if they're taking drugs or doing things we don't approve of. Who are we to judge who the angels would go to? Their actions might not have a good effect on others or even themselves. But to label everything as good and bad is putting things into black and white, and that doesn't work for humans. We're all different shades and our experiences are all different. Most people who take drugs are simply offtrack for a while. And it's not so much that it's bad or good, but it can be a teacher just like everything else. Unfortunately, some people along the way get hurt. I think often people who have ventured out, maybe gone too far with drugs, are those very people who can make really wonderful things happen in life. Because they are willing to take a risk. Taking drugs is risky, right? You almost risk your life every time you do it. So there is that element that they were willing to do something, break out of their chains, they just didn't know what it was yet.

Q   How are angels involved in near-death experiences?

TLT   I've had letters from people who have had near-death experiences, and whether or not an actual angel with wings appeared to them, they were certain that beings of light or of love were there to help the transition between life and death. Many people will say that an angel came to tell them that it's not their time to go yet, and that they have to go back. Sometimes they even get the choice: you could go with us, but you're really not supposed to. I've heard that said. So definitely the angels are around. The angels are definitely around at birth, and I'm certain

Ridolfo Ghirlandaio,
Three Angels, ca.
16th c.

they've got to be around at death, too, to help the transition. The near-death experience is comforting to people because it shows them that life doesn't just end and that's it. They know that there's a reason to this life and birth and death.

Q   Might the angel that people report seeing in near-death experiences be the guardian angel?

TLT   I think there's a good possibility of that. Because we have a guardian angel that's with us from birth through life, and at death, maybe the angel that the people are seeing is their guardian angel.

Q   What about the opposite of the guardian angel—call it the personal demon. Do we sometimes fall hopelessly in the power of our demons?

TLT   I think that God has the last word, basically. God can come in and save someone from the demons' dark forces. However, we have to be part of the process; we have to want to get out of it, and we have to know the right ways to be. We're making the personal choices that are in our realm, but we're not the ones making the world turn. If bad things happen to us, the best thing to do is to say, "Okay, this happened; what can it mean in my life? How can it make me rethink things and get back on the path?"

Q   What about when bad things happen to good people? I'm thinking of the recent incident of that church in Alabama where everyone was praying and they were hit by a tornado and just flattened.

TLT   Do we really know that that was bad? It was bad for the people left behind because they were hurt, but if we start saying that death is bad, we start judging everything as something bad. What if we say, "I don't understand. I don't understand why a whole church full of people would die?" If we looked at the bigger picture, which we're not privy to, we might see that the people left behind were somehow brought together closer. Maybe there was something good out of that. I don't know; I wasn't there, I'm not one of those people who are left behind. But I don't like to judge everything as good or bad because I don't think we have the last word on it. I think God does, and I think the more we judge everything in our tiny little views, the less effective we're going to be. We're going to be afraid of life. Death is not a punishment.

Q   You're saying, just accept it as a mystery.

TLT   That's the best way. You know, I'm thinking of a statement that Anthony Perkins wrote when he was dying of AIDS. He didn't let a lot of people know about the nature of his illness because it was his choice, but right before he died, he wrote a statement he wanted read, and he said that in the end—this is not an exact quote—he learned more about love and compassion by having AIDS than he had in all the years of the cutthroat world that he had lived his life in. He wouldn't trade those moments of love and compassion that he felt and experienced and was able to give. Sure, there was suffering—how could there not be?—but he left it as a positive.

Q   When it comes right down to it, you're such an optimist.

TLT   If the worst thing a demon can do to us is make us suffer and die, we can use that suffering and that death as a positive statement, as a time to love more deeply. That might be the only time in life that we truly have loved and lived. I have heard people say, after suffering through an illness, "I've never understood how precious life was, and what it meant to live deeply, how to walk outside and smell a fragrance and just go 'wow.'" Believe me, they now know what life's about. The demons can't stop you even if you die, for you can go on loving and living.

Whatever happens to you in this lifetime, get back into the saddle and go, because that's your best choice.

Q   What would you do if you felt that a malevolent force was plaguing or influencing your life? How would you act?

TLT   If I personally felt that there was some sort of force after me that I couldn't control, I would go into deep prayer and ask for complete guidance and love from God, and surrender to whatever it was that was happening.

Q   What do you mean by surrender?

TLT   If it's a spiritual problem and we can't solve it ourselves and we feel out of control, the best thing to do is to give it up. We can't really control the whole world, and sometimes it works better when we give up some of that supposed control. So if I felt that I was in a situation where I was out of control, I would stop and go, "Okay, I can't handle this, maybe the higher power can help me."

Q   Would you just appeal to God directly for help?

TLT   Yes, always. You know, the angels never want anyone praying to them. They're pointing us to God, so when we pray, we ask help from God.

Q   Do you think angels are strictly nondenominational?

TLT   Yes. I don't think they belong to any one religion.

Q   So regardless of your belief or lack of belief, you can avail yourself of this kind of help?

TLT   Yes. It's not so much that a person goes to church and believes in a religion, it's who they are, it's the spiritual growth that they experience. That's how the angels help us with who we are. If you go to church and you get something out of it, that's great. If the next person doesn't, it does not mean they aren't wonderful and good and spiritual and that the angels aren't helping them.

Q   They say that Lucifer was the angel of light. What does this mean?

TLT   He was God's favorite brightest angel. Part of the legend goes that he was sent to Earth to test humans—to test how much they loved God, how much they would take. Lucifer then got a little too interested in the humans doing this for him, not for God.

Q   When a bad thing happens, how can you pull yourself out of it? How do you begin?

TLT   If a person encounters something that makes them feel out of control, there are a few things that I think they can do to help create something positive out of it. For one, remember that fear and feeling out of control is the energy that's keeping them in an agitated state. So the first thing to do is to relax and let the fear go and to calm down. Don't get agitated. Does panic ever make things better? No. So relax, calm down, and then try to think things through. Ask yourself, "Why would this happen? How did I get to a point where I'm so out of control with this?" Ask those questions and then the answers will start coming. And you'll start figuring out ways to go beyond it. Relax and say a prayer to God. Many Christians use the name of Jesus or the Christ, and that seems to be something that pulls them back to the center, to the truth, to the light. So if there's a name like Archangel Michael or Jesus Christ or something that is so sacred and holy that it centers you back, then repeat the name.

The next thing you do is you say to yourself, "I need help. What's offered? Where do people get help?" When an alcoholic hits rock bottom we all know where they can get help. You know there's an organization they can go to. So you analyze the situation. What brought you to that point? What could help you?

Go to a counselor. Go to a priest. Go to your minister, your pastor. If you need help, *go get it*. Don't be prideful, don't say, "I can handle this." If you really feel something's gotten out of control and you need help, go get it. Ask for it. Ask God for it. Don't fool around with your life; it's important.

PICTURE CREDITS

ABOUT THE EDITOR

REX HAUCK, a partner of American Artists Film Corporation (AAF), co-produced, wrote, and directed "Angels: The Mysterious Messengers" for television. He has received two Emmy Awards for his writing and directing. Mr. Hauck has also had several motion picture screenplays optioned for production, including " 'Twas the Night" and "Angels of Light." He is a member of the Directors Guild of America and the Writers Guild of America.